ALL ABOUT OPTIONS

FROM THE INSIDE OUT

& Russell R. Wasendorf
Thomas A. McCafferty

IRWIN
Professional Publishing®
Chicago • London • Singapore

This publication is designed to provide accurate and authoritative information in regard to the subject matter covered. It is sold with the understanding that the authors and the publisher is not engaged in rendering legal, accounting, or other professional service.

ISBN 1-55738-434-7

Printed in the United States of America

7 8 9 0

TAQ/BJS

Dedication

For the third time, we must congratulate and thank Geraldine Martinson for her help in preparing one of our books for publication. We also owe much to our families and our associates at Peregrine Financial Group and Wasendorf & Son Company. If it wasn't for all their encouragement, support and insights, we'd still be staring at blank paper. Thanks everyone!

CONTENTS

Preface   vii

Chapter 1: Understanding the Basics, Particularly the Value and Risks
Associated with Stock Options and Options-on-Futures Trading   1

Chapter 2: Learning the Basic Option Trading Strategies (and Uses) to
Solidify Objectives   21

Chapter 3: Forecasting Stock and Futures Price Trends   47

Chapter 4: Option Price Models and Volatility—The Most Important
Consideration for Serious Option Traders   67

Chapter 5: Developing Trading and Money Management Plans   83

Chapter 6: What You Need to Do to Implement Your Trading Plan   97

Chapter 7: What a Difference the Computer Chip Has Made   107

Chapter 8: Selecting the Broker That Is Right for You   119

Chapter 9: Knowing a Little About Federal Regulations Can Sometimes
Smooth Rough Waters   127

Chapter 10: The Single Biggest Mistake New Traders Make—Plus a "Few
Other Common Ones!" (And, of Course, How to Avoid Them)   137

Chapter 11: Getting Started, or the Secrets of Successful Options Trading   147

Appendix 1: Glossary of Terms   155

Appendix 2: Sources of More Information   181

Appendix 3: Long–Term Volatility Charts for Selected Stocks and
Commodities   185

Appendix 4: Exchanges and Options Offered   197

Appendix 5: Description of Option Trading Software   203

Index   209

About the Authors   213

PREFACE

First, we need to address the following questions—

◆ What are options?

◆ Do they have economic value?

◆ How should an investor use stock options and options-on-futures?

◆ What are the pros and cons, risks and rewards?

◆ Is option trading gambling?

Options, in general, are the legal rights, acquired for a consideration, to buy or sell something at a predetermined price by a certain time in the future. Options are very common in real estate, for example. Developers will take options on certain pieces of property as they plan projects. It gives them time to obtain zoning approvals and raise capital. The option locks in the price and buys time.

Real estate and most other options are negotiated from scratch by the two or more parties involved. The buyer and seller need to agree on all the terms or specifications, not to mention price. Reaching an agreement may take anywhere from a few hours to a few months. Negotiations could break down resulting in no agreement or option.

There is another type of option. It is called an exchange traded option and is the province of this book. This type of option differs from the other in that all the specifications are prearranged, except price. For stocks, options generally "cover" one hundred shares of the underlying stock; options-on-futures are on the underlying futures contract. All the other specifications—delivery date, place and type of delivery, quality, etc.—are clearly defined. The only variables are the number of options to be bought or sold and the price.

Since buyers or sellers decide for themselves on quantity, the only thing left to negotiate is price. It is this characteristic of uniformity that makes the stock and futures exchanges possible. The exchanges, in turn, render society in general and the business world in particular a very important economic service—the discovery of price. Trading in options and the underlying stocks or futures contracts tells users, planners, reporters, economists, speculators, investors, government officials, and anyone else interested, the current value of a company's stock or a commodity, along with projected price trends into the future.

If you are a user or processor of soybeans, copper, money, or any one of the over sixty options-on-futures traded in the United States, you can easily check the futures market to obtain the current price and get a good insight into what prices are expected to be three, six or twelve months from now. A look at any of the thousands of stock option prices tells you what savvy traders think about the prospects of individual stocks. Or you might study one of the many composite indexes of stocks, commodities, utilities, foreign currencies, etc. (or the options on these indexes), to get a feel for the price direction of an entire market.

Another possibility might be that your analysis indicates you are facing some serious financial risks. Options could provide some relief. This is the second very important function of the options markets. Coupled with risk management is the ease and convenience of buying and selling options.

Let's use an example. You own a quantity of something. It could be an agricultural product (grains, livestock) or a financial entity (a stock portfolio, Treasury Bonds). Analysis of the price trend indicates it could lose value over the next six months. You don't want to or can't sell the commodity until then. What do you do? You can offset the risk of ownership by taking a short position in an option. You freeze the price through the purchase of the proper option. This is known as hedging and will be discussed in detail in the chapter on strategies.

The important point is that the options markets can be used to pass the risk of ownership of stocks and commodities to someone, the speculator, who wants to accept the risk. The speculator's objective is to make money from the acceptance of the risk. The beauty of using exchange traded options is the ease with which the transfer can be accomplished.

For example, you don't have to go out and find someone to accept the risk. They are immediately available at the exchanges. When you're ready to close out your position, you can do it with a single phone call to your broker.

If you are dealing with a foreign currency or financial instrument, you do not have to worry about setting up an asset custodial relationship in the foreign country. Nor is there a hassle with the transfer of money to another corner of the world or finding an English speaking broker or currency conversion. Additionally, there are ways, discussed later in this book, for trading these markets twenty-four hours a day. This can become important when major economic or political events occur while U.S. exchanges are closed. The fall of the Berlin Wall and the outbreak of Desert Storm come to mind as times when this facility might have been utilized.

We would be remiss in our discussion of the benefits of options if we didn't mention how they can improve the efficiency of your use of capital. Buying an option on any underlying entity can be done for a fraction of the cost of outright ownership of the entity. Keep in mind, when you buy an option, you are only acquiring the right to assume ownership before a given date at a predetermined price. You don't own the entity.

On the other hand, when you're ready to get out of your option positions, it is nothing like selling an entity you actually own and possess. There are no shares to sign and deliver (stocks). Nor do you have to truck it to the elevator (grains) or stockyard (livestock) or remove it from a safety deposit box and have it assayed (precious metals). You avoid all quality and quantity confrontations that can occur when commodities are handled, rehandled, stored and shipped. It is not uncommon for farmers to sell their crops right out of the field and then buy options to replace the actual grain in order to partake of the seasonal price rises that normally occur after harvest. Gone are the worries of spoilage, cracked kernels or rodents—not to mention the hassle of handling and rehandling the crop and trucking it to the elevator.

Limited Risk & Unlimited Reward

So far, we have only briefly alluded to speculators, the people who make the whole system work. Speculators assume all the risk others wish to avoid. Most of you readers will fall into this category.

What motivates speculators to buy options is that they know in advance to the penny what their financial risk will be—but their potential profit is theoretically unlimited. They risk the cost of the option, known as the premium, and the transaction costs, which are brokerage commissions and fees. The reward depends on how much value the underlying entities gain before the speculators take their profits.

A speculator could conceivably buy an option for $300.00 and sell it for $3,000.00 or $30,000.00 within thirty days. This is certainly possible and has happened, although it is not the normal course of business in the options markets. The normal course of business is for options to expire worthless. In other words, the speculator invests $300.00 and loses $300.00. Experienced option traders usually offset their positions before they expire worthless. They'll invest $300.00 and close the position when it has lost $100.00 or $150.00. They'll continue to do this until they choose some winners. We'll talk about this in detail when we discuss how to use the Law of Probability to become a net winner as an option trader.

Even the concept of unlimited profit potential needs some explanation. Theoretically, options have unlimited profit potential. Underline the word "theoretically." But prices for stocks or commodity futures normally do not rise or fall in unlimited amounts. At some price they either become too expensive or too cheap. For example, during the Great Depression, corn fell so low it was cheaper to burn than coal. And that's what some farm families did. On the other end of the spectrum, when corn gets more expensive than wheat, livestock producers feed wheat. The demand and the price of corn eventually return to more reasonable ranges. The same is true for stocks. If the price of a stock drops below the liquidation value of the company's assets, what will happen? Or if the price of a stock rises so high no one can afford it, the market adjusts the price accordingly.

Additionally, there is the profit taking motive to factor into the supply-demand equation governing the price of stocks or commodities. Investors who got in early on a bull or bear move will take their profit at some point. Eventually, the profit takers turn the market around.

What option traders have going for them is predefined risk, rather than limited. On the profit side, they have the prospects of an excellent return, rather than unlimited. Experienced investors seek outstanding risk-to-reward ratios. If they can invest $500.00 with the potential of making $5,000.00 in a few weeks, or a 1:10 risk-to-reward ratio, they'll consider it.

A variation on the predefined risk characteristic of options that appeals to speculators is that it gives them staying power in adverse markets. Buying options-on-futures, unlike futures themselves, does not require margin money or a good faith deposit. The risk is fixed, as previously stated, to the premium and transaction costs. If the markets move against your position, you can hold the option to expiration without having to put more money into the investment. With futures, traders have to replace any money lost when the market moves unfavorably. If you have a very strong conviction that the market being traded will eventually be profitable, an option, if it has enough time to expiration, provides the staying power to hang on to the position.

Is Option Trading Gambling?

Done judiciously, it is not, in our opinion. If investors do not do their homework, arbitrarily buy options, and do not closely follow the markets, you might as well consider it gambling—but wouldn't this be true for any investment?

Serious option traders use the Law of Probability to take advantage of the distortions in the supply-demand situations of stocks and/or commodity futures contracts that regularly occur. Experience, research, and even a little help from a good broker can put the statistical advantage in your favor.

Trading options on stocks and/or futures is complex. The serious investors must invest in books, newsletters, seminars, software and other educational materials. Much time is required to master this investment—but the potential rewards can make the effort a joy.

On the other hand, we have no intention of misleading you. Option trading, like any investment, entails substantial risk. Not every investor is suited for it because it is such a highly speculative venture.

Reading this book is a good start towards understanding options, but please consider it as only the beginning. When you're finished, you should have a solid overview of the subject and a good idea of where you need to turn next in your quest for success in the options markets.

We wish you the best of luck and the offer of any additional assistance we can provide. Don't hesitate to contact us if you have any questions after reading *All About Options From the Inside Out.*

Chapter 1

Understanding the Basics, Particularly the Value and Risks Associated with Stock Options and Options-on-Futures Trading

"Now, on the St. Louis team we have who's on first, what's on second, I don't know is on third."

Bud Abbott from *Naughty Nineties* (1945 film)

Key Concepts

◆ Terminology can be confusing.

◆ What is an option? Puts and Calls?

◆ Differences and Similarities between Stock Options and Options-on-Futures Contracts

◆ Risk versus Rewards of Option Trading

One of the funniest comedy routines of all-time may be the exchange between Bud Abbott and Lou Costello about the names of the players on the St. Louis baseball team in their film *Naughty Nineties*. The name of the first baseman was "Who," the second baseman "What's" and third bagger "Don't Know." When Costello asked Abbott "Who's on second?", Abbott responded by saying: "No, he's on first. What's on second." When asked "Who's on third?", the retort of course was "Who's on first. Don't know is on third." These two comedians go round and round in the hilarious confusion over the players' names.

Options trading terminology can be equally confusing, but not nearly as funny. It is very important to get it and keep it straight from the very beginning. Let's go over a few examples. When you initially open a position, you buy a call or a put. A call gives you the right, but not the obligation, to take a long position in the underlying stock or futures contract at a specific price, called the striking or strike price. When you buy a put, you have the same rights you have with a call, except you can assume a short position in the underlying market.

Now, this is where the confusion often begins. One alternative the trader has is to offset or exit his put or call position by selling an exactly equal, but opposite, position. To offset a call, one sells a call for the exact same strike price and expiration date on the same exchange for the same stock or futures contract.

To offset a put you purchased, you sell one. All the contract specifications—underlying entity, expiration date, exercise or strike price, type (meaning put or call)—must match. One position offsets the other.

For example, you think the price of corn is going to increase substantially over the next 60 days. Since your analysis indicates a price rise, you want to "own" the corn now and sell it 60 days from now at a higher price. To do this, you would go long in the futures market. Rather than do that, you opt to take an option on a long futures contract. That would be a call. Therefore, you buy one corn call option. You now have the right, but not the obligation, to assume a long position in the corn futures market at a specific price, called the strike or exercise price.

Now let's get more specific. The Chicago Board of Trade (CBOT) futures contract for corn, which expires in July, is trading at $3.00 per bushel. Since it calls for the delivery of 5,000 bushels of Number 2 corn in July, it is currently worth $15,000.00. Your analysis indicates it will increase to $4.00 a bushel or $20,000.00 before its delivery date in July. That's a per contract profit of $5,000.00 before paying brokerage commissions or other fees, which are commonly referred to as transaction costs. Transaction costs can range between $25.00 to $125.00 per contract for futures.

Instead of buying a futures contract, you decide to buy an option on one CBOT corn contract. The strike or exercise price you select is $3.10 per bushel or 10 cents above the current underlying corn market. By being 10 cents above the market on a call, the option is cheaper than an option closer to the current trading price of the underlying entity. Let's call it a one-cent premium, or $500.00 (5,000 bu. × $0.01). Also, you want to see the bull move (price advance) begin before you get too committed to a futures position.

The $3.10 corn call is considered a near-in-the-money option, which means it is near the current price of the underlying contract. If you have chosen the $3.00 option, which is the current price of the underlying contract, it would be considered to be at-the-money. The cost of an at-the-money option would be higher, let's call it 2 cents per bushel or $1,000.00 for this $3.00 corn call. A $2.90 corn call would be 10 cents in-the-money.

Now that you have bought a $3.10 July corn call, what do you do with it? You have three alternatives. First, you can do nothing and let it expire worthless. Secondly, you can exercise and assume a position in the underlying futures market. In this case, you would be long one July futures contract at $3.10, which is the strike or exercise price.

Last of all, you could offset the position. This is where the terminology confusion, mentioned at the beginning of this chapter, comes to play. If you wished to offset your position, you could sell one July corn call. The term "sell" also means to write or grant an option. The writer or seller of an option is the trader who agrees to provide a futures contract to an option holder whenever that person decides to exercise the option. In the case of stocks, the writer provides the shares to the option holder when and if the option is exercised. For assuming this responsibility and risk, the option writer of the corn call receives the $500.00 premium. The risk is that the price of the underlying entity will increase. Therefore, a writer will have to deliver a contract that has gained more value than the premium received.

When you tell your broker you want to sell an option, are you offsetting an option position you already own or are you offering to write (as in underwrite) an option someone else wishes to buy?

All this can become even more complicated since options are traded like futures. With futures, you can short the market. This means if you forecast that the price of a certain commodity is headed lower, you sell at a given price and buy back (offset) that position at a lower price. The difference is your profit.

For example, in our corn scenario, let's say you thought corn was headed down $1.00, rather than up. Using the futures market, you would short the market at $3.00 and go long, offsetting your short position, at $2.00. That equates to a $1.00 per bushel or $5,000.00 profit.

You could do the same thing with options. In this case, you buy a put giving you the right, but not the obligation, to take a short position in the underlying futures contract. If your projection of a $1.00 fall in the corn market was correct, you could exercise your option and become short in the futures market. Or you could offset your options position by selling a put that was exactly the same as the one you bought.

Our point is that you must make it very clear to your broker as to what action you wish to take or you'll end up like Abbott and Costello. But the humor may be missing if it costs you money. When in doubt about a term, refer to the glossary at the back of this book. Don't sell a put when you meant to write a call! See Figure 1.1.

While we're discussing terminology, here's a few more expressions you should know before we go any farther. The value or cost of an option is composed of intrinsic and time value. Intrinsic value is what an option would be worth if it were exercised. For example, your $3.10 corn option would have 50 cents per bushel ($2,500.00 per CBOT) intrinsic value when corn is trading at $3.60. It would be said to be 50 cents in-the-money. When corn went from $3.00 to $3.10, your $3.10 option would be at-the-money. While corn was at $3.00, your

Figure 1.1 Comparison of Buyers to Sellers

Option Buyer versus Option Seller

Obtains the Right, but not the Obligation, to Assume a Position in the Underlying Entity	Investment Risk Equal to the Maximum Move the Underlying Entity can Muster
Investment Risk Equal to 100% of Premium Paid for Option Plus Brokerage Commission and Fees	Assumes the Risk of Delivering a Position in the Underlying Entity
Pays Premium	Receives Premium
Pays Commission and Fees	Pays Commissions and Fees

$3.10 corn call was out-of-the-money by a dime. There are also deep-out-of-the-money options, which are far away from the current price of the underlying contract.

When you bought the $3.10 corn call, corn was at $3.00. You paid $500.00. There was no intrinsic value. The $500.00 was time value. The market was saying that the four to six weeks left on the option had a value of $500.00. For this time value to be recovered, corn must go from $3.00 to $3.20 to generate $500.00 intrinsic value or 10 cents per 5,000 bushels over the $3.10 strike price. At that point, depending on what traders thought the market was going to do and how much time was left before the option expired, some additional time value would be added to the $500.00 intrinsic value.

The intrinsic value of a put is figured the same way only from the opposite side of the market. A put has intrinsic value when its strike price is *above* the current price of the underlying contract. For example, a $3.10 corn put would have a dime or $500.00 (5,000 bu. × .10) intrinsic value when corn is at $3.00 per bushel. It may have some time value as well. The longer the time left on an option, from as long as a year to as little as a day, the higher the time value usually is. Or, the more time left on an option, the greater the chances are of the option ending up in-the-money. At least that is the conventional wisdom.

This thinking breaks down somewhat with deep-out-of-the-money options. Each exchange has its own definition of what this type of option is, but the most common description is an option that is two strike prices out-of-the-money plus one more strike price for each month left to expiration. For example, corn call strike prices are a dime apart. If the current futures price is $3.00 and the strike prices for calls were $2.80, $2.90, $3.00, $3.10, $3.20—the $3.20 would be classified as deep-out-of-the-money for the nearby month. The time value—their only value—is usually low, unless the option has a decent amount of time left and there is a lot of price activity occurring.

The reason for this is twofold. First, it takes most markets awhile to move to a point where these distant strike prices begin to become attractive to speculators. Secondly, once the underlying market starts to get within range, the time value builds quickly.

With all this talk about intrinsic and extrinsic (time) value, you may be wondering how option prices are set. Options are traded at various exchanges throughout the world—stock options at stock exchanges and options-on-commodities at futures exchanges. This holds true until you get to some of the options on some of the financial futures contracts. Most are traded on the futures markets, even options on stock indexes, but some options on foreign currencies and stock indexes are traded at stock exchanges. You'll find a review of the exchanges and the option products they offer in the Appendix. Also keep in mind that new option contracts are always being added and unpopular ones are dropped. It's impossible to maintain a definitive listing.

The primary price discovery process utilized by exchanges is known as "open outcry." This is where floor traders in the trading pits (or rings) call out their bid or ask prices to all other floor traders in the pit. When a match is made, a trade is consummated. The "outcry" of orders has its roots in the early rules of the exchanges, going back to the eighteenth century in the United States. The rules required that all orders be shouted out so that any member would have the opportunity of filling the order. As the exchanges grew and became busier, a system of hand signals was developed to augment the oral tradition. The floor brokers record all their buys and sells, referencing the organizational badge of the person on the other side of the trade. All these "deals" are fed into the computer of the clearing firm which balances each day's trading.

Spotters, who work for the exchanges and are located on the perimeter of each pit, transmit via radio the stream of prices generated by the trading. This is the flow of price you see on cable television or price quotation systems. The futures exchanges capture the bid and ask prices, while stock exchanges only transmit fills or consummated sales. With futures prices, you will occasionally see on a screen the price you expected to get only to find out later your order was not filled. This occurs because of the procedure of transmitting both bid and ask prices. The extreme high volume of the futures markets makes this a necessity.

You, as an option trader, call your order to your broker. The broker relays the order to an order desk at the appropriate exchange. From here, it is signaled or a runner takes it to a floor trader in the proper pit. Once the floor trader fills it, the process is reversed. In high volume markets, your order could conceivably be completed and reported back to you in minutes. Slower markets (lower trading volume), particularly for strike prices out-of-the-money or options in the distant months, take longer. There are even occasions when an order cannot be filled.

The exchanges are continuously experimenting with technology to improve the speed and accuracy of options trading. For example, the futures exchanges are developing electronic order recorders to replace handwritten records. Another example would be GLOBEX, which might be characterized as a secondary price discovery process.

GLOBEX is an international electronic system for futures and options trading, which opens when the regular United States markets close. It is a joint venture of the Chicago Mercantile Exchange (CME) and the Chicago Board of Trade (CBOT). The Marche 'a' Terme International de France (MATIF), the French commodity exchange, also participates. The big four New York commodity exchanges, i.e., Coffee, Sugar and Cocoa Exchange, The Commodity Exchange, the New York Cotton Exchange, and the New York Futures Exchange, have agreed in principle to become active. Additionally, several other European and Asian exchanges are very interested.

Another major player in GLOBEX is Reuters Limited. It provides the hardware, software, computer know-how and operates the system. The control center is in Chicago.

The most obvious difference between GLOBEX and the regular exchanges is that orders are matched electronically, rather than via open outcry. It matches orders based first on price and second on time of entry, with orders at the same price being matched so that the order received first at the host computer is matched first.

Another big difference is that it is multinational and multiexchange. The laws controlling the trading activity are subject to the laws of the country of the exchange on which the option you are trading is listed. Therefore, if you're trading the 7-Year ECU interest rate option contract on the MATIF, your trade falls under the laws of France. Additionally, the rules and regulations of the listing exchange govern your rights and the trading rules.

Two other important considerations are liquidity and reliability. You always need to check liquidity. Can you get in and out when you wish? The same goes for reliability. The system has been a long time in development and has a lot of redundancy built into it—but it's not perfect. On July 26, 1992, for example, the system was shut down for a little less than two hours during the trading session to replace a "connector." It is our opinion that more and more trading will be done electronically in the years ahead. Some brokerage firms, for example, accept customer orders electronically already.

Stock vs. Futures Options

There are some important similarities and differences between stock options and options-on-futures contracts. First, both represent a standardized contract. For stocks, it is usually 100 shares of the underlying stock. An option on Exxon, for example, would be an option on 100 shares of that stock. With futures, the option is on one futures contract for that commodity. Any 90-day Treasury Bill option on the International Monetary Market (IMM) contains $1,000,000.00 in T-Bills. All the specifications—namely, quantity, quality, commodity, delivery place and delivery date—are uniform. Refer to the list of futures option specifications in the Appendix. All the traders (the buyers and sellers) need to agree on is price. It is this concept that gives all the exchanges the liquidity needed to be useful.

Another important concept is "settlement," which is the daily procedures for resolving accounts between members. You, as a customer of a brokerage firm, are represented at the exchanges by a member. Therefore, any trades you make must be settled at the end of the day. Once settled, which means your buy or sell tickets are matched with someone else's tickets, the clearing firm guarantees your position. The practice of making the clearing firm one side (buyer or seller) of every trade is what makes the exchanges so liquid. It relieves you of the responsibility for finding a buyer for your sell order and vice versa.

There are two basic methods of figuring account settlements. A stock-type settlement requires that the entity being purchased is completely resolved before profit or loss is experienced by the owner, or gains can be withdrawn from your account. For example, you purchase 100 shares of John Deere stock at $25.00 per share or $2,500.00. It goes up to $30.00 or an increase of $500.00. Later it retraces to $20.00 a share. Eventually, you sell it for $25.00. You broke even, not withstanding commission and fees.

When the stock gained $5.00, you could not take your profit, nor were you asked to make up the $5.00 loss when it sunk to $20.00. Profit or loss is not calculated until you sell the shares.

The futures-type settlement is substantially different. Futures are figured by what is known as daily mark-to-the-market and bought on margin. For example, you are long (it be-*longs* to you) one Chicago Board of Trade (CBOT) silver contract at $5.00 per ounce for 5,000 ounces or a total contract value of $25,000.00. To hold this contract, you have deposited $2,000.00 margin money. Margin is a goodwill deposit, not to be confused with a down payment. Then silver increases to $6.00 per ounce. Your account gets credited $5,000.00, which can immediately be withdrawn if you wish. Or, if silver decreased $5.00 per ounce or $5,000.00, you would have to add money.

Let's say the required margin was $2,000.00 for the silver contract. If the silver contract lost $5,000.00, it would wipe out the $2,000.00 in your account, plus your account would be on debit for an additional $3,000.00. If you wanted to continue to hold the silver position, you'd have to make up the $3,000.00 and add $2,000.00 for margin.

The point of this discussion is twofold. First, if you trade stocks and stock options you settle using the stock-type settlement procedure. If you are a buyer or seller (writer or grantor) of futures options, you settle based on the futures-type settlement procedure.

The sellers of futures options underwrite (or stand behind) the buyers of options. To insure performance, the exchanges require option sellers to maintain enough margin money in their accounts to be able to immediately accept the future position(s) they have sold. When you grant options (sell or write an option), you are told you can be assigned a stock or futures position at any time. If you write calls and the buyer exercises the option, the buyer is assigned a long position and you, the seller, are assigned the short or opposite side of the trade. Sellers in the futures must have enough margin money in their accounts to accept the assigned futures contract; stock sellers need enough money to buy the stock and some firms require 100%. When buyers of puts exercise their options, sellers of these traders are assigned long positions at the strike price of the option.

The term settlement also refers to the final, published price of the day for each stock or commodity contract traded. A committee at each exchange sets the settlement price. When trading volume is high, there can be more than one closing price. This occurs most often in the larger trading pits when a flurry of orders enters the pit just before the bell rings ending trading. A group of traders in one corner may agree on a price different from another group at the other side of the pit. These prices are usually very close, within pennies in most cases. The price settlement committee decides on which single price is most representative of the day's closing activity.

Option traders, as a rule, do not exercise their positions unless they are in-the-money, or at least at-the-money. This means the positions have intrinsic value. To the sellers (writers or grantors), it means someone will be assigned an equal, but opposite, position that is losing money—they are immediately at financial risk. They must stand behind these losing trade(s). Option writers usually react by offsetting these positions as soon as possible. We'll discuss this procedure more in the strategy chapter, which is next.

You may be wondering about the premium the sellers receive. When sellers grant options, the buyers pay the premiums to the sellers, via their brokerage firm. The brokerage firms, which are handling the trades, credit the seller's trading account for the premiums and debit it for the margin that underwrites the options, plus transaction costs (brokerage commissions and fees). If there is anything in excess (the premium is larger than the margin and transaction cost), the writer could withdraw if it is a futures transaction, since sellers of options-on-futures settle based on futures-type settlement procedures. Stock options are handled using the stock-type settlement.

Here's a simple example of a futures-type trade. Trader Jones analysis indicates soybeans will gain $2.00 per bushel over the next 90 days. Soybeans are currently trading at $5.00 per bushel. He buys a call at-of-the-money for $1,000.00. The $2.00 projected gain on a 5,000 bushel contract is $10,000.00. He is risking $1,000.00 to make $10,000.00 or a 1:10 risk-to-reward ratio.

Trader Smith doesn't see it that way. He believes soybeans will trade in a sideways pattern for the next 60 days. He decides to sell or underwrite Trader Jones' call. His account is credited the $1,000.00 premium and debited $850.00 in margin money, a brokerage commission of $45.00 and $5.00 in fees. He has $100.00 excess capital in his account which he withdraws, leaving $900.00 in his trading account.

The following table shows you what happens to the option's intrinsic value and the seller's account.

Soybean Prices	Seller's Account	Intrinsic Value of Option
4.50	900.00	0
4.75	900.00	0
5.00	900.00	0
5.20	- 100.00	1000.00
		(Breakeven Point)
5.25	- 350.00	1250.00
5.50	-1600.00	2500.00
5.75	-2850.00	3750.00
6.00	-4100.00	5000.00

If soybean prices go lower, the seller's premium is protected, but it doesn't gain in value. The maximum profit the seller can expect is the premium.

The buyer has unlimited profit potential, assuming the price of a commodity is unlimited, which of course is an unrealistic assumption. When prices become too high, substitutes are used or users reduce or halt processing the commodity. Nevertheless, soybeans have traded over $10.00 per bushel.

In the previous example, the buyer of the option has two alternatives. Once the option goes into-the-money, Trader Jones could exercise his option and assume a long position in the soybean futures market. At that time, he would have to put up margin money. His second option would be to offset his call. Besides the intrinsic value, there would be some time value depending on how much time was left before the option expired and the volatility of the market. To offset the call, Trader Jones sells a call (not to be confused with writing or granting a call) of the same strike price, same expiration month, same exchange—an equal, but opposite position.

As mentioned at the beginning of this chapter, terminology can be confusing. You offset a call you bought by selling a call. You offset a put you bought by selling a put. You don't offset a call by buying a put. Nor do you offset a put by buying a call. You can short puts or calls and buy them back to offset.

Buying Options

Position	Offsetting Position
Long call (bought a call)	Short call (sell a call)
Short call (sold a call)	Long call (bought a call)
Long put (bought a put)	Short put (sold a put)
Short put (sold a put)	Long put (bought a put)

Selling Options

Position	Offsetting Position
Sold (wrote, granted) a call	Short (Sell) Position in Futures or Stock Market
Sold (wrote, granted) a put	Long (Buy) Position in Futures or Stock Market

There are good reasons, or more correctly strategies, for being either a buyer or writer of options. For now, we need to finish our thoughts regarding the differences and similarities between stock options and options-on-futures. Then we can continue our discussion of terminology.

One of the big differences are the agents who are licensed to broker these two different investments. Brokers usually specialize in either stocks or commodities. There are some who are legally registered to broker both, but they are rare and usually prefer either stocks or futures. The burden of staying current with the enormous amount of information that could influence the direction of all these markets is staggering.

Additionally, the futures and the stock markets are considered by most professionals to be negatively correlated. This means they normally move in opposite directions. When the stock indexes move north, the commodity indexes head south. Being counter cyclical to each other increases the difficulty of trading both simultaneously because the timing of the trend changes is not exact.

There is some middle ground, for example the stock indexes. They are a compilation of groups of stocks. Some are traded on futures markets, while others are traded on stock exchanges. Some stock traders use them to hedge large stock portfolios, a concept we'll detail when we talk about strategies.

There is another very distinct difference between the stock and commodities markets that illustrates just how useful and versatile the options markets really are. There is no futures market for stocks, just options. Some professional stock options traders can't understand why commodities have a futures market now that options-on-futures can be traded. These savvy traders expected the options-on-futures market to totally engulf the futures markets.

Think about it for a moment. Stock options are options on the "cash" or "spot" market for stocks. You buy an option directly on the stock. The option gives you the right to assume a position in the stock market for x-number of shares.

This line of thought provokes these professional traders to ask why not just buy and sell options on cash commodities? The futures market to them seems redundant. An option-on-futures is an option on a contract that is a contract on the cash commodity. Additionally, they reason, options are just as versatile as the futures market with added advantage of predefined risk. They may be right in their assessment in the long run, but for now there is a strong futures market in commodities that you need to become familiar with in order to trade its options.

The markets for options in stocks, futures and indexes are so complex they are beyond the scope of most individuals from an analytical and research point-of-view. For example, the futures markets include the grains, meats, metals, petroleums, food, fiber, debt instruments, financials, and foreign currency complexes. The thousands of stocks available can be grouped by such major categories, such as pharmaceuticals, automobile, steel, retail, manufacturing, etc. We believe you must understand and track the markets you trade to be successful. Therefore, you must narrow your scope and develop a relationship with a broker with similar interest and experience.

Option trading is a specialty within itself. You'll learn, as you study this book, that you shouldn't expect just any broker to supply the special expertise option trading requires. We've seen brokers who refused to trade options because they lack a thorough understanding of them.

Another one of the differences between stock and futures options illustrates the above point. Stock options are basically the same from one stock exchange to the next. Futures options can vary between exchanges. Basically, we're talking about changes in the specifications of the underlying futures contract. For example, the MidAmerica Exchange trades contracts that are approximately half the size of the ones on the other futures exchanges. This may be an exchange to consider when you first start out because of the small size of their contracts—less size, less risk.

Now let's get back to some important terminology you should know to understand the material in the chapters ahead. What if you walked in on the following discussion of strategy between your broker and his manager, as they reviewed your options positions:

"Don't you think you're too long delta? Didn't you want to be delta neutral?"

"I'm just trying to maintain a long gamma. That's what has caused the long delta."

"Your problem is you're trading on price, not volatility, particularly with those out-of-the-money options."

"Okay, okay, I'll get delta neutral at the open. I just hope it doesn't mess up the kappa!"

Does any of this remind you of Abbott and Costello's conversation?

An option's delta factor provides an insight into the relationship between the option and its underlying entity. The delta measures how fast the price of an option changes compared to its underlying stock or futures contract. If a stock price increases or decreases $10.00 per share or a commodity futures price moves 10 cents per unit, how much does the price of the option change?

Deltas for calls range between 0 and 1 and are usually converted to percentages. For example, a delta of 25 or 25% means that the price of a call will move one-fourth as much as the price of the underlying entity. In our example above, if a stock gained $10.00 a share, the option on that stock with a delta of 25 will increase $2.50. The same would be true for an options-on-futures. If the futures price increases 10 cents, the call's premium gains by 2½ cents. If prices decreased, the premium of the calls would decrease at the same speed.

Puts—options to take a short position in the underlying entity—react similarly, except they move in the opposite direction of the underlying entity. As stocks or futures contracts gain, puts move further out-of-the-money. Therefore, they lose value as the underlying entity gains. For this reason, their deltas range from 0 to minus one (-1) or 0 to minus 100% (-100%). If you were holding a put on the stock described above and it gained $10.00, the put with a -25% delta loses $2.50. But if the stock lost $10.00, the put increases $2.50.

In everyday trading situations, most traders don't think in terms of positive or negative deltas. (The exception is when you're hedging calls against puts or vice versa, as we'll get to shortly.) They just calculate the delta and keep themselves aware of where the option is (in, at, or out-of-the-money). They then know a positive move in the underlying entity increases the premium on calls and decreases the premium for puts. A decrease in the value of the underlying entity does the opposite.

The delta factor is calculated by working backwards from market activity. You divide the amount of price difference of your option by the amount of price difference in the underlying entity. For example, if the premium of your option increases a nickel per bushel or $5.00 per share, when the futures price increases a dime or the per share price gains $10.00, you'd have a delta of 50 or 50% ($0.05 divided by .10 or $5.00 divided by $10.00 = 50%). Since the price of the underlying entity is constantly changing, so is the delta factor.

Since much of the premium value of an option depends on whether it has intrinsic value or how close it is to having intrinsic value, the delta of typical options at-the-money will be about 50%. In-the-money options, since they can be immediately exercised for the underlying entity, have deltas at or approaching 100%. Deltas never exceed 100% because they cannot be more valuable than the underlying entity. Options that are out or deep out-of-the-money have deltas from 50% to zero. These options have nothing of value but time.

One small point needs clarification. When we use the term option, we are referring to American style options. These options can be exercised at any time prior to expiration. There are also European style options; these can only be exercised at specific, predetermined periods of time. This may be as little as one or two days prior to expiration. The buyers or holders of a European style option can't exercise them when they get in-the-money or whenever they feel like it. For example, the foreign currency options on the Philadelphia Stock Exchange are of the European style. We do not recommend European type options for novice traders. There is a bountiful selection without them and their restrictions. Just make sure your broker knows you are not interested in any European style options.

The delta factor is naturally influenced by everything that influences the value of an option. Specifically, this is the time to expiration, the price volatility of the underlying entity, interest rates (particularly for options on stocks), and any seasonal factors. But most of all, it is the relationship between the strike price and the current market for the underlying entity that counts.

With all this in mind, it is not surprising that many option traders use the delta factor as a screening tool when selecting which option to purchase. For example, you're considering buying a soybean call. You think between now and the middle of February bean futures will increase by $2.00 per bushel.

When you calculate the delta factor of the two options you are considering, the first one is .50 and the second one is .60. This means that if your price projection of $2.00 is correct, the value of the first option will increase by $1.00 and the second by $1.20. If the second option costs only 10 cents per bushel more, it is probably a better bargain—all other factors being equal—than the less expensive option.

Always keep in mind that delta factors are not stable. They change whenever the price of the option premium and the underlying futures change, which is constantly. But these prices usually move in tandem, except when the option approaches expiration causing its time value to decay rapidly.

There is at least one additional use for the delta factor. Occasionally you may want to hedge an options position against its underlying futures contract or hedge call options against put options. We'll go into more detail on strategies behind these trades later, but now we'll cover how the delta defines the hedge ratio.

First, let's define hedging. Hedging is the practice of offsetting the price risk inherent in any cash market (stocks, physical commodities, or financials) by taking an equal but opposite position in the futures or options markets. The objective is to protect yourself from adverse price movement.

Here are two quick examples. We'll go into more detail when we discuss trading strategies. You own 1,000 shares of IBM stock. Your analysis indicates that it is due for a 20% price retracement. You don't want to sell the stock and buy it back at the "low," but you still want some price protection. You purchase an at or in-the-money put. Then you ride the put down when the stock price falls and offset them at or near the low. You then use the profits from this transaction to help compensate for the paper loss sustained by continuing to hold the stock.

In another example, you use copper or silver in your company's manufacturing process. Therefore, you are following the market very closely. You see a substantial rally ahead over the next six months. You buy enough calls to satisfy your production needs with the idea of exercising these calls for long positions in the futures markets as you need the copper or silver. You can even take physical delivery on the futures positions, if you wished. Or, you can offset the options as prices rise and then buy your needs in the spot (cash) markets, using the profits from the option to compensate for any increases in the cash prices.

The hedger is neutral—long in futures, short in cash or short in futures, long in cash. By being on both sides of the market, the hedger freezes the price. The cost involved amounts to the transaction costs (commissions and fees) that must be paid to do the hedging. Some business executives think of hedging as price insurance.

When you use futures to hedge, you match quantity to contract because futures have a delta of 100%. If your objective is to hedge 40,000 pounds of live hogs, you use one futures contract.

When you hedge with options, you have a different situation. Calculating the delta solves it. Your objective is to stay balanced or hedged neutral. This insures you have dollar for dollar protection. If the futures contract gains or loses, the delta of the option changes. Therefore, the delta tells you the proper ratio to maintain between the two to be neutral. If an at-the-money call has a delta of 50%, the hedge ratio is 2:1. To hedge the 40,000 pounds of live hogs, you would buy two option contracts as opposed to one futures.

This procedure also works for call versus put hedges. Here you want to match the call deltas (positive numbers) with the put deltas (negative numbers) and arrive at zero. For example, suppose you buy three calls with deltas of 40 each or 120 (40 × 3 = 120). To hedge with puts that have a delta of 60, you'd need to buy two (60 × 2 = 120). The strike (exercise) prices and the expirations can vary, but the deltas must add up to zero to be delta or hedge neutral.

The delta factor can also be used to create a theoretical futures position. Futures positions have a delta of 100. If you wanted to get the same price action out of an option with a delta of 20 as you do from a futures, how many do you buy? The answer, of course, is five (100 divided by 20).

One key concept you must always be alert to is that deltas cannot be calculated once or twice during the life of a contract. Once or twice a week, or even daily, may not be sufficient in very volatile markets. Whenever the price of the underlying entity changes, so will the delta. Now, small fluctuations won't seriously affect your hedge ratio, but large ones will. Some traders even plot three-, four-, or five-day moving averages of delta, using each day's settlement price.

Get in the habit of figuring deltas regularly. Plot them on graph paper. Study them to uncover patterns. It's an excellent way of getting a feel for the relationship between an option and its underlying entity.

Building on your understanding of the delta, there are a few other terms related to the delta factors you should be aware of as an option trader. The rate at which the delta changes (gains or loses) is known as the gamma. It is calculated in delta points. For example, if an option has a gamma of 10, for each point increase in the price of the underlying entity, the option's delta gains 10 points. If an option initially has a delta of 25 and the underlying entity gains a point, the delta moves to 35. The value of knowing the gamma is that it will alert you to which options are most volatile. High gammas mean high opportunity—but also high risk. When trading for the first time, we suggest you avoid high gamma options because of the risk involved.

As mentioned earlier, options are wasting assets (Figure 1.2). Eventually all expire worthless. As time runs out, the less attractive they become because their usefulness evaporates. Think of them as a hundred weight of ice in a cooler. The longer it sits, the more it melts. The more it melts, the less it cools. At some point, it is reduced to a puddle of water at room temperature. Then the water evaporates. Nothing is left. That's the life cycle of an option. The beta is the rate at which an option loses its time value. This rate increases as the expiration date approaches.

Options prices are very sensitive to the volatility of the price movement of the underlying entity (stock or futures contract). This is such an important consideration that one of the upcoming chapters is devoted to it. But for now, we simply want to discuss the term used to describe the relationship between changes in

Figure 1.2 Options as Wasting Asset

Options are wasting assets, because they eventually expire. Their time value continually deteriorates as they move toward their expiration date. To make money or conserve losses, you must offset or exercise options before they expire.

volatility of the underlying entity and the price of the option. For whatever reason, the investment industry has not settled on a single name. It has been called kappa, omega, signa prime, vega, or zeta. In this text, we'll refer to it as vega, which seems to be the term accepted by most computer programs that calculate the theoretical price of options.

We touched on carrying costs for futures and stocks earlier. One of the most important of these is interest rates, more so for stocks than futures contracts. An increase in interest rates decreases the price (value) of an option because of increased carrying costs. The term "rho" is used to describe the sensitivity of an options price to interest rates. It is always a negative number. When you begin to run theoretical options prices on some computer programs, you'll be asked for the interest rate. It will be used to calculate the rho as part of the equation.

One simple concept to understand, but a very key one, is market liquidity. Liquid markets are actively traded markets where there is a lot of buying and selling taking place. They are characterized by small price changes or where bid and ask prices are in narrow ranges. The opposite of liquid markets are illiquid ones. The danger with illiquid markets is that your order may not be filled or you'll get a bad fill.

Not getting an order filled can mean missing an opportunity or not being able to exit a market at a profitable position. A bad fill is simply a price worse than you expected. For example, you want to buy a call. You place an order to buy a call at the market when it is trading between 10 and 15. You get filled at 15 or 16, the high for the day. A better fill for a call would have been around the low of the day or 10. If each point is worth $100.00 in this particular market, the difference between 10 and 16 would be $600.00.

You find out about liquidity by checking the daily volume for each market you trade. It is published in financial newspapers, announced on cable television programs, or over electronic price quotation services. Your broker should have access to all three. Daily volume can range from less than 100 to well over 100,000.

You should always discuss liquidity with your broker before placing an order. Be sure to check the volume of the specific strike price you are considering. Strike prices at or in-the-money normally have high daily volumes, much higher than out-of-the-money strike prices. Deep-out-of-the-money options can have little or no volume on any given day.

Exchange rules come into play with liquidity. Some exchanges have a "not held" rule. This means the floor traders are not held responsible for filling every order. In active markets for stocks and futures, any order that's "at-the-market" gets filled. If nothing else, a broker or brokerage firm, designated as a market maker will take an order that is having problems finding a home. But with some of the illiquid options markets, the exchanges protect their floor brokers from having to take a sure loss. This means you could place an option order only to have it come back "unable," even if the bid-ask price is at or around your price.

This normally would not happen if you were trading stocks or futures. You could get an unable ("unable to fill or execute") in these markets, but only if your price was out of the trading range. If you placed an order, for example, to go long cotton at 60 cents a pound or better when it was trading at 50 cents, no one would fill your order because cotton has a 2-cent daily trading range. It cannot run up 10 cents to pick off your order. The market is out of range at this point and the order would be returned as "unable." Option orders can also be returned from the trading pits as unable if a buyer or seller cannot be found.

In the futures markets, there can be limit up and limit down days. These are trading sessions when a particular futures contract is trading beyond the daily limit permitted by its exchange. For example, the daily limit for the Chicago Mercantile Exchange's (CME) live hog contracts is $0.015 or $600.00 (40,000 pounds × $0.015) or 150 points. This means if the contract is bid up $600.00 in a single trading session, trading will be halted. For the record, the hog contract has traded limit up for as many as six days consecutively. This is one of the serious risks faced by futures traders.

When limit up days occur, option prices move wildly because of the high volatility. A put option which is in-the-money by a penny ($400.00) or two ($800.00), quickly loses all intrinsic value. The time value decreases as well because the trend is so violently in the opposite direction. As you can guess, all the in-the-money calls gain value as fast or faster than the puts lose. Competition for calls becomes fierce, moving them into the oversold category.

Since we mentioned market orders and "or better" orders, there are a few other general ones you should be aware of as long as we are discussing terminology. Specific types of orders are used by your broker to accomplish your trading objectives. You don't necessarily need to know each type, but being aware of them helps you plan your strategies. Most traders explain what they want to accomplish with a trade and have their broker decide on the proper order. But you need to know all your alternatives to intelligently plan your trades.

There are basically two types of orders. Those that have no restrictions on them and those that do. Market orders have no restrictions. When floor brokers receive market orders, they immediately execute them. In fast moving markets, you could call a market order to your broker who would relay it to the order desk on the exchange trading floor. Your broker could get your fill back so fast, you could conceivably be still on the line with him.

Speed is the advantage of using market orders. Floor brokers give them the highest priority. You're virtually assured, barring limit up or down days, of being filled.

The disadvantage of market orders is that there is usually no time to stop or change them. Once in the pits, they'll get filled. For example, you're trying to buy a call priced at four cents or $4.00 per unit (bushel, barrel, hundredweight, share, etc.). Your fill comes back at six cents. The two-cent difference occurs due to the speed at which the market is moving. A two-cent difference or a nickel or whatever can sometimes mean the difference between a winning trade and a loser.

The second type of order has some time or price restriction attached to it. Limitations can be attached to the time the order can be executed or the price. For example, there are orders that can only be executed at the opening (Market-on-

Open or MOO) or closing (Market-on-Close or MOC) of a trading session. Each exchange established a specific opening (first 15 minutes) and closing (last 5 minutes) period. Certain orders must be filled right away (Fill or Kill) or canceled. Others are good for various periods of time (Good Till Canceled, Day Orders, Good Through/Time Date).

There are a variety of orders which include some type of price limitation. We've already alluded to the "or better" type order where the floor broker is obliged to meet or beat the price you specify. Then there are stop orders. A stop is a limit, but once reached the order becomes a market order. A Market-if-Touched (MIT) works about the same way as a stop order. Your order is executed if a certain price is touched, but the price you receive doesn't have to be better than the touched price.

The advantage of price limitation is that it prevents your order from being activated until certain conditions are met. Traders often use them in conjunction with their trading system or the forecast of what the market they are trading is expected to do. Or they use them to get a certain price. Much of this type of thinking will become clearer when we discuss price trend forecasting, trading systems, and strategies in the chapters ahead.

The big disadvantage of placing limitations on your orders is that they may not be filled. An "or better" order sounds good, except when you miss a profitable opportunity because the floor broker could not execute it.

The last type of order we are going to cover is the discretionary. You can relinquish the trading discretion in your account to your broker. This can be unlimited, in the case where you sign a limited power-of-attorney for your broker to trade on your behalf, or it can be limited. Limited discretion gives the broker the right to enter a trade in the market based on your prior approval of certain time or price considerations. For example, you discuss your current position with your broker in the evening. You will be traveling the next day and will be out of touch. You decide that you want your position closed out if the market opens higher (or lower or reaches a certain price). The broker only has discretion to make this trade on your behalf. When you give price discretion, it is usually best to place some upper and lower limits on the discretion.

This is by no means an exhaustive discussion of orders. Its purpose is only to make you aware of the alternatives you have to placing a simple market order when buying or selling puts or calls.

When you first consider trading options, be prepared for what we call "options shock." It is sort of like futures shock in that you initially may feel overwhelmed. For example, if your investment background is commodities, you're generally familiar with 40 or so actively traded commodities. There are four to twelve contract months for each and you can go long, short, or spread them.

Let's take something simple, like corn, as an example. It has five delivery month contracts (March, May, July, September, and December). Trading it long or short gives you two other choices for a total of 10. With options, you additionally have to select from at least six strike prices, each with both puts and calls available. Then you can be a buyer or a seller.

Stock traders face a similar maze. There are thousands of stocks with options to choose from, multiple strike prices, and puts and calls for each. Experienced stock traders additionally need to become comfortable trading down trending markets utilizing puts or selling calls.

If this all weren't confusing enough, there are options to consider besides the classic option-on-futures or option on 100 shares of over 7,000 stocks. There are index options of all sorts, including the following:

S & P 500 or 100
Utility Stock Index
Japanese Stock Index
OEX
Value Line Composite Index
Gold & Silver Index
Computer Technology Index
Institutional Index
Major Market Index
Oil Index
National Over-the-Counter Index
Commodity Research Bureau Index
Goldman Sachs Commodity Index

In addition, there are foreign currency options from around the world—Australian dollar, British pound, Canadian dollar, German deutschemark, French franc, Japanese yen, Swiss franc, European Currency Unit. The currencies can be either European or American style, depending on which exchange you trade. Plus they can be full or half-size contracts, again depending on exchange. If this not enough of a selection, the currencies also offer cross-rate options, like German deutschemark-Japanese yen cross.

How long an option do you want to trade? You can trade *Long-Term Equity AnticiPation Securities* (LEAPS) on individual stocks. These give you buying or selling rights on the underlying security for up to two years. Or, you can trade five-day options in the precious metals.

Additionally, you must keep tabs on the day your options expire. There are no uniform methods among the futures exchanges for assigning expiration dates. Some expire on Thursday, others on Friday or Saturday. Most expire four to six weeks prior to the delivery date of their underlying futures contract. Most stock options expire on the Saturday following the third Friday of the expiration date and are set up on a quarterly cycle. Always check with your broker.

Also, make sure your broker knows the rules of the exchange you'll be trading on regarding the expiration of an in-the-money option. On some exchanges if an option expires in-the-money, any floor broker can exercise either side. You could unexpectedly be given a losing trade. Keep your broker on his toes.

Our point is that there is an extraordinary number of options and option combinations to evaluate. For new traders, we recommend trading options-on-futures over an intermediate period of time, for example from 30 to 60 days.

The rationale for this suggestion is that these option markets are liquid and reasonably easy to understand. Further, we ask new traders to seriously consider some of the options traded on the MidAmerica Exchange because they are options on half-size contracts. It often pays to learn to walk before you try to run.

Chapter 2

Learning the Basic Option Trading Strategies (and Uses) to Solidify Objectives

"The happiest time in any man's life is when he is in red-hot pursuit of a dollar with a reasonable prospect of overtaking it."

Jack Billings (1818-1885)
American Humorist

Key Concepts

◆ Power of Leveraging

◆ Law of Probability and Three Rights

◆ Distribution of Winning and Losing Trades

◆ Four Ways to Approach the Market

◆ Twelve Trading Strategies

◆ Writing Puts and Calls

◆ Hedging with Options

Normally a discussion of strategies comes at the end of a book of this nature. We have chosen a more prominent position because we want you to be thinking about your strategies and objectives as you study the remainder of the text. Our expectation is that if you have a good idea of what you want to gain from options trading, all the information that follows will be more meaningful.

In the title of this chapter, we have included the words "strategies" and "uses." These two concepts blend or cross over where options are concerned because options are so versatile. They come in all sizes, shapes, and colors. Some are built for speed; others for dependability and smooth sailing. Still others are very crafty, putting the odds in your favor. Which suits you?

There are basically two types of options traders, namely, speculators and hedgers. The specs are risk takers, while the hedgers wish to transfer risk to someone else. The objective of the speculators ("specs") is to generate profits. Hedgers want to preserve the status quo. We'll probe the role of speculators first, since this is what most traders are. Then we'll tackle the hedging because it can have a dramatic impact on the specs. Some investors who speculate in one market, such as stocks, can manage or hedge that risk in another one, such as the options market.

All speculators are not created equal, but all have the same goal (profits) even though their strategies vary widely. Also, the complexion of the market can strongly influence or change your approach. You must be more flexible than the markets you trade to win.

As you develop your strategies, keep two things in mind—the Power of Leveraging and the Law of Probability. Leveraging allows you to control a large amount of a commodity, or a large number of shares of a stock, with a small amount of capital. For example, let's say corn is trading at $2.10 per bushel and the $2.10 strike price call is trading for $0.055 (5½¢). The contract has six weeks to expiration. You would have control of $10,500.00 worth of corn with an option that costs $275.00 plus $50.00 in commissions and fees for a total of $325.00. Your leveraging ratio would be 32 to 1 ($10,500/$325). A similar situation in the stock market would be the purchase of an AT&T $40.00 per share call at 1⅞ ($1.875) or $187.50 (100 shares × $1.875), plus $40.00 transaction costs. If the stock is at 41¼ or $41.25 per share at the time, the total value of 100 shares would be $4,125.00. Divide this by the total invested giving you a ratio of approximately 18:1 ($4,125.00/$227.50).

Now, what does leveraging do for you? It gives you the opportunity to make a high return percentagewise on your investment. Take the corn example. When corn gains a dime, the total value of the contract increases $500.00. Your $2.10 options is at-the-money. Therefore, its intrinsic value would increase by an equal amount or a 65% return. Additionally, there could be some increase in the time value, depending on how much left to expiration.

You would have a similar situation with the stock option. It's for 100 shares. Therefore, every $1.00 gain per share increases the value of the in-the-money option by at least $100.00 of intrinsic value. A gain of $4.00 per share doubles your investment.

Also, remember we are talking about relatively short periods of time. These options had only six weeks to expiration. There are few investment opportunities that offer the potential of doubling your money in a matter of weeks or months. To make the gains meaningful from a dollar standpoint, serious options investors trade multiple lots of contracts. This would be 10, 20, 50, or 100 options (lots) at a time.

Before you call your broker to make one of these "piece of cake" trades, you need to think it through. The sellers of these options, in the trading pits and all over the world, are not dumb. When you buy a put or a call, someone has to sell it to you (underwrites it). That person expects your option to expire worthless so he or she can keep the premium. To put it more bluntly, the option seller wants you to lose 100% of your investment. Writing (selling or granting) options entails more risk than buying options. The seller can be assigned the opposite side of the buyer's option position any time the buyer decides to exercise it. It would probably only be done when it was in-the-money, which means the seller would be losing money as soon as the buyer acted. The loss could be substantial. Think what would happen to a seller in the futures market who has been assigned a position that is making daily limit moves against him. For hogs on the CBOT, it would be $600.00 per day per contract. After a day or two of limit moves, the daily limit—or the maximum a contract can trade in a single trading session— might be extended to $700.00 or $800.00. Some markets, like the foreign currencies, have no daily limits. It is because of this possibility that the downside risk of selling options is considered unlimited. The upside or profit is limited to the amount of the premium, less transaction costs. Why would anyone enter an investment where the profit potential is limited and the risk of loss is unlimited? This will be covered when we discuss selling options as a strategy. You'll also learn why you may have a better chance of making money in the long run selling than buying options.

Since selling options can be a profit strategy, it insinuates that buying options must be risky. It isn't a "piece of cake." The risk may be limited to your initial investment, but all of this can be lost. This line of thought brings us to the Law of Probability. The strategy you select will have a greater probability of succeeding if it is diversified. This means trading options on a variety of commodity markets or stocks. To be a successful trader, you must be in the right market, at the right time, and on the right side (put or call). You are investing in what you expect to happen in the future—five days, five weeks, or five months from the moment you call your broker and place your order. You have no way of knowing if you will be right or wrong until afterwards.

At the same time, you must protect your risk capital as carefully as possible. This requires sound money management techniques, which is the second part of the Law of Probability. A sure way of ending a trading career abruptly is putting all your risk capital on one or two trades. A "double or nothing" approach to the markets will invariably, in our opinion, lead to you ending up with nothing.

Just as you increase the probability of being in the right market at the right time on the right side by trading several different markets, you'll increase your probability of success by putting no more than 10% of your risk capital on any one trade. This gives you at least 10 opportunities to select one or more trades to pay for the ones that lose or just break even.

You must further consider what is known as the "distribution of wining-losing trades." For example, your distribution might look like this:

Trade Distribution:
   10 trades executed
   5 winners
   5 losers
Of the five winners:
   3 small or break even
   1 modest size
   1 big or decent size
Of the 5 losers:
   4 small
   1 modest

Your objective is to let winners run and cut losers short. If you do an analysis of the trading performance of the most successful CTAs (professional commodity trading advisors), you rarely find a winning percentage higher than 60 percent.

Keep in mind, the prime objective is to make money, not to generate a high percentage of profitable trades. You can be a net winner with a low percentage of winning trades. By low, we mean 40 percent, 30 percent or even 20 percent.

To do this, you must be very disciplined. You develop, for example, strict rules for exiting losing trades (these are detailed later). For example, when a trade

Figure 2.1 Breakeven Analysis (call)

Buying an At-the-Money Call in Futures Market

Assumptions:

Traders outlook is bullish for gold.
COMEX $400.00 call priced at $12.00 per ounce.
Commissions and fees amount to $75.00.

Premium ($12.00 × 100 oz.) $1,200.00
Commissions and Fees   75.00
Total Investment $1,275.00

Breakeven—Gold must increase $12.75 per ounce.

Note: **Analysis does not take time value into consideration, since it is virtually impossible to calculate with any exactitude.**

begins to make money, you place a trailing stop behind it (below a long position or above a short). Eventually this stop position is taken out, offsetting your position. In other words, the market decides for you when to close a position.

As you develop your personal trading strategy, you need to keep all this in mind. Trading several markets takes more time than just one. As does updating a system that is tracking a number of alternative commodities or stocks. On the one hand, you need to be diversified. Equally important is to avoid becoming over extended financially, psychologically, or personally.

Overview of Strategies

We'll begin with a general discussion of option trading strategies and then move to an explanation of specific ones. There will be no attempt to provide a definitive discussion of every possible strategy. But we will explain most of the common ones appropriate for a novice options investor.

There are four basic ways to approach the option markets. First, you can analyze the market you wish to trade and forecast the trend. Or you can use a system that mechanically alerts you to options that are over or under priced. Thirdly, you can be a writer or grantor of options and underwrite the buyers. Last of all, you can use a combination of the three approaches just mentioned. Now, let's discuss each of these approaches.

As a market analyst, you can use fundamental or technical analysis to decide where the market is headed. Fundamental analysis is the study of all the underlying factors that affect the supply-demand equation for a stock or commodity, and thus the price. Technical analysis disregards all fundamental factors. It relies on the study of price action, rates of change in price, volume, or open interest. Prices are often charted and the patterns analyzed. Or it could be computerized, and numerous studies run with the hope of discovering reoccurring patterns. These two alternatives will be discussed in detail in later chapters.

Once you arrive at an opinion of the direction of the trend of a market, you must quantify it. Are you mildly or aggressively bullish or bearish? Are you neutral—do you think the market will trend sideways?

Your second possibility is to adopt some type of mechanical trading system. The most common of these are computer programs (see appendix for listing and descriptions) that evaluate options using a theoretical pricing model. You calculate the price of an option using the amount of time to expiration, market volatility, carrying costs, and current price of the underlying entity (stock or futures contract). Then you compare this theoretical price with the actual market price. This tells you if the option is over or under priced. You then buy or sell a call or a put depending on the analysis. We'll talk in more detail about how this all is calculated in the chapter on volatility.

The third approach is to be a writer of options. Here you have limited profit potential and substantial risk. Again, you have some choices, such as whether you sell covered or uncovered options. Underwriting options is an approach that is rarely recommended to new traders, but it can have an appeal to experienced investors—even if they are new to options.

Lastly, it is common to create trading strategies which utilize a combination of the four basic methods. You can, for example, use the premium you receive for writing an option to buy one. This is sometimes called a "free" trade, since you don't have to pay directly for the option you buy.

Specific Trading Strategies

Now, let's talk turkey. We'll begin with "Raging Bull Strategies." You think the market is grossly oversold—poised for a major move higher.

Let's use silver as an example. It has been trading below $5.00 an ounce for almost two years and under $4.00 for the last 12 months. Your analysis indicates that it is about to make a move from the $3.50 level to over $5.50. Your best estimate calls for $6.00 silver within the next 60 days.

The simplest and most common approach for a new investor is to buy a call. The call gives you the right, but not the obligation, to take a long position in the underlying futures. As the underlying futures gains, so does the call. You can either exercise the option and take your long futures position, or you can offset your option positions at a profit as it gains intrinsic value.

The more difficult question is which strike price to buy. Here are your choices for calls with 60 days to expiration on 5,000 troy ounces of silver:

Call-Strike Prices		Price/Ounce
$3.00	55 cents	In-the-money by 50 cents
$3.25	30 cents	In-the-money by 25 cents
$3.50	5 cents	At-the-Money(current silver price)
$3.75	3 cents	Out-of-the-money by 25 cents
$4.00	1 cents	Out-of-the-money by 50 cents

The $3.00 strike price option has 50 cents intrinsic value and 5 cents time value. The $3.25 strike price is a quarter in-the-market with a nickel time value. The at-the-market option has no intrinsic value and 5 cents time value. The two out-of-the-money options only have time value. The farther out-of-the-money, the less time value.

Studying these values indicates the market doesn't agree with your analysis. Sellers of out-of-the-money options are making them very attractive. A $4.00 call carries a $50.00 premium (5,000 oz. × $0.01).

The at-the-money strike price is very reasonable, if your analysis proves to be anywhere near accurate. At 5 cents per ounce, the call costs $250.00 plus transaction costs of, let's say $50.00, for a total of $300.00. A $2.00 per ounce gain in silver would amount to $10,000.00. The ratio of profit to loss would be 33 to 1.

Another way of looking at this trade would be to calculate the breakeven. How much does silver have to gain just to get your $300.00 back? Each penny gained adds $50.00 to the intrinsic value of the at-the-money option. Therefore, all that is needed is no more than six cents and maybe a little less, if the time value increases as well.

A put works the same way but in the opposite direction. We call it the "Doomsdayer's Strategy." You think, for example, the shares of ABC Company, now at $50.00, are headed south in a big way, maybe even as much as 50%. Checking the paper, or calling your broker, provides the following prices:

Put Strike Prices		Price/Share
$40.00	3/4	Out-of-the-money by $10.00
$45.00	1	Out-of-the-money by $5.00
$50.00	1 1/8	At-the-money (current share price)
$55.00	7	In-the-money by $5.00
$60.00	10	In-the-money by $10.00

Again, the market isn't bracing for a major slide in the price of ABC's stock. It is only asking $75.00 (100 shares × $0.75) for an option with a strike price of $10.00 out-of-the-money and $100.00 for one $5.00 out.

The breakeven for the at-the-money option would be a decrease in the per share price by approximately $1.00 plus 1/8 in time value, or about $1.50 to include transaction costs. The reward to risk ratio, if the shares do drop $25.00 per share before the at-the-money option expires, would be approximately 16 to 1 ($2,500.00/150). See Figure 2.2.

We call these two strategies the "Raging Bull" and "Doomsdayer" because that is the way they are often presented to investors. For these strategies to work, you need a major price move, which is rare. Additionally, you really have only one opportunity to profit and that is if your analysis is absolutely correct. Experience has shown that the odds of this happening consistently are remote.

One of the most expensive errors people new to options make is getting caught up with the excitement a broker may create regarding a trade. "Silver is headed off the charts! Get in now! What can you lose?" The answer is 100% of your investment.

This trading strategy requires you to hit home runs each time at bat. If they pay off big, they are grand slammers! It is for this reason, in our opinion, most option traders, particularly new and/or small traders, are net losers as options traders. There are occasions when you should swing for the fence, but most of the time you should try a strategy with a higher percentage success rate. Unfortunately, most stock and futures options traders never get beyond this point in the learning curve.

Base Hits

Attempting to get walks, singles, or doubles consistently is a much higher percentage play—consider the spread trade. Spreading simply means trading both the long and short sides of a market at the same time. The spreader attempts to make a profit by anticipating the amount of change in the price movement between

Figure 2.2 Breakeven Analysis (put)

Buying an At-the-Money Put in Stock Market

Assumption:

Trader's Outlook is bearish for stock.
ABC's stock's $50.00 per share puts are priced at $4.00 per share.
Commission and fees amount to $50.00.

Premium ($4.00 × 100 shares) $400.00
Commission and Fees   50.00
Total Investment $450.00

Breakeven—ABC stock must decrease $4.50 per share.

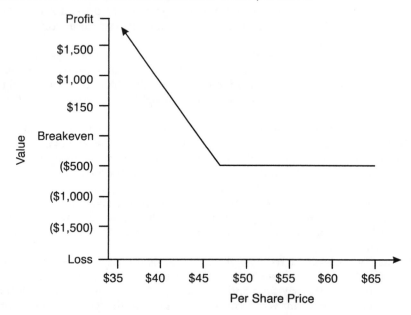

options. The price differential between the two markets is the spread, thus the name.

There are various types of spreads. They can be described by market (exchange), commodity, or delivery month. You can trade "inter" or "intra" types of spreads or combinations of the two. Inter means between two different entities; intra means within the same entity. See Figure 2.3.

Volatility Spreads

Volatility spreads are one of the simplest and most useful options spreads to learn and use. The spread trader buys a put and a call at the same strike price. For example, let's say corn is trading at $2.52 per bushel. You buy a put and a call at a strike price near or in-the-money at $2.50, for example.

You do this with the expectation the corn prices will become more volatile. For example, this situation can occur at the time of the release of an important crop report, such as "Farmer Planting Intentions." You may not be sure if the report will be bearish or bullish, but you expect it to cause a lot of excitement—therefore, price volatility!

This situation can occur in the stock market, when there is news of a take-over, new product introduction, or major stock split. If this happens, the premium value of both your options could increase. Or, if the market takes off north (bullish), your call becomes more valuable. If it goes south, your put premium goes into the money. Your net position should improve one way or the other.

If the impact of the news is already in the market with prices and volatility unchanged, you lose. You must then decide whether to hold your spread in hopes of future volatility or take your loss. A little added advantage of this spread is that the premium is usually lower than the sum of the premium costs of both a put and a call purchased separately. A put/call spread purchased at the same time at the same strike price is called a special double, and it will be discussed as a separate strategy later.

Time Options

Another popular option spread is the time spread. It involves options with the same strike price but different expiration dates. The prime objective of a time spread is to take advantage of the tendency of the time value of an option to decline at a very rapid rate before finally disappearing just prior to expiration. Typically, a put or call with a nearer expiration date is sold (written), while a put or call with an expiration date that is more distant is purchased. The option sold and the option bought both have the same strike price.

The intent is to sell time. The more distant put or call loses its time value at a slower rate, which limits the risk of such a position by removing the potential for unlimited loss on sharp upside moves.

Figure 2.3 Types of Spreads

Long Corn/Short Wheat	Intercommodity
Long CBOT Wheat/Short MN Wheat	Intermarket/Exchange
Long July/Short Sept.	Interdelivery
Short CBOT Corn/Long CBOT Corn	Intermarket/Exchange
Short July Corn/Long Sept. Corn	Intracommodity

The Price Influencers Strategy

The price of the underlying entity is the prime determinant of how much an option spread will profit. If the spread position is established by selling the nearby option and buying the more distant when both options are at the money, the spread will be profitable if the futures or stock prices remain relatively constant. It will tend to lose money if the prices change.

The spread will be at its widest when the price of the underlying contract is closest to the exercise price of the option. The spread will narrow as the price moves away from the exercise price in either direction.

Bull Spreads

Spreads can also be described as bull or bear spreads. A bull spread is usually long the nearby delivery month and short a more distant delivery month. Or we could buy an option at a price close to the current price of the underlying entity and sell one that is at a higher price. The expectation of the bull spreader is that if the price of the underlying entity rises, the effect will be felt strongest by the closest delivery month or the option closest in price to the underlying option.

Let's say May silver is now at $4.50 an ounce and a $5.00 strike price (50 cents above an out-of-the-money) call has a 25-cent premium, or $1,250. But we really don't want to take that much of a risk by simply buying a call. Silver has been somewhat lackluster over the last few months. We feel that it is headed higher; however, we're not sure of the timing or how far it will go. On the other hand, we don't totally want to miss what we think is an opportunity.

An alternative would be to write (sell) a call with a higher exercise price and buy the nearby option. In this case, the $6.00 silver call could be sold for about 14 cents or $700. The spread between the two options would be an 11 cents debit. Such a spread is called a bull spread and the risk in the position is limited to the amount of the original debit.

Risk limitation does not occur without giving up opportunity. If the risk is limited, so is the profit potential. The maximum profit in a price spread is computed by subtracting the original debit from the difference between the exercise prices of the two options. Here's the mathematics:

Difference Between Option	1.00
Debit	.11
Maximum Profit/oz.	.89

Maximum Profit (5,000 oz. x $0.89) = $4,450.00

In our example, the debit or net premium cost is 11 cents and the difference between the exercise prices is $1.00. You are risking 11 cents to make $1.00. At the expiration, a silver price of $6.00, for example, would mean the $5.00 call would have gained $1.00 per ounce or $5,000.00, while the $6.00 call you wrote would be exercised. This means you would lose the premium of 14 cents, but you would also be closed out in the market. You would be long and short one silver contract. If the price of silver dropped below $5.00, both options would expire worthless and you would experience the maximum loss of 11 cents.

Bull Spread Rules

The rules concerning option bull spreads that you must keep in mind are as follows:

◆ A bull spread profits only when the spread widens.

◆ The maximum profit on the bull spread is the difference between the strike price minus the debit (the amount of the cost of the long side exceeds the proceeds or the premium received for selling the short side).

◆ The maximum loss is the debit or the net premium paid.

Now let's discuss the bear side of spreads.

Bear Spreads

Basically, they call for an opposite market opinion of bull spreads. You use them when you believe the market is about to move lower.

If you project a declining silver market, you could sell (write) a put at a lower strike price option, e.g. $5.00, and buy one at a higher one, say $5.50. At the time the options expire, if the price of silver never goes below $5.00, the put you write will not be exercised by the person who bought it—you keep the premium. The put you bought at $5.50 may gain depending how low silver goes. At $5.00 silver, at expiration, your $5.50 put has 50 cents intrinsic value or $2,500.00. Additionally, you would pocket the premium of the $5.00 put you underwrote. This would be your maximum profit.

If silver continued to trade lower before expiration of these options, your profit would not increase. The reason is the owner of the option you sold would exercise it. To protect yourself and end your market exposure, you exercise the put you bought. You would be long and short the silver market or neutral (one position offsets the other).

The rules for bear option spreads are as follows:

◆ A bear spread profits when the spread narrows.

◆ The maximum profit on a bear spread is the credit (the amount the proceeds from the short side exceed the cost of the long position and the transaction costs).

◆ The maximum loss on a bear spread position is the difference between the strike price less the credit and transactions costs.

Bull Time Spreads

Just as you can trade bullish or bearish price spreads, you can trade bullish or bearish time spreads. A bull time spread would involve buying a deferred month and selling the nearby month.

If on the other hand you were bearish, a bear time spread would entail buying the nearby expiration month and selling a deferred expiration month. For example, buy a July ABC Company call option and sell an October call option. The rules cited earlier apply to bull and bear time spreads, as well as bull and bear price spreads.

Straddle Strategies

We will continue this discussion of spreads with a variation called the straddle. It is similar to a spread in that you trade both sides of the market at the same time, but there is a difference. A straddle is a type of spread that entails the purchase of a put and a call (called a long straddle) or the sale of a put and a call (called a short straddle). Previously, we bought and sold either puts or calls, not combinations.

Earlier we concentrated on bullish and bearish trading strategies. These are valuable tools when we know (or think we know) where the market is headed. What do we do when we think the market is going to take off, but we don't know which direction? Or even more puzzling, how can we trade a trendless market?

The answer is the straddle. The long straddle, like the volatility spread discussed earlier, is a trading strategy to take advantage of dramatic market moves, even when we're not sure of the direction.

The Long Straddle

In its simplest form, the long straddle involves the purchase of a put and a call that share the same expiration date and strike price. To be successful, a big market move must occur before the options expire.

Let's use the corn market again as an example. The primary growing region is the Midwest. In this scenario, it has been in a drought for the past two years. As we head into the planting time, the subsoil moisture has not been replenished.

Last year the crop got by with a series of timely rains. Just enough rain occurred when it was desperately needed. The year before the farmers were not as lucky. What will happen this year?

The U.S. rarely has two down years of corn production in a row. Additionally, the price of corn is very price sensitive, often referred to as elastic. When supplies are scarce, the price skyrockets. When supplies are plentiful, the price plummets. When supplies are adequate, the price moves sideways.

This year we think one of two things is going to happen—either there will be plenty of rain or a drought. A full measure of rain will wash out prices. A drought will fire prices to new highs. How do you trade these fundamentals?

Table 2.1 Long Straddle

Future Price	Call Price	Put Price	Total	
1.40	(20.0)	80.0	60.0	
1.60	(20.0)	60.0	40.0	
1.80	(20.0)	40.0	20.0	
2.00	(20.0)	20.0	0.00	
2.20	(20.0)	0.00	(20.0)	
2.40	(20.0)	(20.0)	(40.0)	Max. Loss
2.60	0.00	(20.0)	(20.0)	
2.80	20.0	(20.0)	0.00	
3.00	40.0	(20.0)	20.0	
3.20	60.0	(20.0)	40.0	
3.40	80.0	(20.0)	60.0	

(In Dollars)

If we think the price range could be anywhere from a low of $1.40 to a high of over $3 per bushel, we might decide to use a long straddle. We'll buy a near-in-the-money put and call, at say, $2.40. See Table 2.1.

As you can see, the money is made with this strategy on the extremes. The more the market declines, the more valuable the put becomes. The opposite is true of the call. At some point before expiration, the savvy trader would abandon one leg and exercise the other. The point is you're in good shape to take advantage of a bull or bear run without knowing which will occur before hand!

You lose, of course, if the market trades trendless from the time you enter until expiration of the options. The maximum you lose is the two premiums paid for the put(s) and call(s) and the associated transaction cost. The upside is theoretically unlimited. We say "theoretically" because all bull or bear markets eventually end.

The Short Straddle

The opposite trading strategy to the long straddle is the short straddle. Rather than going long a put and a call, you short or sell a put and a call. This is the ideal strategy to use when you think the market is going to be flat and lifeless for the duration of the options sold.

Let's use the same corn scenario described above, only we now think the rains will be normal, crop production normal, and the market will trend sideways until our options expire. Rather than buy a $2.40 call and a put, we sell them. See Table 2.2.

You find the short straddle attractive because it allows you to take advantage of the normal decline in an option's time value as it approaches expiration. In this case neither option is exercised, which means you retain the full premium on both sides. The danger is a serious price move, which could be very expensive.

Table 2.2 Short Straddle

Future Price	Call Price	Put Price	Total	
1.40	20.0	(80.0)	(60.0)	
1.60	20.0	(60.0)	(40.0)	
1.80	20.0	(40.0)	(20.0)	
2.00	20.0	(20.0)	0.00	
2.20	20.0	0.00	20.0	
2.40	20.0	20.0	40.0	*Max. Loss*
2.60	0.00	20.0	20.0	
2.80	(20.0)	20.0	0.00	
3.00	(40.0)	20.0	(20.0)	
3.20	(60.0)	20.0	(40.0)	
3.40	(80.0)	20.0	(60.0)	

(In Dollars)

As with all trading strategies, you begin with a strong opinion of where the market is headed. Always be prepared to adjust your position(s) whenever you discover that all or part of your underlying analysis has changed or is incorrect.

Strangling the Market

The "strangle" is a type of straddle. It differs from the simple straddle just discussed in that both legs do not share a common strike price and are out of the money. They are similar in the sense that you are trading both sides of the market and you can trade a long or a short strategy.

Another critical characteristic is different: the return curve. With the simple straddle, the maximum return was available at only one price point. Refer to Tables 2.1 and 2.2. With the strangle, the maximum return is available at several price points. See Table 2.3.

Strangles also differ from straddles when it comes to the usual position taken by traders. The short strangles are more commonly used; you'll usually find straddles to the long side.

Why Use a Short Strangle?

The basic strategy is the same for the short strangle, as it is for the short straddle or the volatility spread. You see a market that you expect to trade flat until the expiration of the options. The strangle strategy becomes particularly attractive if there is a history of unexpected volatility in the market you plan to trade, or perhaps some seasonal patterns that might come into play. The short strangle insulates you more from this kind of threat than does the short straddle or volatility spread.

Table 2.3 Strangle

Future Price	Call Price	Put Price	Combined Total
66	$1500	($4500)	($3000)
68	$1500	($2500)	($1000)
69	$1500	($1500)	0
70	$1500	($500)	$1000
72	$1500	$1500	$3000
73	$1500	$1500	$3000
74	$1500	$1500	$3000
76	($500)	$1500	$1000
77	($1500)	$1500	0
78	($2500)	$1500	($1000)
80	($4500)	$1500	($3000)

The short strangle finds favor with traders over the short straddle because it further reduces risk. To begin with, you are trading different strike prices and they are out-of-the-money. Therefore, the underlying contract must move farther than with a short straddle, which has the same strike price and is in or near in-the-money, before someone will exercise one of the options you write.

As with most any investment strategies, less risk means less reward. This is true here since the premium for out-of-the-money options is comparatively low.

Let's use an example. Your analysis for this scenario indicates the bond market will be stable for the next six to nine months. Therefore, you enter a short strangle by selling a 74 out-of-the-money call and an out-of-the-money put at 72. The underlying futures contract is trading around 73:00. To simplify this example, let's say both options have the same premium, $1,500. The premium you receive would then be $3,000, less any transaction costs. Table 2.3 demonstrates a variety of market price changes and their impact on your investment.

Notice how the maximum income increases from one price point on the straddle tables (Tables 2.1 and 2.2), to three price points on the strangle Table 2.3, specifically between the 72 put to the 74 call strike prices. Between these two points, both options are still out-of-the-money. When both options expire out-of-the-money, you retain the full premium. This, of course, is the maximum profit you could expect. If one of the legs of the strangle expires in-the-money, then your profits diminish proportionally.

Prices can, at least theoretically, increase indefinitely and can decrease to zero. When prices move dramatically against one leg of the strangle, the option represented by that leg is likely to be exercised. This means you'd be assigned an equal and opposite position in the futures market. For example, if you are short a put, you will receive a long futures position if the option is exercised. Since the market is moving against you, it could quickly become expensive.

Calculating Breakeven

For this reason, strangle strategists often calculate their breakeven point. It is slightly different depending on the direction of the market. For example, if prices go over the call strike price, it is likely the short will be exercised. But, it is only when the loss exceeds the net premium received that you become a net loser. You can define the breakeven point by adding the call strike price to the net credit (premium received). Our 74 call strike plus the $3,000 premium, or 3:00 adds up to 77:00 as breakeven.

The downside breakeven is determined by subtracting the premium from the put's strike price. Once this price is exceeded, you begin to lose money. In our example, you would reduce the 72 put by 3:00 which comes to 69:00.

The Long Strangle

Most of this section was devoted to the short strangle as opposed to the long strangle. Our reason is that a long strangle is rarely used. Everything mentioned about the short strangle is true for the long—only in reverse.

The Long Synthetic

In options trading, you can use a strategy that utilizes options only, but creates the same effect as trading the underlying contract. The strategy is called the synthetic long or short. Let's talk about the long first.

You create a synthetic long position through the purchase of a call option and the sale of a put option, where the two legs of this position share a common strike price and expiration date. Just as the name implies (long), you must be strongly bullish on the direction you expect the market to head.

Here's an example. You do an analysis of the stock market. Your conclusion is that the Dow is headed much higher—you think nothing can stop it. Instead of taking a position in an underlying futures, like the Standard and Poor 500, you opt to trade a synthetic long. This means you will buy a call and sell a put. For this example, the S & P 500 is trading at 350. We'll assume, for simplicity's sake, that the call and the put are in-the-money. It costs you two index points to buy the call and you are paid two index points for selling the put. Therefore, you break-even, less the transaction costs. Some brokers call this a "free" trade.

You decide to hold the synthetic long position until expiration. If prices shoot up as you forecasted, the call gains value and the short expires worthless. You win on both by closing out or exercising the call and collecting the premium on the unexercised put.

What happens if prices drop? In this case, you lose double. Your call expires worthless causing you to lose the premium you paid, and the trader to whom you sold the short exercises it. You are required to deliver a short futures position that is in-the-money.

The third possibility is the market moves sideways. Here you break-even, less transaction costs. You keep the two-point premium you received for selling the put and lose the two-point premium you paid for the call. Keep in mind that the transaction costs are doubled on this strategy, compared to just taking a position in the underlying market. Table 2.4 illustrates the three scenarios described.

Now, both options do not have to be at the same strike price. If the call is in-the-money and the put is not, you have a deficit since the premium you receive for the put will not cover the call. On the other hand, if the put is in-the-money and the call is not, you'll have a credit. The only problem with this is that the underlying entity will have to move farther in order for your call to start making money.

The Synthetic Short

You can trade a synthetic short, just as you could a synthetic long. For the synthetic short, you buy the put and sell the call. Again, you should use the same strike price and expiration date. This strategy mimics taking a straight short position in the stock or futures market.

The same risks mentioned for the long are experienced if the market goes against you. In this case, you are looking for a bearish price move. If prices go up instead of down, your call will be exercised and your put will expire worthless.

As with any investment, you must do your prognostication first. If you call the market correctly, you win the brass ring. If you are wrong, you pay the piper.

The Special Double

A very unique trade, alluded to earlier, available to options traders is the "special double option," or sometimes just referred to as a "double option." This is a combination of a put option and a call option at a fixed strike price. The premium

Table 2.4 Long Synthetic

S&P Index	P/L Call	P/L Put	Combined	Futures
346	4	2	6	6
354	2	2	4	4
352	0	2	2	2
350	(2)	2	0	0
348	(2)	0	(2)	(2)
346	(2)	(2)	(4)	(4)
344	(2)	(4)	(6)	(6)
342	(2)	(6)	(8)	(8)

This table illustrates how the synthetic options position (row 4) mirrors the performance of a straight position (row 5) in the futures market. Negative numbers are in the parentheses.

cost of a double is usually close to, but slightly less than, the sum of the premium costs of both a put and a call purchased separately.

The only stipulation of the double option is that only one side of the double can be exercised, but both sides can be traded as many times as desired. All the trading techniques discussed earlier with regard to puts and calls will work equally well with either or both sides of the double.

The double has an additional advantage which places it in a special category far and above other strategies. It frees the holder from his dependence on market direction predictions. The double option, being the combination of both a put and a call, can be profitable regardless of whether the market advances or declines. You may often find it easier to determine that there is going to be some price volatility, rather than the direction the market will go next.

Just think about it for a minute. Let's say you notice your favorite commodity or stock beginning to trade in a tight coil or triangle formation. The coil gets tighter and tighter. You know the commodity is poised for a breakout.

But will it go up or down? You're not really sure. All you know is it can't trade much longer without committing itself. This is the opportunity you're looking for to trade the double. When the breakout occurs, you close out the losing side and ride the winning side to the next point of resistance. Then decide if you wish to take your profits or not.

Like any trading strategy, it is not without risks. For example, the breakout could fizzle. You could end up holding worthless options. The key is correctly evaluating the degree of volatility, which we'll discuss in a later chapter.

Butterfly Spread

Here's a useful strategy for quiet markets. All it takes is patience and low price volatility. The term butterfly comes from the schematic that is often drawn to illustrate the relationships of the various legs or sides of this spread. You can execute either a long or short butterfly spread. The long spread is most common, so we'll describe it.

The long butterfly spread entails the purchase of a high strike price and a low strike price option and the writing of two intermediate price options. All the option legs are calls in the long butterfly and puts in the short. For example, you could buy a $7.50 call (high) sell two $7.25 calls (intermediate) and buy a $7.00 call (low). Naturally, multiple contracts could be bought as long as the relationship is kept in balance.

With this strategy, you realize your profit if the market hovers around the short strike price level. Assume that the $7.50 call (out-of-the-money) is acquired for $800.00, the two $7.25 calls for a total of $2,300.00 (at-the-money), and the $7.00 for $1,800.00 (in-the-money). Combining the purchase prices and the premiums paid, this butterfly costs you $300.00 plus transaction costs. If everything goes wrong, the options offset each other. The purchased calls are exercised to counter balance the ones written and exercised. This is your maximum risk. What could happen is the market could become heated and the price of the underlying entity could sink well below the low priced call or rise above the intermediate options ($7.25) triggering their exercise. If it stays in the range of the intermediate options, the low price option would gain 25 cents in value. If the contract is for silver or soybeans containing 5,000 ounces or bushels, this would be a gain of $1,250.00; less the $300.00 debit for a $950.00 net profit times the quantity of spreads you put on.

Spread Risk

Before we leave the subject of combination trades (spreads, straddles, and strangles), we'd like to alert you to some of the special problem areas you could encounter. First is the problem of getting a good fill on all legs (sides) of the combination trades. Some spreads that are very liquid (heavily traded) have floor brokers that make a market in them and your order can be placed as a spread. Your broker places the spread by ordering the price spread desired. Each leg of less common spreads have to be put on separately, sometimes in different trading pits. In these cases, you have less control over the actual spread you eventually receive.

If your combination trade includes selling one or both legs, you could get exercised on the option(s) you've written. This would usually only happen if the sell side was losing money for you. Your strategy would be disrupted and the remaining leg may or may not be profitable.

There is always the possibility that both sides of the combination could be unprofitable. These combination trades depend on both sides of the trade reacting somewhat in unison to the same news, so that they close or widen together. There is always the possibility that unexpected or unknown factors will influence one leg and not the other, therefore disrupting your strategy.

When you decide to unwind (offset) your combo, one leg may be more liquid than the other. This particularly happens with out-of-the-money options close to expiration. If this occurs, you may only be able to offset one side. This would leave you holding the other leg as a net long or short position, which may or may not cost you money. Lack of liquidity can be more of a problem with individual stocks than commodities. With either, it is a very serious consideration that can be checked out in advance. Before leaving the subject of spreads, you may want to study Figure 2.4. It explains how you calculate profit and loss.

Writing Options

Keep in mind we are discussing American-style options, which can be exercised (therefore assigned) at any time, as opposed to European, which can only be exercised at a predetermined period just before expiration. This is a very important distinction, as we begin our discussion of writing options.

If you choose to write options, the fear or risk is that you will be unexpectedly assigned a losing position. And, as we said previously, the holder of the option is not likely to exercise until the option is in-the-money. This means that the opposite positions assigned to the writer or grantor are losing money.

Figure 2.4 Calculating Profit/Loss from Spreads

Strategy:

To profit from a mildly moving market at the least cost.

Assumption:

Trader buys one leg of the spread and sells (writes) the other.

Both options are for the same underlying entity and are both calls or puts.

Calculations:

If premium for the option bought is larger than the premium received for the leg written, the result is a debit in the trader's account.

Futures Example: $.15 premium paid less $.10 premium,
received = 5-cent debit.

Stock Example: $4.00 premium paid less $2.00 per shared,
received = ($2.00)

Debit is then multiplied by the per unit quantity of the underlying entity.

Futures Example: $.05 debit x 1,000 oz. (silver) = ($500.00)

Stock Example: $2.00 debit x 100 shares = ($200.00)

Profit/Loss:

If the underlying entities move the opposite direction of the options (down for calls or up for puts), all the options expire worthless and the trader loses the amount of the debt.

If the underlying entities move in the direction favorable of options (up for calls or down for puts), the profit generated will be limited by the strike price of options written. When that is hit or exceeded, the holder of the option will exercise it and trader must exercise his/her option to offset.

Explaining the assignment of an option to a customer by a broker can be a tricky situation. The reason is each exchange has its own rules governing assignments. The Securities and Exchange Commission (SEC) for stocks and the Commodity Futures Trading Commission (CFTC) for futures require the assignment process to be fair and unbiased.

Exchanges use various random selection processes to assign positions, after they learn from their clearing operation, (usually an independent corporation), how many option buyers have given notice to exercise options. It can take a day or two before all this works its way back to the writer of the option. Your broker could call and say: "By the way, you're on margin call. Two of your options were exercised the day before yesterday. Please wire $2,000.00 by today's close of business."

That's the risk—what's the reward? The benefits of options writing depend on motivation. For some, it can just be a way of increasing the return from a stock. An investor, for example, owns a block of a well known stock on which options are traded. The return in dividends and appreciation amounts to 10%-12% per year. To try to push this up to 15%, the investor decides to write some covered options on half the block of stock. The expectation is that the options will never be exercised.

A covered option writer, as you must have guessed by now, is one who owns at least the amount of the underlying entity (stocks or futures contracts) upon which he or she is offering options. An uncovered option writer writes options without owning the underlying stock or commodity. If exercised on, they must pay the brokerage firm for the underlying entity which is purchased on the open market.

As with all options traders, the writer must have an opinion of market direction. Will it be up, down, or sideways? Will it be a strong or mild move? The advantage writers have is that they can win without being accurate.

For example, let's say your analysis indicates the price of a stock or a commodity is going higher. You decide to sell a put. You would win (collect the premium)—if the market trades sideways, if higher, or even if it only goes down (against your position) a little. Part of this calculation depends on which strike price you selected. Option writers only have to be near right to earn the premium, while the investors who buy puts or calls have to be very, very right for the underlying entities to move far enough to pay back the premium, transaction costs, and then a little more to prompt them to exercise the option. Sellers win with singles; buyers need homers, or at least triples!

There is another drawback in addition to the risk of selling options. The profit potential is fixed. All the seller can hope for is the premium, less the transaction costs. The exercise price of the option is the ceiling of profitability for option sellers of covered options. Beyond this point, the option buyers will exercise their right to the underlying entity, taking it away from the seller. The underlying entity could be a stock, foreign currency, debt security, or commodity for covered option. For uncovered, it could additionally include a wide variety of indexes. As mentioned earlier, option writers are uncovered or naked when they write options without owning the underlying interest. Indexes are all uncovered because there is no practical way to own an entire index in the cash market.

An example or two might bring this concept into sharper focus. We'll start with a covered call stock option. ABC, Inc.'s stock is currently trading in a $30.00 to $35.00 a share range. You write a 40 call and pocket the $4.00 (100 shares × $4.00 = $400.00 less $40.00 transaction costs of $360.00) premium. Before the expiration date arrives, the stock increases to $47.00 and the buyer exercises. Your total return would be the $40.00 the buyer pays you for the stock, the $4.00 premium (less commission and fees) and any dividends that may have been paid to shareholders of record prior to date the option is exercised. You do not get any of the gain in stock value between $40.00 and $47.00 and you no longer own the shares.

What if you made this same investment, but you didn't own the stock? You would sell a $40.00 option on ABC, Inc. naked. When the option is exercised at $47.00 a share, that's what you have to pay to get the shares to meet your obligation to the buyer of the option. If the stock jumped to $50.00 or $60.00 a share on news of a merger before exercising, you have to meet the market.

With covered options, you have a predetermined price for the underlying security or commodity. With uncovered options, your cost is whatever the market happens to be when you are assigned (exercised upon) a position or when you go to the market to cover the option you wrote. It is for this reason that the risk of selling uncovered options is considered greater and is characterized as unlimited.

Many security firms require new customers to maintain 100% of money needed to fulfill the obligation to deliver the stock for uncovered options. This is called a cash secured option. These funds are usually held in an interest bearing account. In the futures markets, you must maintain the proper amount of margin money to be able to immediately accept the assignment of a futures contract(s). The premium you receive from the buyer can be used to meet all or part of the margin requirement. The futures-type settlement procedure allows you to withdraw excess equity, if the funds (premiums, etc.) exceed the margin requirements. Interest isn't usually paid on futures margin, unless it is held in the form of a Treasury Bill, which usually requires a $10,000.00 minimum.

Two related questions come to mind as we discuss the risk and reward of options writing. First, if you write uncovered options, as most speculators do, how do you protect yours from the danger? And, which options are most attractive?

Taking the latter question first, the most desirable options to write are usually the most risky—specifically, options that are at or very near in-the-money with a short amount of time remaining to expiration. These options normally have the highest premium because they are the ones buyers think will be in-the-money soonest. They are actively being bid for, which means they are liquid (plenty of buyers).

In response to the first question, you protect yourself by not being greedy or getting married to your decisions. Greed sometimes causes a trader to hold positions longer than they should. Traders who become enamored with their analysis have difficulty admitting they are wrong. Thus they hold onto their positions too long.

You protect yourself by dumping losing trades fast. In the industry, we say: "Cut your losers short, let your winners run." If you have written (sold) an option, you offset by buying an option. You were paid a premium to write the option. When you offset, you pay the premium back to another trader who is writing (underwriting) the option. When you are offsetting a losing position, the premium you pay to "buy your option back" is normally more than what you were paid—thus you lose.

It's common for traders to use what are known as stop loss orders. These are orders to buy a position(s) opposite theirs when a certain price is reached in the market. That certain price is the amount they are willing to lose on a given trade.

Theoretically, this can be done with options. The problem a trader can experience is that many of the options markets are illiquid. In the markets, a stop loss order becomes the bid or ask price, depending on the direction of the market. The stop loss can be prematurely hit. Another problem is that stop loss orders are "not held" orders for floor brokers on most exchanges. In the very liquid markets, stop loss orders can be very effective.

Another alternative is to transform a naked option to a covered option. You do this by buying the entity that underlies and offsets the option. For a stock option, you'd buy or sell 100 shares of the stock. With an option-on-futures, you acquire a long or short position in the underlying futures contract. Be sure to offset properly. If you wrote a put, you need to buy a long futures contract to offset.

Many traders rely heavily on their brokers to protect them from losses related to adverse market moves. Brokers follow the markets minute-to-minute. They keep an eye on volume and price activity. They have a good feel as to whether a good fill can be obtained during certain trading sessions. The traders may give the brokers some limited discretion on the time or the price at which to place the offsetting order. This permits the brokers to act fast, if necessary. Promptly exiting losing positions is a characteristic that distinguishes the novices from experienced traders.

As mentioned earlier, the most sought after options are often at or in-the-money with little time left to expiration. But they are not the only game in town. There are a lot of out and even deep-out-of-the-money options bought. And, someone has to be writing these options.

A futures option that is out-of-the-money with 60 to 90 days to expiration may only sell for a penny or two. Are they good deals for writers? A copper call, a dime out of the market with three months to expiration, may pay the writer a premium of $0.017 or $425.00 (25,000 lbs. × $0.017). A lot can happen in the four months to expiration. The big question is whether copper will gain the 10 cents needed to make it worth exercising by the buyers. Every one cent move in copper amounts to a $250.00 change (25,000 lbs/100 cents) in the intrinsic value of an in-the-money option. Therefore, copper must really move about 12 cents before the option writer begins to lose.

If copper begins a move, gaining a nickel...then up seven cents—what do you do when it's at-the-money? When do you close your position? The answer depends on your trading system, which we'll discuss later. Our point is that you cannot always sell an option, collect the premium, and passively wait for the option to expire worthless.

Although it is true most options expire worthless, you never know for sure how many times they changed hands before expiration. Many novice traders don't think about this. They believe they can sell options and simply wait for them to erode into nothingness. This can be a very dangerous and costly point of view.

One last thought. The serious sellers of options trade multiple lots. When they sell, they do it in bundles of 10, 20, 50, or 100 options at a time. A hundred lot of the copper options described earlier brings premiums of $4,250.00. The margin required would be $9,000.00 to $10,000.00. If the trader kept a $10,000.00 Treasury Bill on deposit and rolled the three-month position over four times in the course of a year, the trader would more than double his margin money each year. Plus the T-Bill would be collecting interest.

Are we recommending a selling strategy to new traders? No, for these reasons. Before attempting this strategy you need to have a "good feel" for the markets you are going to trade. Good feel means knowing how the market is likely to respond to market news and noise. For example, what is the historical range of price volatility? If you study the long-term price volatility charts, you get an insight in the maximum size price move you could expect. Some traders think about this as the maximum risk, when evaluating the different strike prices. This concept is so important a later chapter has been devoted to it.

Next, for your protection, you must have a solid working relationship with a successful options broker. It takes time to find and nurture such a partnership. Also necessary are reliable trading and price forecasting systems. All of these subjects will also be covered in detail in future chapters.

Our point is—because of the serious risk and predefined reward—writing options should wait until a trader has gained some experience. Even then, covered options or spreads, which include writing one leg, should be experimented with first. Now, let's discuss the other major type of options trader.

Hedging with Options

As mentioned at the beginning of this chapter, hedgers wish to transfer the risk of owning something (cash corn, stock shares) to someone who wants to speculate on the price of that something. Hedgers straddle the price fence, thus the term.

For example, an Iowa farmer normally produces 150 bushels of corn per acre on his best 500 acres, or 75,000 bushels. By June, his crop looks good and the futures price for December corn is at $3.75. The farmer wants to lock in some of his production at this price. So he decides to hedge 50,000 bushels or 10 contracts of 5,000 bushels each.

Since he will have physical possession of the corn in December after harvest, he is already long. To hedge or become neutral he must short the market or sell 10 December corn at-the-market puts. This locks in the $3.75 (less his commission cost for the option contract) per bushel price on 50,000 bushels.

If the price of corn falls, the farmer's puts gain in value to compensate for the loss in the cash side of the hedge. The key is knowing the delta or hedge ratio of the strike price selected so the farmer will be 100% hedged or neutral price wise. If the strike price had a hedge ratio of 0.50, the farmer would buy 20 puts instead of 10.

This example could have used copper, silver, foreign currencies, or stocks. With stock portfolios, the hedger uses the stock indexes that most closely reflect

Figure 2.5 Soybean Hedge

	Cash	Option
May Prices	$5.75	Buy Nov. $6.00 put at $0.25/bu premium
Sell Cash at Harvest (Nov.) Price:	$5.00	Sell Nov. $6.00 put at $1.00 in-the-money
Strategy: Sell (buy a put) Profit:	$0.75	
Cash Received	$5.00	
Option Premium Received	$0.75	
Total	$5.75	

Soybean farmers can use options to lock in price while crops are still in the fields. If prices were to increase, instead of decrease, cash commodity gains value and put option expires worthless. Hedger ends up with same results.

the composition of the portfolio. For broad based portfolios, consider the S & P 500 or the New York Composite Index; the Value Line for portfolios of small stocks; the Over the Counter Index for nonlisted stocks; or the Major Market for portfolios similar to the Dow Jones Industrial Average.

To protect against a price rally, the hedger buys calls. They gain in value as prices of the underlying entities gain. If your company had to pay a Japanese manufacturer in Yen for a piece of equipment 60 days or six months from now, and you were afraid the Yen was going to rise against the dollar, you might buy Yen calls to "freeze" the current conversion factor. Or, if your business uses large quantities of a commodity, like copper, silver, corn, soybeans, cattle, money, foreign currencies, etc., and you wanted to protect yourself against a price increase, you could buy puts at your price, convert them to futures contracts, and take delivery when the contracts matured. You would be removing the price risk factor from these transactions.

Hedging with options is like buying price insurance for the commodity you own or must acquire in the future. Figure 2.5 provides an example of how a hedge can work for a farmer.

Market Opinion

All of the strategies discussed have one key element in common—the trader must have an opinion as to market direction. We'll now discuss how one arrives at an opinion.

Chapter 3

Forecasting Stock and Futures Price Trends

"*Question:* What are the desirable qualifications for any young man who wishes to become a politician?
Mr. Churchill: It is the ability to foretell what is going to happen tomorrow, next week, next month, and next year. And to have the ability afterwards to explain why it didn't happen."

Sir Winston Churchill
(Adler's *Churchill's Wit*, 1965)

Key Concepts

◆ Basics of Fundamental Analysis

◆ Understanding the Five Primary Technical Approaches to Market Analysis—Bar Chart Analysis, Trend Following, Structural, Character-of-the-Market, and Other Approaches

◆ Pros and Cons

◆ Which Works Best, When?

Option traders must have strong opinions to deliberately invest in what they think stock or commodity prices will be tomorrow, next week, next month, and next year. When they are wrong, they must have the ability to reevaluate and correct their analysis—and then get right back in the market! This chapter and the next one deal with the most common approaches taken by traders to solidify their thinking.

First, we'll discuss how to forecast the price trends of the underlying entities. These trends dictate the price movements of the options on those entities. In the next chapter, we tackle the concept of volatility and theoretical option price modeling compared to the actual bid-ask prices.

There are two basic schools of thought on price forecasting—fundamental and technical analysis. One utilizes the right side of our brain; the other the left. One is more intuitive; the other more rational. One looks for the reasons why prices will change; the other directs its attention to past patterns in its search for future direction.

Fundamental and technical analysis are used to anticipate price trends for both stocks and commodities. Most techniques were initially developed for stocks, since they have been trading longer on organized exchanges in the United States

(Philadelphia Stock Exchange was founded in 1791; Chicago Board of Trade in 1848). Analysts choose their approach based on their education, background, experience, past success, and temperament. Some combine the techniques. If you plan to trade options in an organized fashion, you will probably find yourself primarily in one camp or the other.

Fundamental Analysis

We'll begin with fundamental analysis because most people find it is easier to understand. It is basically common sense. All you do is study the factors that can change price and anticipate their impact. For commodities, when supplies become scarce, prices rise. When plentiful, prices recede.

Analysts build a model that represents the supply-demand equation. Think of it as a tug of war with supply on one side and demand on the other. The bigger, heavier the supply side gets, the easier it is to pull prices down. If demand grows bigger and faster than supply, it will pull prices higher. Here's the basic supply-demand equation for a commodity:

Existing Stocks plus Production less Usage = Supply

The supply is then evaluated as being adequate (sideways price trend), inadequate (bullish market), or overabundant (bearish projection).

Fundamental analysts get gray hair from unexpected events. They project a drought that will reduce production of a grain, only to see rainfall records set. Or an Iraq invades a Kuwait upsetting the world supply of crude oil. Strikes, government actions, changes in consumer preferences, new inventions, etc.—all these can ruin an otherwise brilliant analysis.

Another perennial problem for the fundamental commodity analysts is gathering and analyzing all the possible variables. Just getting all the information (weather, political activity, government programs, usage, currency, yields, input prices/supply, demand, etc., etc.) from all over the world can be prohibitive for most individuals. This is exaggerated when other countries are uncooperative or deliberately misleading to improve their country's situation.

You must also consider the fact that fundamental analysis is usually of a long-term nature. When you begin to access supplies, like the planting intentions of farmers, the impact of this information will not be totally felt until harvest. In addition, a lot of other events will occur in the intervening six to eight months.

Fundamental analysis of the stock market is somewhat different. The supply of shares of a stock doesn't change from one season to the next. And when the supply changes, as in a split, the price usually reflects the change.

Demand for stocks is more closely related to the general health of the economy. Fundamental stock analysts often study business cycles. As Charles Dow taught—when the tide rises, all the ships in the harbor rise. As the Dow Average rises, so do "all" stocks. By knowing when the economy is about to change direction (heat up or cool off), the analysts can anticipate general demand or lack of interest.

One of the key factors are the indexes prepared by the Bureau of Economic Analysis of the Department of Commerce. The indexes were chosen from all the data the Department gathers based on the following six characteristics: Economic significance, statistical adequacy, consistency of timing at business cycle peaks and troughs, conformity to business expansions and contractions, smoothness, and prompt availability. Analysis indicated combining certain of these individual indicators into indexes was more reliable than depending on them individually. Below are the results of this research.

Leading Indicators Index:
Average workweek
Average weekly jobless claims
New orders for consumer goods
Vendor performance
Contracts/orders for new plants/equipment
Building permits
Change in unfilled durable goods orders
Sensitive material prices
Stock prices
Money supply (M2 in 1982 dollars)
Consumer expectations

Coincidental Indicators Index:
Employees on nonagricultural payrolls
Industrial production
Personal income less transfer payments in 1982 dollars
Manufacturing and trade sales in 1982 dollars

Lagging Indicators Index:
Percent change of labor costs per unit of manufacturing output
Ratio of manufacturing and trade inventories to sales in 1982 dollars
Average duration of unemployment
Ratio of consumer installment credit to personal income
Commercial and industrial loans outstanding in 1982 dollars
Average prime rate change by ranks
Change in consumer price index for services (smoothed)

The indexes are distinguished by their timing characteristics. The Index of Leading Indicators historically reaches its cyclical peaks and troughs before general business cycles does. The Index of Coincidental Indicators makes its turn around at roughly the same time as the business cycle does. The statistical indicators that make up the Index of Lagging Indicators typically hit their highs and lows after business cycles have turned.

If you study the composition of each index, you can see that they cover just about every aspect of the economy. You find labor, production, management, consumers, financial, and even stock market statistics included. Most importantly, these specific statistics were selected because they so closely tracked the ups and downs of business cycles.

The rule of thumb is that turning points in the economy are signaled by three consecutive monthly readings in the same direction. For example, if the Index of Leading Indicators records a +0.2% in July, a +0.4% in August and a +0.3% in September, we would be theoretically headed out of a recession, if we were in one. The opposite is equally true—three negative monthly readings in a row indicate a recession on the horizon. These indexes are not 100% accurate. Most economists are happy with a 70% to 80% reliability. Much also depends on momentum. Large, consistent changes are more meaningful than weak, inconsistent ones.

Stock Market Reaction

These indexes seldom have immediate market impact when released. The reason is simply that the components are known to the market before they are compiled into indexes. Serious analysts watch the individual statistics as they are released. It's easy for them to predict the movement of the indexes based on changes in the components.

Like everything else associated with options trading, there are occasional surprises. These usually involve unexpected changes in degree, rather than direction, of the indexes. When these occur, the reaction of the market is the same as it would be towards any other macroeconomics indicator. For example, higher or more positive numbers in the Index of Leading Indicators foster the expectation that economic expansion is just around the corner. The bulls in the market begin buying, while the bond traders prepare to short their markets.

Analysts must put the numbers into the perspective of the business cycle. Sometimes strong leading indicator numbers can be received negatively. This occurs when they are released late in the business cycle. At these times, they are seen as harbingers of growing inflation. They are telling economists that the economy may be about to expand too fast. Inflation may be out of control.

Also, there are times when these three indexes give contradicting signals. One or two may indicate the economy is expanding, while the third suggests the opposite. These types of circumstances are common to traders. It tells them to stand aside until all three synchronize. As with any market prognostication system, you must know when to bet the factory and when to stay on the sidelines. Always remember they are called "indicators", which doesn't denote that they are expected to give you the absolute direction of each upcoming move in the economy.

Once the overall direction of the trend of the stock market—as reflected by the business cycle—is clear, the fundamental stock analysts evaluate those stocks they feel will most benefit from the trend. It is common at this stage to look at the subindexes, such as the Dow-Jones Industrials, to see which subcategory is displaying the most strength. Earnings of stock classified by industry (pharmaceuticals, insurance, publishing, etc.) can be checked. There are 97 industry groups in common use.

The last step is selecting individual stocks and making specific recommendations. At this stage, analysts study earnings per share, talk with executives, project growth of the industry, and calculate liquidation value. There are literally hundreds of ways to fundamentally pick the stock(s) with the most growth potential. Most individual investors must rely heavily on their brokerage firm to do the exhaustive task of research and analysis.

Technical Analysis

Technical analysis (TA) is completely different. Pure technicians totally disregard everything but the signals generated by their technical system. The theory is that every fundamental factor affecting supply and demand reflects in the price. Therefore, if you study the stream of prices flowing from the trading floors and the related statistics, such as volume, open interest, and momentum, you can uncover trends and anticipate future price objectives.

Don't let technical advocates mislead you. Technical analysis tracks the past; it does not foretell the future. Technicians rely on history repeating itself. There is one thing TA does very well and that is quantify market sentiment. It provides an excellent technique for counting all the votes of everyone trading.

Think about the stock and futures markets as public polls. Brokers are the pollsters. They go out and survey the general trading public. "Where do you think the price of the S & P is headed? In your opinion, is the price of IBM too high or too low?" The answers to all the questions are communicated to the trading pits, where they are processed. The results are published daily in various financial papers in the form of price gains or losses.

Keep in mind that the people who answer these surveys are very sincere about their answers—they have backed their opinions with money. Collectively, they represent all the thoughts, research, and emotions surrounding the entire financial community. The people polled may have been influenced by the media, their personal financial situation, a computer program, or what has and is happening in the world.

The voting results show up on price charts, momentum oscillators, and on other technical analysis tools. It is a way of measuring the temperature or tone of the markets. New behavior patterns manifest themselves in new price chart formations. Your task, as a technical analyst, is to make sense of them. When you start this process, you join the rest of us in attempting to guess at what will happen tomorrow.

Technical analysis is often referred to as a self-fulfilling prophecy. This evolves from the fact that its use is so widely accepted, particularly in the futures markets. For example, one of the simplest techniques is drawing trendlines on price charts. The most common example of this is the up or down trendline. Every technical trader is taught that when a major trendline is broken, it's time to reverse one's position. And, just like lemmings, when prices break the trend, "all" the traders reverse their positions—fulfilling its prophecy. For this reason alone, anyone trading options should know the basics of chart analysis, if nothing more than to anticipate what other traders can be expected to do.

One of the most compelling reasons for having faith in technical analysis is the enormous amount of trading equity controlled by technical traders. We have, for example, access to a database of over 100 professional commodity trading advisors managing hundreds of millions of dollars. Of this group, most use some type of technical analysis in their trading.

The reason for this is simply the enormous amount of information required to trade successfully using fundamental analysis. The natural consequence of acquiring gigantic amounts of data is not having the time and resources to do the analysis.

Another little quirk of fundamental analysis is that it is not self-correcting. For example, if a trendline is broken, or a support-resistance level penetrated, the technical trader views this as a reason to reverse or abandon a position. But what does the fundamental analyst think, if he thought corn was a good buy at $2.00 per bushel and it drops to $1.50? Is it a better buy? When does one reverse one's position? When do you "know" you're wrong?

Before we go too far, we want to stress the fact we are not belittling fundamental analysis in any way. There are major grain companies and well-known professional traders (CTAs) who use it as their primary analytical technique. It is also very common for all types of traders to use fundamental analysis to determine the basic trend or the overall direction of the market. Then, technical analysis is used to select specific exit and entry points.

Another problem with fundamental analysis is unknown factors. We have seen many unexpected political moves in recent years—the fall of the Berlin Wall, the Iraqi invasion of Kuwait—that have sent the market reeling uncontrollably. How do fundamental traders handle these? Ideally, they would utilize protective stops.

Technical traders will see the market breaking a trendline or generating an exit signal of some sort, and react. Technicians have "reasons" to reverse or stand aside (not trade) the market(s).

Please don't get the impression technical analysis is a panacea. Traders can, unfortunately, lose money just as easily and just as fast with technical analysis as they do using fundamental analysis. The big difference is there are technical analysis systems that are manageable by small traders.

One thing we have learned over many years of options trading is that it is not the system alone that generates success for traders. If there were one or two perfect systems, we'd all know about them and they probably wouldn't work any more. But there are hundreds and thousands of systems.

To make a system work, you must combine it with sound money management techniques and stick with it. The most valuable aspect of a trading system may be that it "forces" you to make a trading decision by flashing a signal. By constantly fine-tuning a system, you can make it work for you. Your system's and your money management rules must make you a disciplined trader—one who can survive the inevitable losses you will sustain.

Types of Technical Analysis

We divide technical analysis into five basic types—bar charts of prices, trend-following, structural, character-of-market, and "other." Price bar charting is probably the most common for commodities. Daily, weekly, and monthly prices are charted and the formations analyzed. An example of trend-following technical analysis is moving averages, which combines a series of prices and smoothes them mathematically. Structural analysis assumes the market moves in established, recognizable patterns—like seasonal, cyclical, or wave patterns. Probably the most sophisticated is character-of-market. This type of analysis attempts to exactly measure the "quality" of a price movement, then takes a position opposite the momentum, anticipating where the market is headed next.

As you might guess, our last category, "other," is a collection for all types of analysis that are not easily classified. This could be anything from something as simple as trading contrary opinion to insights gained from studying the phases of the moon. We'll now provide an overview of each type.

Bar Charts

Since there are only 40 or so commodities (with four to twelve monthly contracts) actively traded compared to thousands of stocks, it is easier for a publisher to create a chart service for them. Additionally, most stock traders hold their positions longer, which reduces the need and value of a daily charting service. Nonetheless, charts of stock prices can easily be located. Options charts can be found in some advisory newsletters devoted to options traders and can be generated by some software programs. (Refer to the index for specific names, addresses, and telephone numbers.)

Current charts are so important to traders, most electronic price quotation services provide them—even for online data. Brokers commonly follow electronic charts showing every price tick, within seconds of when the trade occurs.

Figure 3.1 shows the basic element of the price bar chart, the price tick. The vertical line represents the unit's (day, week, month) trading range. The top is the high and the bottom is the low. The short horizontal line on the left denotes the opening prices and the one on the right (as you face it) is the close. Not all charts include the right or opening price tick. Most price charts show only a closing tick. The vertical axis of the chart represents price and the horizontal time.

Daily, weekly, and monthly bar charts are depicted similarly with the high, low, and close represented by a vertical line above the date. Nontrading days, weekends, and holidays are not depicted, so there is no break in the pattern.

Long-term charts of commodities, covering months and years of price activity, periodically show price distortions up or down. Careful analysis often reveals these are places where the contract rolled over from one contract month to the next. For example, the June silver contract expires and the chart service continues the chart using the December contract. In this case, there could be a price gap or distortion between the two contract months. The reason is simply that, as the June silver contract approaches expiration or delivery, trading heats up driving

Figure 3.1 Price Ticks

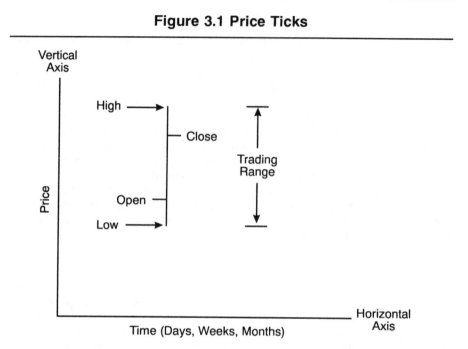

The Price Tick is the basic element of commodity price charts. The vertical line denotes the price range for the period (day, week, month). The left horizontal tick mark indicates the open, and the right horizontal tick the close.

prices a little higher or lower. The far out contract, December, trades with less volatility and prices remain steady. Our point is that the rollover from one contract to another can sometimes cause a distortion depending on the factors influencing the different delivery months. These longer-term charts are often referred to as "continuation" charts.

As a rule, the longer term the chart, the smoother the pricing pattern. This means that the price patterns on weekly charts are usually smoother than those on daily charts, and that monthly charts are smoother than weekly ones. Also, the longer the term of the chart, the more reliable the pattern is considered. For example, an area on a monthly chart that has given support to prices (we'll be discussing specific price patterns shortly) would be expected to be stronger (or more reliable) than the same formation on a weekly or daily chart. This is generally true for all formations or chart signals.

Across the bottom of most daily charting services (see Figure 3.2), you'll find a record of the trading volume and open interest for that day. Volume indicates the total number of contracts traded. Open interest measures the number of contracts held at the conclusion of a trading session. These are very important figures because they tell you the degree of activity of traders, or the momentum

Figure 3.2 Daily Price Charts of a Futures Contract

COTTON (CTN) MARCH 1993 c/LB.

Here is the daily price activity of a futures contract. Weekends and other nontrading days are omitted to provide a smoother picture. Daily volume and open interest are plotted across the bottom of the chart.

Chart courtesy of "Pocket Chart"

of the market you're studying. We'll be discussing these in more detail as we discuss specific price patterns.

Chart Formations

You could fill a good size bookcase with full-length texts discussing interpretations of bar charts for stocks and commodities. Several of the better ones have been cited in the bibliography. Highlighting some of the more common formations gives you an insight into how a trading system based on bar chart analysis might work.

The most common and significant formation is the trendline. It can be either an up or down trendline. Trendlines require at least two points to touch the line and are considered more reliable the closer they are to 45 degrees in incline or decline. A parallel line is sometimes drawn to indicate a channel or trading range. Uptrend lines are drawn below the price ticks and downtrend above. The higher degree or steeper the trend lines are, the likelier they will be broken and the trend will reverse. See Figure 3.3.

Figure 3.3 Uptrend Lines

Trendlines indicate the overall market sentiment. It could be bullish, bearish, or neutral. The steeper the trendlines become, the more likely a trend reversal will occur.

Chart courtesy of "Pocket Charts"

All technical analysis is built on the premise that history repeats itself. When a trendline is established, technical traders expect it to continue. When it gets too steep, they expect the trendline to be broken. When a trendline is broken, they expect the trend to reverse. This mindset is part of what makes technical analysis work; what makes it a self-fulfilling prophecy.

Technical analysis also works because it is based on sound psychological principles, the most basic of which is herd psychology. When the trading herd sees a trendline, they trade it until it ends. When it ends, they look for the next trend or formation and trade it.

No one knows what the future will bring. It is a total unknown. Therefore, people (traders) who risk their money on anticipating where commodity prices will go next are uncertain, uncomfortable. When people are uneasy, they stick together. This basic need of man is responsible for history repeating itself and the meaningfulness of chart formation. Just like anything else in life, none of the formations are anywhere near 100% reliable.

Support and resistance areas are very common and significant. There are places where down trending markets come to rest repeatedly or up trending markets tend to stall repeatedly (Figure 3.4). For example, a market rallies and

Figure 3.4 Areas of Support and Resistance

Areas of resistance slow or stop uptrends; support levels retard or halt downtrends.

then falls back to a previous price level, from which a second rally is launched, only to decline back to the same price level again. This is a support area. The opposite, where a market rallies time and again only to stall out at a certain price level, is a resistance area.

Areas of support and resistance are "zones of error". Thus, once a support area is penetrated, it becomes a resistance area because there are traders who bought at the support level and still hold their losing positions. They'd be happy at this point to get out at breakeven. These traders offset their losing positions which props the opposite side of the market.

Closely related to support and resistance formations are multiple tops and bottoms. Take the double top as an example. A market rallies, reaches an area of resistance, stalls, and begins to decline. After a short retracement, it rallies again, only to stall at the exact same resistance area. The chartist would call this a double top or "M" formation and consider it a sign of weakness. It would be a signal to short the market. The risk, of course, is that a triple top could develop. The trader who shorted the double top would be whipsawed by the market. Whipsawing is when you reverse your position only to have the market turn against you. You lose twice, once on your original position and again on your reversal. Multiple bottoms are the opposite of multiple tops.

More complex versions of the multiple tops or bottoms is the head and shoulders and inverted head and shoulders formation. They resemble the silhouette of a person and are very important for several reasons (Figure 3.5). First, they are considered very reliable by professional chartists. Furthermore, they foretell a major reversal in trend. Last of all, they can predict the length of the next move or the reversal.

A head and shoulders formation usually consists of the following five key phases:

1. Left shoulder.
2. Head.
3. Right shoulder.
4. Neckline penetration.
5. Prices often retrace and bounce off the neckline before heading toward their first price objective. This provides a second opportunity to short the market.

The first price objective is measured from the top of the head to the neckline and projected downward from the point where the neck was broken. A second, or even third, objective of the same distances can be projected depending on the

Figure 3.5 Inverted Head and Shoulder Formation

WASENDORF GRAIN INDEX, 1977 = 100

Head and shoulder formations resemble the silhouette of a person. Note how this one signals astute technicians of a major upcoming price move.

velocity of the market as it reaches the first objective. Inverted head and shoulders work just the opposite.

Another formation that is considered very reliable by chartists is the rounded bottom. These are long, drawn out formations that can take months to mature. They are often called "saucer" bottoms because of their shape. When the saucer bottom matures, it signals a long-term uptrend.

The reason for this is that while the rounded bottom is maturing, the price of the commodity is relatively low. It is at the bottom of its price range for a long time. While this occurs, it is not uncommon for new uses to develop that increase the long-term demand. For example, while corn was making a rounded bottom in 1986-1987, new uses for it, as gasohol and corn sweeteners, were developed. When it finally began a price rise, it had a stronger demand base and a long-term bull move developed.

There are a lot of other bar chart patterns used by chartists, such as triangles, boxes, key reversal days, etc., but we can't cover them all. If you're serious about trading, you need to spend some time studying all the formations—so you'll at least know what other traders are likely to do.

Trend Following Techniques

The second category used to classify technical analysis techniques is trend following. We'd like to quickly review two basic approaches. The first is moving averages.

These can be calculated for any period of time—3, 5, 7, 30, 200-day, whatever. Once calculated, they can be charted (Figure 3.6). To prepare the moving average, you can use the high, low, open, or close. The latter is most common. Naturally, you must consistently use the same one. Here's an example of how a 3-day moving average is constructed:

Day#	Closing Price	Total of Last 3 Days	3-Day Average
1	2.40		
2	2.42		
3	2.45	7.27	2.42
4	2.50	7.37	2.46
5	2.53	7.48	2.49
6	2.55	7.58	2.53
7	2.53	7.61	2.54
8	2.49	7.57	2.52
9	2.45	7.47	2.49

You can see that this procedure smoothes out the price volatility. The moving average lags the current price activity both on the way up and the way down.

Some traders have developed trading systems from using combinations of moving averages. For example, you could use a set of moving averages of different lengths, a 5 and a 10-day. The slowest moving average, the 10-day in this case,

Figure 3.6 Price and Moving Average Chart

Note how this 3-day moving average lags the daily prices. Moving averages are used to smooth price action as a means of clarifying trends.

gives the long-term trend. The faster moving average, the 5-day, provides the buy-sell signals. The rules are simple:

1. A buy signal occurs when the faster average crosses above the slower.
2. A sell signal occurs when it crosses below.
3. Offset long positions when daily price closes below either moving average.
4. Offset shorts when daily close is above either moving average.

The challenge is to uncover the set of moving averages that work best for the stocks or commodities you wish to trade.

Another sample of a mechanical trend following system is the Point-and-Figure Chart. It is based on the theory that long periods of price consolidation are required to generate a significant price move. This system totally disregards time and concentrates solely on price movement.

Chartists use "X"s to denote upticks and "O"s for downticks. Therefore, much interday information is required and a scale must be set. Computer optimization programs are available to select scales. The only rule of thumb is that the scale must be larger than the minimum price fluctuation of the contract being charted. A popular scale for commodities is one cent value to each block with a three cent reversal. This simply means that an X or an O is put on the chart for each one cent move up or down. Once three consecutive Xs or Os are recorded against the current trend, the trend is considered reversed and positions are offset or reversed (Figure 3.7).

With this system, 45-degree angle trendlines and channels are considered to be even more significant than on bar charts. Other formations, like double bottoms and triangles, are also used in the analysis.

Structural Analysis

Technical analysts who use this type of analysis, believe in the "Natural Law." The sun rises in the east each day. The seasons rotate from Spring, Summer, Fall, and Winter. Patterns and respective cycles can be found everywhere. Physical sciences are based in this fact. Why not stock and commodity prices? The structural analysts search for these patterns. A discussion of a few of the more prominent schools of thought follows.

Figure 3.7 Point and Figure Chart

The "X"s denote positive price moves and the "O"s negative. These charts can be used as a mechanical trading system within themselves.

Seasonals

Seasonal patterns are the easiest to understand, especially if you consider the agricultural commodities. The seasonal price trends these commodities undergo reflect the regular annual changes that take place in their supply-demand equation.

Think about a typical crop year. First, we anticipate planting intentions. Then we worry and fret through the weather markets of the growing season. Finally we usually have an abundance of supply at harvest time.

Studies have shown, for example, that 70 percent of all seasonal tops occur between April and July for soybeans, while 80 percent of the time soybean prices bottom between August and November.

How can you use this information? If you know the seasonal patterns for the stock or commodity contracts you trade, you can use these patterns to confirm signals you get from other methods of analysis. Some traders will not trade against reliable seasonal patterns without having a very strong reason for doing so.

Cycles

Cycles are similar to seasonal patterns, but they can be longer than 12 months or extremely short in duration. Cycles are built on the observed phenomenon that events have a tendency to repeat themselves at reasonably regular intervals. The business cycle described earlier would be good examples.

As previously mentioned, much of man's life is governed by repeatable patterns or cycles. Since man made and drives the markets, it seems fair to assume that the markets would also possess definable cycles.

Cycles measure the time between each high or low (peaks and troughs). By knowing the time span between each high and low and the previous high and low, you are in a better position to anticipate the next high or low. Time is usually measured in calendar days, as opposed to trading days. Calendar days are used for the simple reason that people and nature do not take weekends off—money continues to change hands, as do events affecting cycles.

A long-term cycle generally lasts a year or more; intermediate less than a year; short-term ones last a few weeks or days. As a rule, allow approximately 10% leeway in the length of a cycle when establishing your expectation for the next top or bottom.

Elliott Wave

The Wave Principle states that social and market behavior trends and reverses in recognizable patterns. These patterns or waves reoccur. Prices unfold in "five waves" of crowd psychology when moving in the direction (up or down) of the primary trend. Then they move against the trend in "three waves." The wave pattern reflects life's starts, stops, false starts, reversals, etc. Progress is made in a jerky, saw tooth pattern, rather than a smooth up or downtrend.

Isolating the exact position of the current price activity within the wave patterns allows the trader to profit by anticipating the market's next move. Once your trading becomes synchronized with the wave pattern, you can successfully ride the economic waves of the markets. This technique is most commonly used to analyze the stock indexes and the Dow.

Gann Numbers

The best known of all structural analysts is probably W. D. Gann. His 1942 book, *How to Make Profits Trading Commodities,* was the first important treatise on this subject. He believed that precise mathematical patterns govern everything, particularly the stock and commodity markets. More importantly, he believed these patterns could be uncovered and exploited. Since his price predictions became legends in his own time and he claims to have made millions in the market, we can only assume he discovered many of them.

Integral to his trading system are Fibonacci Numbers—again a throwback to natural law—and angles of price trend movement. Together, his numbering system uncannily alerts traders to highs, lows, support-resistance areas, and reversal points. His work should be studied by every serious trader.

Again, this is not a definitive list of structural analytical systems, merely an overview. Now we'll take a glance at character-of-market type systems.

Character-of-Market Analysis

Character-of-market analysis is very sophisticated because it attempts to measure the quality of a price movement, and then take a position that may be opposite of the current trend. The other types of analysis discussed so far try to spot existing trends or certain formations that are reliable harbingers of future price activity.

With character-of-market analysis, the technician seeks what are known as "overbought" or "oversold" conditions. If the market is found to be overbought, it is sold. If it is found to be oversold, it is bought. This approach is a 180 degree turn from the trend-following approaches, where a strong market is bought and a weak one is sold.

The psychology behind character-of-market analysis is simply that when markets become too top heavy, they fall. Or when everyone gives up on prices ever rising again, they will. It is a contrarian approach to technical analysis.

The trick is determining when a market is overbought or oversold. Here are some of the better known approaches.

Oscillators

Oscillators are concerned with price changes over a period of time. Simple oscillators utilize the difference between two moving averages. The departure between them indicates overbought and oversold conditions.

More complicated ones use the difference between daily prices. It can be the settlement, high-low, or opening price. Take a simple five day settlement price oscillator as an example. It is computed by subtracting the settlement price of the fourth previous trading day from the current settlement price. If the settlement price has risen, you get a positive remainder. A negative remainder occurs if the price has fallen. If the remainder is exceptionally high or low, the analysts will consider the market overbought or oversold and take the opposite position. Analysts using oscillators employ more complicated ones than this simple example, but the basic concept is the same.

Relative Strength Indexes

These are indexes that attempt to quantify the momentum of the market. When certain price levels are reached, a market is said to be overbought or oversold and, therefore, due to reverse its trend.

This approach works well in choppy, zigzagging markets. If you use them in a long-trending market, you may get burned badly. You need many tools on your technical analysis workbench. These are excellent ones to have when the market appears to be confused or erratic—but never rely on just one approach for analyzing all markets and all the varying market conditions.

Other Approaches

We can't spend a great deal of time on "other approaches" to technical analysis for two reasons. First, there are simply too many of them. Secondly, most of them are too complex to be easily described. The best we can do is just to make you aware of a few of the possibilities.

Astrological Analysis—Astrology is the study of the aspects and positions of planets and other heavenly bodies to predict future human events. There are a number of books, and even a newsletter, devoted to price analysis based on astrology. Lunar phases, planets, and even sun spots have also been used.

Correlation Analysis—This is the study of the relationship of a specific stock or commodity with a related or nonrelated entity in the hopes that a correlation between the two (or more) will indicate future trends. A simple example is the correlation between gold and paper currencies, gold and the U.S. budget deficit, a particular stock and the advance-decline numbers.

Fibonacci Numerical Progression Analysis—The classic name for this mathematical phenomenon is the golden ratio. It was originally recognized by the ancient Greek mathematicians and popularized in the 13th Century by Leonardo of Pisa, known as Fibonacci. The numerical series is created by starting with 1 and adding the results of each addition to the previous one—0, 1, 1, 2, 3, 5, 8, 13, 21, 34, 55, 89, (89 + 55 = 134) 134, etc. Using these numbers in various calculations as divisors or multipliers generate the golden ratio, which is 1.618 or 0.618. This ratio was called golden by the ancients because it appears widely in nature (branching of trees, flowers, sea shells, etc.) and is appealing to the eye. It was used in such varying structures as the Egyptian pyramids and the Sistine Chapel.

If it exists in nature, is used commonly by man, and creates a pleasing design or formation—technical analysts postulate that it should then appear in price charts as well. When it does, they give special emphasis to price advances or retracements that reflect the golden ratio. These technicians look for moves up or down of 62%, or angles of this degree between critical points. No one is absolutely sure why this ratio is important, but in many cases it appears to work and generates meaningful projections. W. D. Gann, as mentioned earlier, made extensive use of the golden ratio in his work.

Contrary Opinion

One last type of analysis you should be aware of is sometimes referred to as contrary opinion. It simply states that the masses are usually wrong. If the crowd or herd thinks a specific market is headed higher, it is probably ready to make a move lower.

The stock, commodity, and options markets are very fast moving, very emotional markets. Traders are called on to make split second decisions, often involving large sums of money. Additionally, these decisions are not necessarily based in cold, logical analysis of facts. Often, as you probably gathered from this discussion of fundamental and technical analysis, the decisions are more based in faith than anything else. This is only natural, since we're dealing in future events.

For this reason, you need to guard against being caught up in a stampede of bulls or bears. You must walk the line between following a trend and getting caught up in a ground swell of emotion that keeps you in a market too long. Namely, beyond the point where it turns dramatically against you generating substantial losses. Contrary analysts believe that by the time the herd reacts, it is too late and things are about to change. Contrarians can base their decisions on either fundamental or technical analysis.

Combined Approaches

Using one type of analysis, even if one approach is technical and the other fundamental, does not preclude using others, even several others. The most common example is the analyst who uses a fundamental system to determine the long-term trend and one or more technical systems for the short term. The fundamentals tell you why the market is moving; technicals signal when. This is sometimes referred to as the Market View Approach.

We specifically said "one or more" technical systems for the short term because certain systems work better in certain types of markets and for certain stocks or commodities. For example, at times the markets in general, or a specific stock or futures contract, may have the tendency to trend up and down for long periods of time—three or four months or longer at a stretch. When this occurs, trend following systems (moving averages, etc.) work well.

But what happens when the markets get very choppy or trendless? Trend following systems suffer severe whipsawing in nontrending markets. You probably want to use a character-of-the-market type of system in these very erratic types of markets.

Our point is that there is not a single trading approach that will be successful in all market conditions. If the activity of a market doesn't suit your system(s), you should change markets or stand aside until more favorable conditions return.

Applying Your Analysis

The purpose of technical and/or fundamental analysis is to solidify your opinion of where, and how strongly, the market is headed. You select your option trading strategy based on your degree of bullishness or bearishness. There is at least one other alternative, which is the subject of the next chapter.

Chapter 4

Option Price Models and Volatility— The Most Important Consideration for Serious Option Traders

"Most of the change we think we see in life is due to truths being in and out of favour."

Robert Frost's *Black Cottage*

Key Concepts

◆ Using a Theoretical Option Price Model

◆ Determining if an Option Is Over, Under, or Fairly Valued

◆ Random Walk Price Theory

◆ Calculating and Quantifying Stock and Commodity Price Volatility

◆ Analyzing Historical, Seasonal, and Implicit Volatility

◆ Combining Volatility Analysis with Fundamental and Technical Forecasts

In our survey of technical analysis, we neglected to mention one very important tool—Theoretical Option Price Modeling. Our reason is simply that a full chapter needs to be devoted to the subject.

Option prices, as determined by open outcry on the various stock and commodity trading floors, are either fairly priced, over, or undervalued. They must be one of these three. Therefore, if we could compare what the price "should be," given the current facts, with what it is in the pits, we could come to a logical opinion regarding the most advantageous trading strategy.

For example, if your analysis indicates the option being evaluated is fairly priced and that it will remain that way until expiration, you might consider writing the option. On the other hand, if all indications are it is grossly undervalued and poised to make a major move higher, you'd look for the best bullish strategy. The opposite, or a bearish strategy, would be called for if you are confident the option is currently overvalued by the marketplace.

Another important use of price modeling is strike price selection. Your fundamental or technical analysis alerts you to a major bullish or bearish move—but which of the five or six strike prices available offer the most profit potential? Price modeling provides a rational, quantitative answer. In other words, price modeling can be used in combination with other types of analysis, as well as a stand alone trading technique.

Part and parcel of this concept of over and undervalue is price volatility. How widely will prices swing in the next 12 months, quarter, month, week, or day or two? Once you know the volatility and the option's price relationship to the current market, you're in great shape to select a strategy and/or strike price(s).

The best way to begin is to introduce you to the Black-Scholes Option Pricing Model. It is not the only model available, but it is the best known and most widely used. The model was developed in the 1960s for stocks and modified in the mid-1970s for options-on-futures by Myron Scholes and Fischer Black. Both men are legends in academic circles and the investment community.

The formula for the Black-Scholes Model is complex, beyond the scope of this book. Option traders use computerized versions requiring the input of four variables. The software program solves for the fifth. These programs are widely available, even affordable and virtually all brokers who trade options have access to them (see Appendix). The variables used are:

1. Time to expiration of the option
2. Price of underlying entity (stock or futures contract)
3. Exercise or strike price of the option
4. Carrying charges (interest rate, dividends for stocks)
5. Volatility of the price of the underlying entity

If you were evaluating an option, it is easy to see that the first four items are given. You can count the days to expiration. The current price of the stock or commodity comes from the paper, quote screen, or your broker. You select the strike price(s) you want to evaluate and the carrying charges are assigned or, with the case of dividends, they are announced in the financial press or can easily be estimated. With interest rates, it is usually recommended to use a rate that is closest to the time to expiration. For example, if there is three months to expiration, you use the 3-month Treasury bill rate.

The last item, volatility, causes all the grief. It is the one input item that can be wrong, resulting in an incorrect value. This could be very costly. For this reason, we will discuss volatility in some detail. To understand price volatility and the Black-Scholes Model, we must back up a little and talk about how prices change and the assumptions on which the model is based.

Random Walk

An enormous amount of study has been done over the years by some very intelligent and well-equipped economic scientists in hopes of discovering what causes prices to change. To the best of our knowledge, no one has discovered the secret.

As mentioned in the last chapter, traders and analysts use fundamental and technical analysis in their quest for discernible price trends, but they are by no means 100% reliable. Most market participants would be ecstatic with a reliability factor anywhere near 100%. Computers offer the promise of becoming the market tamer. Their capability of making thousands of calculations per minute, of easily handling the most complex equations, of manipulating millions of bits of data in econometric models is the hope of economists who dream of predicting tomorrow's prices today.

To date, there is no definitive price modeling methodology for futures, stocks, or options. But isn't this what excites us about these markets? Try as we do, our success rate is limited. The better we do, the harder we try—the more frustrated we become. Sounds a lot like golf, doesn't it?

Not being able to predict prices or price trends into the future with any certainty leads to the conclusion that price movements are random in nature. An additional conclusion is that prices cannot be artificially manipulated, at least for extended periods of time. By this is meant that the few attempts at cornering a market failed. The most recent example was the Hunt Brothers' assault of the silver market in 1979-1980. They bought, bought, bought silver until it approached $50.00 per ounce, only to watch it, and the family's wealth, plunge. Cornered markets are the rare exception that proves the rule.

More importantly, there are some price movements that appear to occur regularly and can be predicted mathematically. This characteristic of pricing allows us to determine the probability of future price action. The key word is "probability." It will never, in our estimation, be possible to unequivocally forecast prices. If traders or investors knew, as opposed to think they knew, what tomorrow's prices were definitely going to be, they'd discount the impact of inflation and everyone would agree on a price. There would be no need for exchanges.

The factor known as inflation is an important component of price determination because it modifies the concept of normal distribution of prices. If prices were absolutely distributed normally, they would be evenly scattered on either side of the mean, or average price. Inflation challenges this logic. A normal distribution curve is symmetrical, allowing for values of from below minus to infinity. Therefore, it is logical to expect negative commodity or stock prices? A symmetrical pattern also suggests there is an equal chance for an asset to go down, as well as up, in price. Inflation tends to improve the chances for price increases the farther we project into the future. This, of course, does not eliminate the strong possibility of a commodity or a stock losing money or going down in price. Nor does it remove the possibility of the percentage of growth to be lower than the inflation rate, resulting in a *de facto* loss of value. Nonetheless, the price of virtually all commodities and stocks gain over the long term.

What price analysts do is skew the results a little toward the positive side of the mean as they build their equations. This is accomplished through the use of a lognormal distribution curve. It calculates price changes in percentages, rather than dollars and cents. Prices move up or down as a percentage of the current price. A stock or commodity currently priced at $100, for example, experiences a

5% move. That puts it in a range of $95 to $105. At $50, the 5% move is $2.50. As the entity approaches zero, the changes become nearly meaningless, just as it is illogical to expect the value of a stock or commodity to go to zero. At some price, someone will find a use. Corn, for example, during the Great Depression was used as fuel. When stock prices go "too" low, someone buys the stock and liquidates the company. As prices go higher, the dollar increments become greater, even if the percentage remains constant.

At this point, let's summarize the conclusions of this discussion about price changes:

1. Price changes appear to be random, since there are not any analytical tools that are anywhere near 100% reliable. At best, fundamental and technical analysis systems are only partially successful.
2. Prices defy artificial manipulation over the long term. Eventually, supply and demand come into balance.
3. Prices move up or down. No one can accurately predict with any certainty which way they will move next.
4. Price changes, in dollar terms, should be skewed toward a positive side of the mean to be realistic using lognormal distribution because of inflation and other upward pressures.

These are the assumptions behind the Black-Scholes commodity and stock option pricing models. Most other theoretical pricing models also use these assumptions.

Now, let's build on these assumptions. Since price changes are random, we need to have an understanding of how prices are distributed randomly. This in turn leads to an appreciation of how to locate the mean (average price) and how to calculate deviations from the mean (volatility). We'll begin with a quick review of the theory of probability.

The Flip of a Coin

If you ever have been forced to take Statistics 101 in high school or college, you probably have been exposed to a discussion of the odds of getting a head or a tail when flipping a coin. Extensive experiments have documented that no matter how many times you flip a coin, there is always a 50-50 chance of getting a head or a tail. If you toss 10 straight heads in a row, you still have a 50-50 chance of getting a head on the eleventh try.

This axiom is the cornerstone for the concept of normal distribution of random events. For example, let's flip a penny 225 times—15 separate series of 15 tosses each.

Each time you repeat this experiment, you may or may not get the exact results shown. But what will happen is that the majority of the time you will get very similar results. The theoretical results follow.

Series Results	# Heads	# Tails
1	1	14
2	2	13
3	3	12
4	6	9
5	8	7
6	7	8
7	10	5
8	11	4
9	9	6
10	5	10
11	6	9
12	4	11
13	2	13
14	1	14
15	0	15

Specifically, you'll most often get the results—assume the coin is properly balanced—in the middle of the spectrum. It would be very unusual (32,000:1) to get 15 straight heads or tails. Or only one or two tails and the rest heads. Or all heads and no tails. Normal distribution describes what is likely to happen with random events. Charting this on a graph generates the well-known bell shaped curve.

We have additionally assumed that we need to use lognormal distribution. This skews the results to the positive side of the mean to account for inflation and the unlikely event of a commodity or stock price going to zero. Making this adjustment to our curve produces a bell shaped curve slightly leaning to the right, as you face it.

The bell shaped curve is the distribution curve. The one produced by flipping a coin repeatedly is "normal" or moderate in appearance, but the shape can change. Erratic data produces a flat arc because the data points are scattered. Data representing a slow moving market results in a curve that is very steep or narrow, since the data points are close together. (See Figure 4.1.)

The key concept is that the flatter the shape of the distribution curve, the more volatile is the market being evaluated. What we want to learn to do is plot price changes for various markets to generate distribution curves, so that we can quantify market volatility. Once we do this, we will be able to make statistically valid estimates of what price moves can be expected from these markets.

Underline the words "statistically valid estimates of what can be expected." This is the best we can do when we are attempting to forecast prices. On average, or normally, we'll be correct. This doesn't mean we'll always be right. We'll still be wrong some of the time.

What it will do is put the odds in our favor, giving us an edge. It should provide an excellent insight in market volatility, allowing us to answer questions like:

Figure 4.1 Volatility Curves

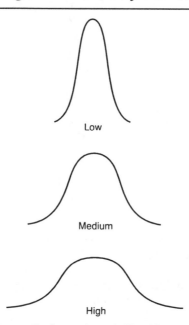

Low

Medium

High

The closer price points are, the lower the volatility. Highly volatile markets are characterized by wide or flat curves, since the data points are spread out.

"How much of a price move can we expect?"

"What are the chances of this market making a limit move?"

"Can we expect a certain futures contract or stock to make enough of a move during the life of the option we plan to buy to generate a profit from the option?"

This type of analysis provides educated guesses to these questions. It is the basis behind the computer programs that calculate the theoretic value of options, as an example. By running these programs, the software ranks the option alternatives telling you which ones are under or overpriced. It may even create strategies to take advantage of the given market conditions.

This statistical analysis won't tell us which way a market will move. Don't forget, we are discussing volatility of what we have classified as RANDOMLY moving prices. We will be able to figure the odds statistically of a market making a $2.00 move over the next 35 days—but will it be up or down?

That information won't come from this type of analysis. The answer—or more correctly best estimate—comes from other types of analysis, such as the fundamental or technical already discussed.

Now, let's take a closer look at the mean and the concept of standard deviation. The mean is simply the average of the price data and is the peak of the bell curve. The standard deviation describes the arch of the curve. Flat curves represent fast moving markets; steep curves reflect low volatility.

For purposes of illustration, let's go back to our coin flipping example. We made 15 series of 15 flips. To find the mean, you multiply the number of either heads or tails (only one side need be calculated) in each flip by the number of that flip and divide the total by the total number of heads (occurrences) recorded.

Flips	×	# Heads		
1	×	1	=	1
2	×	2	=	4
3	×	3	=	9
4	×	6	=	24
5	×	8	=	40
6	×	7	=	42
7	×	10	=	70
8	×	11	=	88
9	×	9	=	81
10	×	5	=	50
11	×	6	=	66
12	×	4	=	48
13	×	2	=	26
14	×	1	=	14
15	×	0	=	0
TOTALS		75		563

563 ÷ 75 = 7.5067

The mean or average for 15 coin flips is 7½, which is logical since we expected the normal flip of a coin to be a 50-50 proposition. Therefore, approximately half the data points will fall on each side of the bell curve, if we were to plot the results of all the flips.

Calculating the standard deviation is somewhat more involved, utilizing very complex algebraic formulas beyond the scope of this book. What you do need to know is the meaning of the standard deviation. In our coin flipping example, the standard deviation calculates to approximately 3.00. Standard deviation tells us two things about the data, namely how scattered or diverse it is and the probability of any specific outcome. In the case of a futures contract or stock price, this means we can calculate how fast a market is likely to change (volatility) and the chances of a certain price being hit or surpassed.

Please don't worry about not being able to mechanically calculate the standard deviation. Any trader who uses it regularly nowadays relies on computer programs. The function for figuring it is built into most advanced spread sheet programs, for example. Naturally, it is part of the software that runs the Black-Scholes formulas.

Actually, what is normally done is to calculate more than one standard deviation. It is common to figure one, two, and three standard deviations from the mean. These standard deviations are on both sides (plus and minus) of the mean. They tell us what percentage of the occurrences (coin flips, closing prices, rates of return) being evaluated will fall on either side of the mean. Here's a guideline:

◆ Plus or minus one standard deviation includes 68.3% or two-thirds of all occurrences.

◆ Plus or minus two standard deviations includes 95.4% or 19 out of 20 occurrences.

◆ Plus or minus three standard deviations includes 99.7% or just about all occurrences.

This simply means that if the result we are expecting, known as occurrences, falls within one standard deviation of the mean (average or midpoint of the bell curve), we would have a two out of three chance of that happening. Don't forget this is plus or minus one standard deviation, which means the result could be positive or negative because we have made the assumption that price movement is random.

For example, we want to know the probability of a certain commodity making a limit move or a stock price doubling. By running a standard deviation of the price activity, we could calculate the probability of that happening. But there is some "Kentucky windage" involved. How much data do we use to calculate the standard deviation? Do you use only last week's, month's, quarter's prices? Life of that particular contract or stock? All the data on record? This is a judgment call on your part based on experience. Consider taking two or three snapshots of the volatility using current, near, and longer term data. Is the volatility increasing or decreasing? This provides a feel for the price activity so you can make your judgment.

Does this analysis guarantee the results? No, definitely not. Even at the third standard deviation level there is 0.3% chance that the next occurrence (settlement price, etc.) will be outside the range.

To get back to our coin flipping example, the mean is 7.50 and the standard deviation is 3.00. Therefore, the first standard deviation ranges from plus or minus 3.00 of 7.50 or from plus 4.5 to minus 4.5. This would be a line (refer back to our table of results) between Flips #4 and #5 and Flips #10 and #11. Therefore, all the combinations of coin flips from 5 through 10 would have a two-thirds probability of happening. If we were to flip a balanced coin from now until eternity, the law of probability states that 68.3% (approximately two-thirds) of the results would fall within the above stated range.

Now, we'll discuss an actively trading market. What we will be doing is taking a snapshot of the current price activity and making some projections. When we do this, there are three things that can go awry. First, even if we use the third standard deviation, there is a one in 369 chance the next data point will be outside the parameters. Secondly, we could anticipate a positive move and actually experience a negative one. In other words, our analysis of the direction of the next move could be incorrect. Thirdly, we could be using an incorrect volatility value.

The volatility value changes whenever a new data point is added. The change may be virtually immeasurable if the new data point falls near the mean, but it occurs nonetheless. It is for this reason we think of price modeling as a snapshot or single frame of the price discovery process. Underline the word "process," for price discovery is indeed an ongoing process.

The first step in analysis of a trading market is to establish the mean. In most option price models, such as Black-Scholes, the current price is the mean. These pricing models assume the expected return from the underlying position (a futures contract or 100 shares of a stock) is zero. The apogee of the bell curve is the current price. To adjust for the expected return, carrying costs and dividends are added. For futures, there are no carrying costs of consequence, because the interest on the "small" margins, combined with the short period of time these positions are usually held, is not significant. And, futures do not generate dividends.

For stocks, it is a different story. At least half of the cost of a stock purchase must be anteed up when a position is opened on margin and interest must be paid on the other half. Additionally, dividends may be paid during the life of the option on the underlying stock. Therefore, the carrying cost and dividends are added to the current price.

Once you have the mean, you can proceed to calculate the standard deviation or volatility. This volatility figure represents one standard deviation of price change at the end of one year. For example, let's say gold is trading at $400.00 per ounce and has a volatility value of 20%. Over a year, you would project its trading range as plus or minus 20%, or from $320.00 to $480.00 per ounce, approximately 68% of the time. Calculating the second standard deviation (20% x 2 = 40%), projects that 95% of the data price points will range between $240.00 and $560.00 per ounce. The third standard deviation forecasts a range of $160.00 to $640.00 per ounce, which should account for 99.7% of prices "discovered" by open outcry in the pits over the year in question.

In most cases, using calculations based on a year isn't much help. Few options are liquid enough to be traded over a full year and even fewer option traders wish to hold positions that long. Sometimes even a month or a week seems like an eternity for in-the-money options. Therefore, we must convert the volatility to shorter periods of time. The Black-Scholes Model handles this by dividing the annual volatility by the square root of the number of trading periods in that year.

Here's an example of adjusting the yearly volatility rate to a daily rate. The usual figure used for the number of trading days (exclusive of weekends and holidays) is 256. This number is used because it is very close to the average in any given year and has an even square root, namely 16. Therefore, if the annual volatility rate is 20%, the daily would be 1.25% (20 ÷ 16). This means our $400.00 per ounce gold contract would have a daily volatility of $5.00 or a projected daily range of $395.00 to $405.00 per ounce. Of course, this is for the first standard deviation or two out of three days or 68% of the time. At the second standard deviation level, we could expect a $10.00 per ounce swing up or down one out of 20 days. A $30.00 per ounce move could be expected one out of 369 days, which would be the third standard deviation.

How do we project this probability out for a week? Stocks and commodities trade 52 weeks a year. The square root of 52 is 7.211. The annual volatility of 20% divided by 7.211 is 2.77%. This figure times $400.00 per ounce equals $11.08, which is the maximum weekly price change we would expect two-thirds of the time. Only 5% of the time would we project a change of more than $22.16 on a weekly basis.

From what we've discussed so far, it is clear how you can calculate the anticipated dollars and cents price range for a commodity or stock given any time period and volatility rate. For example, what would the price range of a $100.00 per unit commodity or stock share be for the next 25 days with an annual volatility rate of 35%?

365 day ÷ 25 day = 14.6 trading periods
Square root of 14.6 = 3.82
35% volatility ÷ 3.82 = 9.16%
9.16% × $100.00 = $9.16
The price range would be plus or minus $9.16 or from $90.84 to $109.16
for 68% of the time.

The beauty of this mathematical exercise is that you can work backwards, as well as forwards. Given the volatility value and our projected price change, how good a probability is it that we'll see the price change we project? Let's say, you need a $30.00 price change on a $200.00 per unit futures contract or stock between now and expiration, just 50 days away, with an annual volatility rate of 20%.

365 ÷ 50 = 7.3
Square root of 7.3 = 2.7
20% ÷ 2.7 = 7.4%
7.4% of $200 = $14.80

This tells us that our $30.00 target may be unrealistic from a law of probability standpoint. We should expect a $14.80 swing 68% of the time. If we divide $30.00 by $14.80, we get 2.02 or approximately 2 standard deviation. Therefore, we have approximately a 1 in 20 chance of a $30.00 move. Do you offset your position faced with this scenario and salvage what you can or continue to hold? The answer depends on your money management skills and your approach to risk.

Which Volatility?

As mentioned previously, the amount of the data used to calculate volatility varies. For example, a week or a month or a year's worth of data can be inputted in the equation. Also, any particular price, such as the open, high, low, or close, can be used. The standard approach is to use the settlement price, which is the daily price at which the clearing houses settles all accounts between clearing members for each contract and contract month. The settlement price and the closing price are not always identical.

In other words, there is some discretion required when selecting the data. Two traders, one using the settlement prices and the other opens, could calculate different volatility factors for the same contract over the same period of time. The same is true for the two other analysts, where one uses the settlement price for the last five days and the other uses 200 days of data.

You must also be aware of the fact that intraday price movements or daily price ranges can be greater than one standard deviation price change on any given day. Let's say you calculated one standard deviation for a certain contract as 50 cents a day. You calculate from settlement price to settlement price. Your calculation of volatility could be right on the money, yet the daily price range could be $1.00 or more. (As a side note, there have been other methods explored to figure volatility besides the standard deviation, but none have caught on.)

Continuing this line of thought, you may calculate the daily volatility of a certain $50.00 commodity or stock at 1.25% or a dollar value of 62½ cents. For the next five days, you monitor the following price changes: +.55, -$1.25, -.05, +.25, +.75. With one standard deviation of 62½ cents, the law of probability indicates that 68% of the time the price change of the commodity should range between a plus 62½ cents and a minus 62½ cents. In the above series of price changes, three out of five or 60% are within the range.

What should an analyst conclude from this information? First, the data only covers five days. Therefore, there is no reason to immediately assume the volatility rate is incorrect. Secondly, the percentage of price changes within one standard deviation is close, 60% versus 68%, to expectations. The one figure that might concern the analyst is $1.25, which is over twice one standard deviation. The expectation would be for a price change of this magnitude to occur one in twenty times, rather than one in five.

The first thing the analyst would do is look for a reason why one of the price changes ranged into the second standard deviation. This often occurs when a government report exceeds market expectation. For example, let's say this example was the live hog market and was trading at $50.00 per hundred weight. USDA (United States Department of Agriculture) then released hog numbers 10% or 20% below market expectation, driving up prices the $1.25. If this was the case, there would be a good reason for the surprise price change. If no reason for the change can be found, the analyst might consider changing the volatility rate.

The correct nomenclature for the volatility rates calculated using current market prices is implied volatility. It is the rate of price change implied by current trading. If this is what implied volatility is, what kind of volatility have we been previously talking about? Up until now, we have been discussing historical volatility. It provides a consistent view of an option over a period of time. For example, a service providing daily historical volatility charts would use the daily settlement price, or they might use each Friday's settlement price to produce weekly charts,

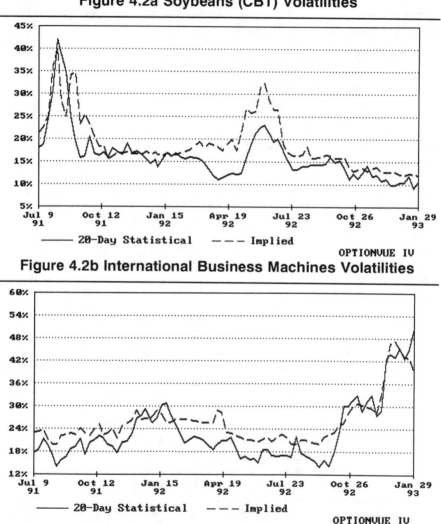

Figure 4.2a Soybeans (CBT) Volatilities

——— 20-Day Statistical   — — — Implied

OPTIONVUE IV

Figure 4.2b International Business Machines Volatilities

——— 20-Day Statistical   — — — Implied

OPTIONVUE IV

or the settlement price of last trading day of the month for a monthly chart. Refer to Figure 4.2 and Appendix 3 for examples of volatility charts.

The value of the historical charts is they can give you the overview or the long-term perspective. Let's say you calculate, using the Black-Scholes Model, that you need a volatility factor of 30 in order to have a shot at making money or breaking even on an option you are holding. Perusing the historical volatility charts for the underlying commodity or stock reveals that volatility has never exceeded 25. Is there any reason to expect a new high to be made? If not, it may be time to offset your position to salvage as much time value as possible.

Seasonal Volatility

Volatility is the quality of being volatile, which means changing readily and repeatedly, changeable, fickle, or transient. From our experience, this definition suits the grain markets to a tee at certain times of the year. It also holds true for several other market groups, such as petroleum and softs, that have pronounced seasonal patterns.

The rationale for this behavior is simple. The more widely scattered prices for a commodity, let's say corn, the higher the volatility. Think back to the bell curve. If prices are scattered in a broad pattern around the mean—as opposed to a tight pattern or narrow price range, the curve will be flatter. The flatter the curve, the higher the standard deviations.

Broad price ranges in the corn market are the result of uncertainty regarding the supply-demand situation at key times of the year. The first spurt of volatility occurs when USDA releases its initial estimate of the planting intentions of farmers. How many acres will be planted? Factored into this figure will be any federal acreage reduction or set aside programs.

Once the crop is in the ground, a series of weather-generated volatility rallies usually occur. Spring rains bring the risk of delayed planting. But if it doesn't rain, there is the fear of low germination rates and that the chemicals (primarily fertilizers, herbicides, and pesticides) won't be activated. After the corn is as high as an elephant's eye, the farmers begin to worry about a drought or pollination problems. Then the worry warts struggle through a wet fall that could hamper harvest, early frosts that may reduce yields and snow cover which could keep the combines out of the fields.

So far, we've only discussed the supply side of the supply-demand equation. The demand leg has its own seasonality, primarily tied to livestock numbers, prices, and demand. If ethanol ever gets wide acceptance, corn demand may influenced by the seasonality of gasoline production and demand.

Price rallies naturally stimulate volatility rallies, if prices are widely scattered. It is not uncommon to see the volatility jump by 3%, or even as much as 10% to 15%, in a very short period of time. The obvious result of these swings is rapidly accelerating prices for calls, particularly strike prices in or near in-the-money. They are being influenced by both the direction of the market, which is increasing in intrinsic value, and the improved volatility, which makes it more attractive to traders.

An informative exercise is to repeatedly run the Black-Scholes Model changing only the volatility rate. Keep all the other variables—namely, strike price, time to expiration, underlying futures contract price, and interest rate—the same. This provides an excellent insight into the impact of volatility. We recommend at first varying the volatility by five points each time. Then duplicate the drill at just one point intervals.

When attempting to trade seasonal volatility, keep in mind that the influences on one contract month may not apply to another. For example, a contract that extends through the July and August drought months, such as the November contract, should be assigned a higher volatility rate, than the May contract that doesn't. You might give November a volatility factor of 5% more, compared to May.

When you begin to assign or adjust volatility rates, you are entering the area of forecast volatility. There are advisory services that publish volatility forecasts. These numbers can be valuable guides, but they have the weakness associated with any analyst's attempt to foretell the future. Therefore, you should only use them as a guide, the same way you use historical volatility. Personally, we place more weight in historical numbers, particularly the highs, lows, support, and resistance levels.

Moving Averages

The analyst or trader seriously relying on volatility can use simple averages, weighted averages, or moving averages to get a better feel for what value to use when running simulations. Let's say you are planning to enter an option position. You want to run the Black-Scholes Model, but you're not sure of what volatility factor to use.

Your first step should be to look at the historical values. The current historical (over the last year or 250 days) volatility is 15%, for example. Checking the last quarter or 60 days shows a figure of 22% and the current figure, say the most recent 10 to 15 days, is 20%.

Volatility for the last quarter is 46% above the historical value. You should find out why. It could be a normal seasonal pattern, since the nearby rate appears to be returning to the historical level.

A simple average of the three values is (15 + 22 + 20 = 57/3) 19. This could be used. Or, you could give more weight to the historical factor by calculating a weighted average. If you plan to buy and hold an option for the long term, you would give more weight to the historical perspective. Short-term traders would give the emphasis to the near term. For example:

Long Term:
    15 x 5 = 75
    22 x 3 = 66
    20 x 1 = 20
    161 ÷ 9 = 17.8

Near Term:
    15 x 1 = 15
    22 x 3 = 66
    20 x 5 = 100
    181 ÷ 9 = 20.1

Moving averages are an excellent tool for filtering out market noise and uncovering trends. Long, medium, and short-term moving averages can be compared. This often provides a valuable method for uncovering trend changes.

Estimating Volatility

So far, we have used historical, seasonal, and implied volatility to get a fix on what volatility rate we should use in the Black-Scholes formula. Additionally, we have experimented with simple and weighted averages. Now we'll compare the volatility characteristics of related futures contracts.

Over a decade ago, we developed a proprietary set of indexes that track the physical commodity markets. It is known as the Wasendorf Composite Index and its four subindexes, namely the grains, meats, metals, and food/fiber. Experience with these subindexes has demonstrated to us that the volatility of the commodities within each group is similar. For example in the grains, when the rate of change in prices for oats becomes active, we look to this excitement to spread to corn, soybeans, meal, oil, and wheat. Oats are usually the least liquid, meaning they have the lowest volume and open interest of the grain complex. For this reason, it takes less price activity to generate price movement. The more price movement and the more scattered it is, the higher the volatility. It is extremely rare to have a lot of trading volume with pricing held to a tight pattern.

Equally true, when one or two markets within this group are inactive, most of the others are also. The reason is the interrelationship of these commodities. Oats, corn, soybeans, wheat—all are used for feed and food. If oats or corn become expensive, compared to wheat, livestock producers feed wheat. If cattle numbers are on the rise, so will the demand for corn and soybeans. When soybean prices are active, it affects meal and oil prices. For these reasons, these different commodities share similar volatility characteristics.

The following is a list of the commodities in the other three sub-indexes of the WCI. The commodity with the asterisk indicates the volatility leader of the group.

Meat Sub-Index: Live Hogs, Live Cattle, Pork Bellies, *Feeder Cattle
Metal Sub-Index: Silver, *Platinum, Copper
Food-Fiber Sub-Index: *Cocoa, Coffee, Sugar, Lumber, Cotton, Orange Juice

Naturally, these behavior patterns are not limited to just these commodities. For example, the volatility rates of the European currencies tend to move in unison, as do the base metals (lead, zinc, aluminum, copper, etc.) and the debt instruments (bonds, notes, interest rates, etc.).

Therefore, when you are estimating the volatility of one commodity, you can look to the volatility of like commodities for clues or verification. Let's say you're trying to get the feel for the volatility of corn. You check oats and find that it is at the high end of its volatility range and in an uptrend. With this information, you might increase the rate you plan to use for corn by a few percentage points.

Traders who specialize in trading certain commodity groups often chart the historical volatility of the entire group on a single graph. From a chart like this, you can more accurately gauge the relationship between the volatility rates of commodities in the group.

T-Bills/Bonds

Don't forget some futures, like Treasury Bills, Bonds, and Eurodollars, for example, are indexed by 100. This must be taken into account when we calculate the daily or weekly volatility. To do this, we assume that interest rates will never be a negative number, just as we previously assumed that the price of a physical commodity would never go to zero or below. If T-bills were trading at 98.00 and it's annual volatility was 16%, the daily volatility would be .98 (16% / 16 × 98.00 = .98). This appears to be a bit unrealistic. Therefore, we use 100-98.00 or 2.00 in the equation (16% / 16 × 2.00 = 2), which is more plausible.

Summary

Volatility is the primary measure of how wide of price swings a futures contract or stock will make over a given period of time. An annual volatility rating of 20 indicates the price of the commodity being studied has the potential of ranging from a plus 20% to a minus 20% of the mean price, which is the current price for futures. For stocks, it is the current price plus dividends and carrying charges.

To make an intelligent decision regarding whether an option is oversold or overbought, and therefore whether it is a good investment opportunity, most option traders calculate a theoretical price. This price is compared to the current market price and trend.

The calculation of the theoretical price of an option uses the following inputs: 1) time to expiration; 2) underlying futures or stock price; 3) strike price; 4) interest rate (dividend for stocks if paid before expiration); 5) volatility. All of these are given—except for volatility. Since volatility is the only factor that must be estimated, it becomes extremely important. Traders use historical records, comparisons, and other techniques to estimate the future rate of volatility. But no matter what approach is used, it is still an approximation. This again underscores the importance of understanding volatility.

One last note to emphasize just how important volatility is to the professional trader is the fact the Chicago Board of Options Exchange (CBOE) has developed a CBOE Volatility Index. This index measures the potential price variations in blue-chip securities traded on the U.S. stock markets and allows you to hedge the value of options on benchmark stocks caused by fluctuations in volatility. The S & P (Standard & Poor) 100 stock index was used as the base because it is the most liquid option index in the world. A mathematical formula calculates the probability of prices moving 20 percentage points above or below a target price over a year's time. If you plan to trade stock options, you'll want to track this index. You can use it as a guide when you need to estimate volatility or as a checkpoint to second guess estimations.

Chapter 5

Developing Trading and Money Management Plans

"When schemes are laid in advance, it is surprising how often the circumstances fit in with them."

Sir William Osler (1849-1919)

Key Concepts

◆ Putting Your Plan on Paper—Goal Setting

◆ Gut and Financial Checks

◆ Selecting which Markets to Trade

◆ Trading Plan Checklist

◆ Nine Money Management Rules

◆ Twelve Psychological Trading Rules

◆ Thirteen Trading Rules

Now we'll get down to using what we've learned. So far, you should have a general overview of options trading, terminology, strategies, and approaches to price forecasting. Where do you go from here? How do you get into the market?

First of all, we strongly recommend you develop a plan—and put that plan on paper! A written plan does two important things for you. It forces you to make concrete decisions, which we'll go over in a second. A hard, document provides you with something you can measure your progress—and more importantly, your discipline—against.

It's sad to see the number of traders we've seen over the years who have waffled from one approach to another without any clearly stated plan. They wander in and out of the market, often making the same mistakes over and over.

Your written plan need not be fancy. It's not a formal proposal. It could be as simple as answers to the question we'll be discussing shortly. But it will help you decide what you are going to do, how you are going to do it, what you need from outside sources, and what you expect to gain.

When you get to the point of selecting specific trades, try using the technique known as visualization. It first became popular in sports, particularly on the olympic level. We use it to improve our golf game. You visualize a shot before you swing. In your mind's eye, you see the ball arc high, eventually dropping onto the green near the pin.

With trading, you create the perfect trade in your mind based on your analysis. The Yen moves higher for the next 30 days. Corn follows its seasonal pattern from its harvest lows, peaking mid-summer as the results of a drought scare. The rationale is that if you don't have a clear picture in your mind of where a market is going on the price charts, you're not ready to enter the trade.

Just like our golf, not every shot or trade is perfect or near perfect. We don't shoot par any more than we make money on every trade. But in both cases, after we visualize how things should be, we know early on when they are not. This technique helps us cut our losses short and let our winners run for all they are worth. You'll also be asked to keep a trading journal, which will be described in the next chapter.

Writing Your Plan

Step one is describing your trading philosophy and general goals. This can be done in one or two sentences. Here are a few examples.

Example #1
"I plan to trade for medium to long term, holding positions for 60 to 90 days. My primary strategy will be spreading."

Example #2
"I'm a short-term trader. I seek options in or near in-the-money close to expiration and plan to hold these positions no longer than a few weeks."

Example #3
"My approach will be to write covered options. I'll concentrate on options one or two strike prices out-of-the-money."

Example #4
"I plan to hedge my stock portfolio. I'll buy puts in the S & P 500 when I think the market is in a bearish trend."

These are only examples and reasonably conservative examples at that. A very aggressive trader could have written: "I plan to trade my brains out whatever the risk...trying to double or triple my money every month."

By jotting down your general approach to the market, you set the tone for the rest of the plan. It helps you answer the questions to come.

What are your goals?

We all want to make the most we can. If we didn't, we'd be looking at certificates of deposits or Treasury Bonds. Your goals dictate your strategies and must reflect your philosophy. A goal of 200% or 400% return to equity per annum requires a different strategy than a goal of 25% to 50% per year. If these return objectives seem high to you, compared to other types of investments, remember options trading is very speculative. High return; high risk. No pain; no gain.

Let's go back to the point of matching investment goals with strategies. If your return objective is on the high side, say 200% per year, it is unrealistic or impossible to reach it using a "conservative" spread strategy, such as the buy call spread. This type of spread, as illustrated in the strategy section, has a predefined maximum profit and predefined maximum loss. The maximum profit is nowhere near 200%. To have a shot at 200% return requires a much more offensive strategy, like buying in-the-money puts and calls. The risk, of course, is if the underlying entity trades sideways or in the wrong direction; your options will expire worthless.

Once your overall goals are set, you should break them down to per trade goals. For example, let's say you are starting with $10,000.00 in trading equity. Your goal is to double it this year or a 100% return. That means you need to generate $10,000.00 in net profits over the next 12 months or $834.00 per month.

If one of your money management rules is to never invest more than 5% of equity in any one position, you have at least 20 trades or one or two per month. Let's use two trades per month, assuming that some will make money giving you the extra four trades per year. You, therefore, have two trades to make $834.00 or $417.00 each, net of commissions and fees. If each option you buy or sell takes $500.00 of your equity or the 5%, your basic approach is a dollar per dollar risk to reward ratio, which is low for options or "conservative."

Additionally, you know in advance that not every trade will make money or even break-even; some will be losers. For this reason, you look for trades with a 1:3 risk to reward ratio. The key to success is the discipline to focus on specific, achievable goals.

This line of thought brings us to the subject of risk. When attempting to measure or quantify risk, economists use the term "utility," which is a measure of personal satisfaction. If something generates a feeling of greater satisfaction than whatever it is compared to, it is said to have greater utility.

You need to seriously think about how much risk you are psychologically prepared to accept. Do you classify yourself as adverse, neutral, or an aggressive risk taker? For example, a risk adverse person may not be interested in a trade that projects a dollar return for every dollar at risk. These traders want to take little or no risk and are comfortable with low but dependable rewards. The buy call spread and covered writing strategies appeal to them. The neutral and aggressive risk takers are willing to take greater and greater risks to get higher and higher utility.

Playing into this concept is your personal financial situation and responsibility. A single person with a handsome six-figure income can afford to take some risks. On the other hand, the bread winner of a large family in a middle income tax bracket should be more conservative.

As you probably guessed, you must factor into the analysis your personality. Will you be a good trader from a psychological standpoint? Options trading requires optimism, good judgment, and the ability to make good decisions under a lot of financial pressure. Excitable types rarely do well—nor do worriers. Additionally, it helps to have a life free, as much as possible, from other major personal problems that can distract you from the markets.

After sorting through all these thoughts, it's time to set specific return goals that you will shoot for—

5% per week

10% per month

50% per quarter

150% per year

Set the amount and term to match your strategy. Long-term traders evaluate themselves on the long term. Short-term investors need to do their evaluation more often.

At this point, you are setting targets. You can revise these marks higher or lower the longer you trade. Within a year, you should have a real good feel for what you and your trading system can do.

Which Markets?

One of the next questions is to determine which markets. This decision starts with your price forecasting approach. If you anticipate using fundamental analysis, you should choose markets that you are very familiar with, ones that you understand intellectually and intuitively. This is because there are so many variables that can influence prices, there is no way to measure all of them. Even the most sophisticated econometric models come up short. Investors with farm backgrounds can trade the agricultural options, for example. Or serious students of the stock market should trade the stock index options.

If you're a technical analyst, you seek markets in which you can get signals you are confident are reliable. Not every tech system works on every market. Nor are technical systems dependable in every type of market, such as trending and nontrending.

The traders interested in using price volatility to spot over or undervalued options, either as their sole analytic tool or as a supplement to another approach, should probably consider a computer program. As you'll see when we get to the chapter on automated trading (plus the Appendix), there are several very good programs available.

Related to the question of "which markets," is the question of how many different stocks or commodity markets you should trade at any one time. This is the concept of diversification. As you read the following, think back to our earlier discussion of the Law of Probability.

One of the benefits to selecting a full portfolio is diversifying your risk over as wide a spectrum as possible. The theory is both offensive and defensive. It's offensive in that it is designed to put you in the right place at the right time. By taking a position in several commodity markets or stock issues, you have a greater possibility of catching a major market move. No one—absolutely no one—can anticipate exactly when a given share or market will make its next big move up or down. Therefore, the more alternatives you are covering, the greater the chance you will be successful.

From a defensive stance, by spreading your investment capital over a wide variety of markets, you won't be caught in the wrong market at the wrong time or even the right market at the wrong time. Option trading is a lot like fly fishing. You're constantly casting your line with the objective of making a big strike. If a trout doesn't hit, you reel your line in and try again. Option traders let their profits run and cut losses short. A good, successful trading system often has more losing trades than winners. The difference is the overall gain from the winners exceeds the losses from the losers.

Additionally, experience has taught us that the different stock or commodity groups are normally negatively correlated. That means they do not move up and down in unison. When one group is bullish, another is bearish and a third may be moving sideways. For example, if grain prices are high (bullish) and going higher, it puts pressure on livestock producers because it cuts their profit margin. More livestock are subsequently sent to market sooner and livestock prices become bearish, moving lower as the cash market is flooded with animals. Understanding negative correlation can help you from getting caught with all your eggs in one basket.

Once you begin to reach some preliminary decisions on how, which, and the number of options you can afford to trade, it's time to consider what you want or can invest in options trading. In this section of trading plan, we're talking in general terms. The rule of thumb is the amount should not exceed 10% of your risk capital, which in turn is defined as money you could afford to lose without incurring a change in your lifestyle.

Experienced investors invest a small portion of their risk capital in highly speculative investments, like options, with the idea of generating a very high return. The purpose is twofold. First, the bulk of their net worth is held in more conservative investments for protection. And, secondly, the hope for high return from options trading gives their overall return on investment a boost.

Here's a checklist of what questions should be answered in the introductory or overview section of your written trading plan.

1. What is my option trading philosophy? Am I a long, medium, or short-term trader?
2. What are my goals? Have I broken them down into per month and per trade goals? Are they realistic?
3. Am I psychologically and financially suited for options trading?
4. How do I plan on keeping a trading diary?
5. How do I plan to select trades? Close out or offset trades? What is my analysis technique?
6. What strategies suit my resources?
7. How many and which markets will I trade?
8. Are the answers to all of the above questions consistent?

As you write your plan, keep in mind that it is a living document. It will change as your experience increases, as markets change, and as new option products are introduced.

You should also begin at this stage to prepare a list of your limitations and needs. This can be anything from something personal, like discipline, to something physical, like quotation equipment, to something intellectual, like research on the underlying entities. Later, we'll show you how to use this list of shortcomings in your selection of a broker and brokerage firm.

Once you've written general, almost philosophical, answers to the eight questions listed, you should prepare a list of specific trading rules to live by and trade by. The purpose of these rules is to instill discipline into your trading. Your trading decisions are business decisions—treat them with the same cold logic you would use to address the refinancing of your home or business.

To help organize these rules, we have divided them into three general categories—money, mind, and management. You need to sort through our suggestions and extract the ones that particularly pertain to you. Then tailor them to your financial, personal, and trading style.

Of the three groups, we personally believe the money management principles are the most important. Our reasoning reflects the Law of Probability already discussed. Good money management allows you to survive the losing trades you will invariably encounter so you will still be trading when you are in the right market, with the right strategy at the right time.

Nine Money Management Rules

1. *The first and simplest thing to do is divide your risk capital into at least 10 parts, preferably 20.* To put the Law of Probability at your back, you want to be able to make 10 or more trades. You're attempting to have the normal distribution of winning and losing trades make you a net winner dollar-wise. If you do not have enough risk capital to make 10 trades with a reasonable good chance of succeeding, seriously consider waiting until you do. If, for example, you only have $1,000.00 in risk capital, and decide to buy 10 deep out-of-the-money options, the odds are so far out of your favor you would probably be better off at Churchill Downs. Buying 10 deep out-of-the-money options is not "investing" in options in our opinion.

2. *Always calculate the transaction costs as part of the risk-to-reward ratio.* The major component of this is the brokerage commission. Don't overlook it. If you over trade your account, commissions can draw down your equity, just like losing trades do. We'll discuss the negotiation of brokerage commissions in detail later.

3. *Never forget what you are trading.* Options are wasting assets—eventually they will expire worthless unless offset or exercised. Think of your options as one hundred pound blocks of ice. The time to expiration is the ambient air temperature. The food in the icebox is the portfolio of underlying entities. The purpose of the ice is to keep the stock or commodity options fresh until you are ready to use

them. But the longer you wait, the more the ice melts and the less time they'll stay fresh. The closer you get to expiration the faster the ice melts, as the temperature rises. At expiration if you don't do anything with the options, you'll have a puddle of warm water and a pile of "spoiled" underlying entities. In other words, you forfeit 100% of the premium you paid for the options.

To conserve your risk capital, offset or exercise before expiration! All too many new traders allow options to expire worthless—pros rarely do.

4. *Always know what your risk-to-reward ratio is.* Divide what you expect to make in profits from an option by your total cost (premium, commission, fees). If it is not at least 3:1, you may want to look for a better opportunity. Exceptions can be certain strategies, like the buy-sell spreads, that have a fixed down side risk with high probability of reaching the upside objective.

5. *Be very careful of pyramiding.* This is the practice of buying additional positions with unrealized profits. It increases your leveraging but also increases your risk.

6. *Avoid letting a profitable position become a loser.* This sounds obvious, but it is a common mistake of new traders. It is often caused by a trader taking his own analysis too literally.

Here's what can happen. A trader forecasts a move in an underlying entity (stock or commodity) and buys an in-the-money option. The move occurs as predicted but ahead of schedule or with more momentum than expected. Instead of placing a trailing stop loss order to protect profits or promptly offsetting, the trader holds the position too long waiting for a certain target price to be reached. While waiting, the positions make a negative move and the option eventually expires worthless. Markets usually fall twice as fast as they rise.

7. *Diversification of positions into several different classifications should be included in your money management rules.* For example, you might have a rule that no more than 25% of your positions are in any one stock or commodity group.

8. *Don't forget the biblical parable about seven lean years following the seven bountiful years.* Option trading often follows a similar pattern. You find yourself with a string of winners, only to be followed by a string of losers. Our recommendation is to siphon off profits to an emergency account when available.

Another good approach is to withdraw your original investment from your trading account as soon as possible. Then you are trading with profits only. This sometimes relieves much of the pressures traders feel when they lose their "own" money.

If you can withdraw some profits on top of your original investment as well, it helps you stick to your original plan which obviously was successful. Do not automatically reinvest all profits in the market. A "go for broke" mentality is very dangerous in this arena.

When a losing streak begins, take a trading vacation or cut the size of your trades in half. If you are trading ten lots of a certain spread, reduce trades to five lots. If losing trades continue, cut down to one or two lots. Eventually, you'll recover, but you can't if you have traded away all your equity.

9. *From time to time, you may be approached with a strategy that makes good sense from a tax situation.* Do not let this be the reason for taking the trade. Take the time to do your regular analysis to assure yourself it is a good trade on its own merits.

Twelve Psychological Trading Rules

Now let's discuss some psychological rules you might want to incorporate into your written trading plan. To paraphrase a famous Yogi Berra baseball saying: "Options trading is 90% mental and the other half is knowledge, experience, and skill."

1. *Rule numero uno is to follow all the money management rules.* Money at risk is, of course, a very serious source of stress. If those rules are violated, following the ones described below will not do you much good.

2. *Experiencing losses in the option markets is not failure.* It's the normal course of business. You can equate it to trying to hit a baseball. A hitter who has a .300 batting average gets a hit about every third time at bat. Two-thirds of the time he loses. Worse yet, of the three in ten hits, only a small percentage of them are home runs. An even smaller percentage of the home runs are grand slammers. A lot of the hits are singles.

In option terms, singles break even and may pay, or partially pay, the transaction costs (commissions and fees).

The batter who hits .300 or has a lifetime average that high will be a success. So will the options trader whose every third trade is profitable. The law of probability will see to it that he gets a few homers and an occasional grand slam.

3. *Don't run your mind through the wringer on every trade.* Once you make up your mind on a position, stay with it, unless you uncover some overwhelming reasons to abort the trade. Avoid listening to the advice of others once your mind is made up.

4. *Closely related to number three is the ability to live with your trading decisions.* You must accept full responsibility for them and that's that!

5. *At the same time you're accepting responsibility to live with your trading decisions, stay impersonal.* Be prepared to cut losing positions early through the use of stops.

6. *When you feel the market is dragging you down, walk away for awhile.* Take a vacation from the markets.

7. *Take pride in yourself and your trading skills.* It is the only thing that keeps us going sometimes—the market can be a "great humbler." Therefore, you need to control your reaction to success and stay humble. Pride often induces over trading which can result in serious financial damage.

8. *Trade as "James Bond" would—with cold, calculated precision, once you have decided what to do.*

9. *Maintain the maximum amount of self-discipline.* Set concrete rules for yourself—for example, stop trading for a day or a week after taking two consecutive losses—and stick to them.

10. *Master yourself.* As part of your diary, include remarks about your behavior. Then work at correcting any flaws. You must work against natural instincts to be stubborn, emotional, and inflexible. Find your character flaws and overcome them.

11. *Be well aware of who you are.* Know your level of risk tolerance; you won't make sound decisions when you're way over your head financially. Nor when you're too tired or ill or not prepared to trade. Don't be afraid of missing an opportunity by taking a day off. Believe it or not, there are always great new trades in the offing. Learn to be patient; pick and choose your trades carefully.

Match your personality and temperament to your trading system. If you're not a detailed person, use a system that requires as little detail as reasonable. If you're very excitable, avoid day trading. Consider being a position trader, and once you put a position on, let it alone until you're ready to offset it.

12. *Try not to overtax your resources, particularly time.* Carefully evaluate how much of a commitment in time, money, and mental resources you can make. Part-timers should limit themselves to tracking three to five markets and trading only two to three. The markets should be ones that you have some prior experience with, a special interest in, or are knowledgeable of through your profession or life experience. For example, traders with farm backgrounds often have a good feel for the agricultural markets. Trading markets you're fond of makes the research easier.

Thirteen Trading Rules

The last set of rules deals with actual trading. Here we suggest certain things you should or should not do. These axioms come from the real world of options trading.

1. *Rule Number One contradicts all the ones that follow—Be a Doubting Thomas!*
First off, don't believe anything you hear about trading. Use all you learn as a guide, and find out what works for you as an individual. This frame of mind spills over into what your broker and fellow traders tell you is going to happen in a particular market or their advice in general. We have seen a lot of people make a lot of money in the options markets, but we've only seen few, if any, who made money consistently by listening to someone else. You need to distinguish between useful information about the markets and someone's opinion. The basic rules, combined with your education, experience, and understanding of your markets, blend into a unique approach. This is your trading system, which includes money management and psychological restraints, as well as your trade entry and exit decisions.

2. *Be totally open.* Be open to new ideas, new strategies, new markets, new information, and new forms of trading and communicating. Never forget you're attempting to predict what will occur at some point in the future. Most traders assume price patterns repeat, but exactly when and how closely the patterns mirror past ones is unknown. Look for the old, but trade the new.

Your approach to the markets should include the flexibility to change your mind, trade the short side of a market as well as the long, make adjustments in your money management or trading system, and consider markets you haven't previously traded. A successful trader is often the one aware of the most alternative paths. He or she has the flexibility of a master chess player to adjust to the unexpected.

3. *Place your markets in their historical perspectives.* Even if you don't use them as signals or indicators, you should know the historical highs and lows of the markets you trade. Additionally, you must have good understanding of the seasonal patterns and major cycles. Why? Simply because a large number of technical traders will trade based on these patterns. You must take their anticipated reaction into account as part of your overall trading analysis. If, for example, you buy a corn put at what are the normal seasonal lows (at harvest), you better have good reasons or deep pockets.

4. *The same reasoning, expostulated in Number Five, applies to developing a sound knowledge of technical analysis.* It is often called a "self-fulfilling prophecy" because so many traders see the same technical signal and react in unison. For example, an uptrend line is broken alerting technical traders that the current uptrend is now a downtrend. Just like a herd of longhorns heading for water, they stampede to the short side of the market.

5. *Don't spit into the wind, trust a junkyard dog, or trade contrary to the trend.* There are good financial and psychological reasons trends are created and maintained. For instance, would you pay more for something you intended to resell if you didn't think it was going to increase in value? Of course not. You buy a call because you believe you'll be able to sell it for more in the future. The same is true of a down trending market. You buy a put because you think you'll be able to offset your positions at a lower price.

The amazing thing is that this is nothing but human nature. We all feel this way. Just about all traders trade this way, causing markets to trend.

Therefore, you need to know the trend of the market you are about to enter before you open a position. You can either go with or against the trend. If you go against the trend, you need a good reason—such as it is about to enter an area of resistance you feel it cannot penetrate, or you become aware of some fundamental information that is not yet in the market but has the potential of turning it around. Either way, you want to know what the herd is thinking. This is the trend.

6. *Develop a definite plan or strategy for entering and exiting trades.* For example, you might enter a market with limit orders and exit by continually moving your

trailing stops closer to the trading range until they are hit. The danger you want to avoid is not carefully planning entry and exit points. All too often, traders get in markets too late and exit too early. Or novice traders get filled "unexpectedly" and have no idea what to do next, nor any strategy planned to exit the trade. They just let their options expire worthless.

7. *A corollary to the previous rule is to avoid closing positions prematurely.* We've seen experienced traders very orderly open a position and precisely close it when their price objective was hit. We tell our customers: "You can't tell how far a market is going up (or down) by how far it has gone already." The only true way of knowing is when it changes direction and is no longer going up or down. Following positions with protective stops also corrects this problem.

8. *Learn the art of placing protective stops.* It is easy to tell you to place stops, but it is not as easy to tell you how or where. It requires much experience with the specific markets you trade and a good feel for the current and expected volatility.

You need to place your stops close enough to where your position is trading to protect yourself from losing what you've gained so far, yet not so close that you get prematurely stopped out. A good place is just beyond a technical barrier and outside the daily maximum volatility target. Avoid points known to be the target of floor traders because they'll stretch the trading range to reach the orders in their deck.

Stops are particularly important for options traders because you are trading a wasting asset, which will expire worthless if you don't do something. Let the stop salvage something out of a losing position, if the markets move against your positions.

9. *Plan and develop rules for taking profits.* For example, don't exit a market just because you've become bored with a trade. On the other hand, if a market moves dramatically in your direction and you have no idea why, take your windfall profit or at least put a tight stop behind the position. You want to avoid any situation you don't understand. You'll never forgive yourself if you take a serious drawdown on a trade you didn't understand.

10. *Learn to trade puts as well as calls.* Most traders buy only calls. They neglect the short side of the market.

The high number of trades on the long side of the market is particularly noticeable among stock option traders. The reason for this may be they feel guilty about "letting down a company," if they trade the downside. They forget to realize that the company is not directly involved. It's the owners of the shares of stock that are affected. The company only gets money from a stock sales during the initial offering or when they "create" more stock.

11. *Never hedge "trade" or try to spread out of losses.* True hedging occurs when you are on both sides of a market. The correct way to do this is to be on one side of a cash market and on the other side in options or futures. For example, a farmer has 5,000 bushels of soybeans in a storage bin or growing in his fields. In other words,

he is long 5,000 bushels. To hedge, he sells 5,000 bushels or buys a put option on the Chicago Board of Trade. He is now neutral price wise. When the commodity contract is about to expire, he can deliver the beans or offset his position. The rationale for hedging is to pass the risk of ownership to a speculator and lock in an acceptable profit.

Some option traders, when faced with a losing long position, buy a put at the same strike price on another exchange. They call it hedging, but it isn't. It's more like an intermarket spread. This is bad trading. When faced with a losing position, offset it and take your loss. If you wish to trade spreads, do so. Look for spread opportunities when the relationship between two related contracts is, by your analysis, misaligned. If you decide to reverse your position, do it. But do it as a completely new trade.

12. *Never buy a call just because the underlying entities' price is low or a put because a price seems high.* Traders often get trapped by the logic that if the underlying entity is very low it must go higher. This may be true in the long run, but it sure isn't in the short to medium term.

Remember the old onion futures contract that went below the cost of the bags in which the onions were packaged. Also, silver is often a by-product of lead and other base metal mining. Its production can continue after its price drops below production costs. Even the cattlemen continue to produce livestock when in the red because it takes two and a half years from the time a cow is bred until a steak is produced from its offspring. This process can't be turned on and off at will.

Another example was shorting the silver market in early 1980 (or buying a put) because it was "too high" at $30.00 an ounce. You would have cried when this commodity shot up another $10.00 more an ounce. That's $50,000.00 more profit per contract.

13. *Never leg out of a spread, unless this was your original strategy.* Legging out of a spread means selling off one side and continuing to hold the other. You should be in a legitimate spread for legitimate reasons. Therefore, when you close out this position, you should offset both legs.

We summarize this section by emphasizing the biggest "secret" of options trading—it is self-discipline, the ultimate key to successful options trading. If you learn nothing else from this material, this is the most important single aspect. Here are a few tips:

◆ Create a comprehensive trading strategy. This includes money management as well as a trading system. Put it in writing.

◆ Money management is the more important of the two.

◆ Never trade when you are sick—physically or psychologically.

◆ Follow your own trading system. Avoid the advice of others. If you want someone else to make your trading decisions, give them the discretion (limited power of attorney) to do it.

◆ Only trade your own trades. If you are trading someone else's, you'll lack the conviction to stick with them, if the sledding gets tough. And, only make trades that are clearly defined, both the entry and exit points.

◆ Set break periods. For example, if you have three or five losses in a row, it's time to back off for a while.

◆ Keep a journal explaining why you entered each trade, why you exited, the results, and a critique of your performance. Compare what you actually do to your initial money management and trading strategy. We'll have more regarding your journal in the next chapter.

There is one more way to think about options trading. It is summed up in an old market axiom: "The markets are always right!" In other words, they move up, down, or sideways—despite what our analysis indicates. You need to be disciplined enough to take advantage of what the market gives you. We'll have a little more to say about discipline shortly because it is such a key to successful options trading.

Chapter 6
What You Need to Do to Implement Your Trading Plan

"This very remarkable man
Commends a most practical plan:
You can do what you want
If you don't think you can't,
So don't think you can't think you can."

Charles Inge (*Weekend Book*, 1928)

Key Concepts

◆ What is a Trading System?

◆ Types of Systems

◆ Discipline and Your Trading System

◆ The Value and Use of a Trading Journal

◆ Dealing with Your Pride, Greed, Fear, and Hope

After reading through the lists of rules, the chapter on price forecasting, and the section on strategy, you might be wondering what a trading system actually is. How do you put one together and what do you need to do to make it successful?

These are not simple questions, and there are no definitive answers. To properly deal with them, we need to digress for a minute. In the chapter on volatility, we discussed the random nature of prices and several times we referenced the Law of Probability. These two concepts converge when you attempt to develop a trading system.

First, you must resolve in your own mind the dichotomy between random price movement and your ability to forecast prices into the future. If price changes are truly random, what good is a trading system based on the expectation of knowing at least the direction prices will go, not to mention being able to predict specific target prices days or months into the future? And, all systems do attempt this in some degree or fashion.

Here's how to deal with this dilemma. We hope we made it clear earlier that neither technical nor fundamental analysis is anywhere near 100% accurate. Additionally, each specific analytic technique is further limited based on the specific characteristics of each underlying entity and the trading pattern of the market being studied. For example, a character-of-the-market technical forecasting method does better in choppy markets than a trend following system.

Our approach is to pick and choose the technique based on the underlying entity and market conditions. It is not uncommon to use more than one, even several, at the same time. You get a signal from a price chart and look to an RSI (relative strength index) for confirmation. Or, you may use fundamental or chart analysis to isolate a trend and Japanese Candlesticks for market entry and exit points.

You need to think of your analysis as an estimate. If price changes are truly random, it is an estimate or an educated guess. If price changes are not random—which implies they follow discoverable patterns or rules, why haven't extremely reliable trading systems been developed? Carrying this logic farther—if dependable forecasting approaches can be uncovered, there would be no need for option markets, nor stock or futures markets. More importantly, if these laws governing price activity can be uncovered, why not the laws of human behavior? No need to stop here, why not the future? Man has been attempting to foretell it since verbal communications began—but to no avail. Despite what ardent promoters of seasonal, cyclical, Elliott Wave, Gann Numbers, and hundreds of other analytical approaches say, their forecasts are only educated guesses at best.

If you develop a way to accurately forecast the future, would you share it? Would you sell it to all comers for $99.95, $495.00, $10,000.00 or $100,000.00? If everyone had the system, would it still work? Would you sell it and take that risk?

In other words, the ability to foretell the future is not currently available, at least we can't share it with you at the moment. This is where your price forecasting approach becomes part of your total trading system.

Since your opinion of the direction of prices is only an estimate, you need to learn how to manage the risk of investing in your market opinion. This is done many ways. The use of trading techniques, such as stop loss orders, is one. Refer back to the money and trade rules in Chapter 5 for others.

Another important part of this defensive stance is selection of strategy. As we saw when we discussed specific types of trades, some are more conservative than others. Or, we could say some are more risky.

At the point where you have settled on a specific trade, you need one more input from your trading system. We are referring to entry and exit points. How (and when) do you plan to get into and out of your trades? This must be addressed before trades are put on. You can always make adjustments as conditions change, particularly if they are favorable to your position. We are just saying the most successful traders we know trade with a definite plan in mind—better yet, on paper.

Try thinking of your trading system as a three-legged table—one of the legs is your opinion of market direction or if an option is over/under priced; leg two is management, monetary and psychological; and three is the mechanics of the system, meaning the selection of such things as entry and exit points. To be structurally sound, all legs must contribute to the support of the table. If one of the legs comes up short, the system topples and falls.

What Type of System Is Right for You?

There are basically two types of systems, namely, mechanical and intuitive. The system that is 100% mechanical would theoretically make all the decisions for you. You would incorporate all your rules for money management, stock/commodity market analyses, and trade selection. The system takes all the data you feed it and "tells" you the best opportunity.

A purely intuitive approach is just the opposite. Unfortunately, too many traders select trades this way. They just do what they feel like doing or what their brokers get them excited about. Occasionally this approach works for very experienced traders.

Most successful individual traders we have dealt with, find a middle ground between these extremes. They will, for example, have a set of money management rules they never violate. For trade selection, they may use a computer program or some other type of mechanical process. The mechanical system analyzes the current markets, selects the best opportunities, runs break-even tables, risk array scenarios, and ranks the trades indicated based on their risk-reward criteria. This information is combined with experience, generating the trade decision.

To make this type of system or any other work requires a good deal of discipline. By discipline we mean training intended to produce a specific pattern of behavior or, more simply, controlled behavior. You want to train yourself to do something as nearly perfectly as possible.

Let's forget trading for a moment and examine the concept of discipline from another perspective. What if you wanted to lose 30, 40, or 50 pounds? Knock 6 inches off your waist? Go down 2 or 3 dress or suit sizes? More importantly, once you lost the weight, you wanted to keep it off.

What steps would you have to take? Cut down on your caloric intake and increase the number of calories you burn each day. Eat less, exercise more. That takes care of our first goal of losing 40 pounds. To successfully maintain the new lower weight, you have to permanently change your eating patterns.

To do this, you're talking about a major commitment. It's one thing to give up chocolate ice cream for 30, 60, or 90 days. It's quite another to give it up forever. That's behavior modification!

Success in this endeavor also requires you to become more specific and follow up on your progress. This calls for written goals and menus. Then you must weigh yourself regularly, record the results, and honestly evaluate how you're doing.

Most people gain back what they lose because of lack of commitment and discipline. Most options traders do the opposite—they give back what they gain for the same reason. Written goals, written plans, follow-up procedures—it's all fine, but without the wholehearted commitment to making money from the options markets, it means little.

Now, let's get back to the three areas you, as an options trader, must train your behavior. The first is your trading system. Studies seem to indicate there are a wide variety of systems that can make money in the markets.

All trading systems have a few functions in common. They usually give specific trade entry and exit signals, along with some type of a timing mechanism. Your function is to take the appropriate action.

If this is carried to the limit, the ideal trading system would be totally automatic. You'd hook it up to a computer order placing system and have the profits wired to your bank.

We don't think this would work because even the most automatic of systems need the human touch to adjust to the idiosyncrasies of the market. A good analogy might be a plane with the guidance system of the cruise missile. It's great as long as the ride is smooth, but what happens when the hydraulic system blows or an engine stalls? You sure want a pilot or two on board then.

On the other hand, the human touch must be gentle and timely or we face the dreaded "operator error" syndrome. It's discipline that keeps us on the straight and narrow. Discipline also makes sure you do your homework—updating the system regularly, reviewing it, and following the signals.

Money management is the second critical area. We hit this hard when we discussed money management rules. The only thing needed here is to be sure we adopt those rules that are applicable to our trading style. Put them in writing and keep them in front of you.

The last area refers to our personal performance. You must discipline your emotions—particularly your pride, greed, hope, and fear which we'll discuss shortly. These are the emotions that lead you back to your old losing ways.

How Do You Stay on Track?

You begin with honesty. If you want to lose weight, you need to say to yourself: "I'm fat and I'm going to lose 40 pounds in the next 3 months." If you want to win in the futures market, you must say: "I'm going to enter some losing trades— there's no avoiding that. But I'm not going to let that bother me because I'm going to follow my trading system's rules, my money management rules, and my personal emotional rules. I'm totally committed to making money in the options market and keeping it!"

From here, you develop specific strategies to accomplish your mission. For example, following rules can be made easier if you set a firm schedule. Update and review charts daily by 7:00 p.m. every trading day. Discuss markets with your broker at 8:00 p.m. each night. Think about recommendations overnight and call your broker in the morning to place orders. Update your trade journal before leaving for work. Check the market at noon.

Back up your schedule with checklists so nothing gets overlooked. It helps to match your homework with your personality. If you are not the type to do a lot of detailed number crunching each night, you need a simple system that doesn't require it or can be automated.

If you flat don't have any time, you shouldn't be trading. Successful options trading requires a lot of work on somebody's part. If you aren't up to it, consider an alternative approach to the markets, like an account managed by a professional trader or a fund.

Follow Your Road Map

Your trading system and written plan is your road map to success in the options market. Discipline is your navigator that keeps you on course. Be sure to listen to your navigator so you'll end up where you want to be.

One of the best ways to assure you're on the interstate highway system to success is to keep a trading journal. Unfortunately, far too many traders neglect this valuable tool. They often say: "Why should I bother? Don't I get a monthly statement recapping all my trading activity?"

The most important piece of information missing from your monthly statement is the reason you got into the trade in the first place. What did you expect to happen? What was the risk-to-reward ratio? What alternative trades did you turn down in favor of the ones you took? What signals—fundamental or technical—triggered your trading decision? What attracted you to the trade initially?

How does the old adage go? "Those that forget the past are condemned to repeat it." Trading is an extremely personal and emotional endeavor. Our minds interpret the ink blots on the price charts. We learn to rationalize our trading decisions. Most good traders talk about their instincts—they can smell a trade when it is still 10 ticks away!

The essence of what these traders are saying is basically believable. But we also know from our experience that writing stimulates thought and clarifies thinking. Researchers who have studied the papers of some of the world-class traders have indicated that their trading wasn't done by the "seat-of-the-pants." The great traders documented what they did—before, during, and after the markets were open.

We learn from our mistakes. Why repeat them? We learn from our successes. Why not repeat them?

The function of a journal is twofold. First, it reminds us why we selected or rejected a trade. It provides an audit trail of our thinking.

We need this historical record because we all have a tendency to mold the past by our perception of the present. If we try to recreate our thinking and our emotional state after the fact, we find ourselves heavily influenced by the results of the trade. This confuses us to a point we can't be brutally honest.

For these two reasons, you should put your thoughts and emotional reasons for each trade on paper before you call your broker. This is needed even if all you have to go by is a "gut feeling that corn is going higher." Record when you first noticed it and what might have triggered it—a new story, a chart formation, etc.

Later on, you may be able to piece the puzzle together and make something more concrete of it.

Reliable instincts are as meaningful in options trading as they are in any human activity. The price trends and patterns of the stock and futures market reflect the instincts and emotional state of every investor that is getting in or out of the market at a given time. You may be instinctively able to sense where a market is going at times, just like fishermen can sense where the fish are.

Your trading journal helps you hone your instincts. You learn to sort out unfounded hunches from brilliant insights. Fine-tune your feel for the market through the use of a journal, just as the professional fishing guides chart their success on the lakes they fish.

What...When...Where?

This brings up the question of what should be included in a trading diary. When do entries need to be made and where do you keep it?

The diary reflects your trading system. First, answer the question: How do I select trades? What are my key indicators? What are my goals? For example, the first thing many traders do is determine if the trend is up or down for the markets they are tracking. This may be your first entry. You would then do the same for the other signals that you regularly check.

Or, you could have your signals listed and just make a check or sign. An "up" arrow for an uptrend and a "down" arrow for a downtrend, for example.

How often do you need to make an entry or update your journal? There are a couple of ways to look at this. First, do you normally trade for the long or short term? Do you trade slow moving markets, like the blue chip stocks, or speed demons, like the S & P 500 Index Option? You should make an entry each time you "check" your markets. By this we mean whenever you evaluate your current position or seriously consider entering or exiting a trade.

What format is best for a trading diary? We've seen all kinds that work, ranging from hieroglyphic notes scratched on a Daytimer to an elaborate record maintained on a computerized word processing program.

The what, when, where, how, et cetera, of keeping a journal is a lot like the question, "How long should a man's legs be?"—long enough to reach the ground. Your journal should satisfy your needs. It is created only to help you trade more successfully. The worst thing it can become is a chore. If you find yourself dreading the thought of updating it, something is wrong.

Simplicity often makes diaries more meaningful. For example, let's say you receive a weekly charting service which you update once or twice throughout the week. You could make your journal entries right on the charts as you are filling in the daily trading ranges. Then cut out the charts you use and put them in a three-ring binder. Once a trade is closed, record the results. Then page back through the chart pages and evaluate your performance. On the last page, write a two or three sentence summary.

The ultimate goal of most traders is to make money. You want to be a net winner. Why not track your progress? Start by dividing a sheet of graph paper into 12 parts, one for each month, 52 for the weeks of the year or 250 to denote the average number of trading days a year. Your selection depends on your level of trading. What we're suggesting is that you plot the "Net Liquidating Value" of your account. You can do it each time you receive a statement from your broker or you can use your monthly statements. Footnotes at the bottom of the graph can be used to record additions and withdrawals. Hopefully, there will be only one initial funding followed by steady growth. A picture of your equity often gives you a clearer insight into your progress. Additionally, the procedure sharpens your focus on your goal.

We also strongly suggest you treat each calendar year as a completely new year. Carry over your year-end equity and begin figuring your gains or losses from month one. The reason for this is that if you had a net losing year, you now have a fresh start. Or, if the past year's trading was profitable, particularly very profitable, you don't get overconfident because you have a big cushion of profits. Stay lean and mean.

The key is making your diary simple, painless, and meaningful. Your objective is to learn how you pick a winner and how you can avoid losers.

Some of the most difficult obstacles for new traders to deal with are pride, greed, fear, and hope. Some market observers, with literary bents, have likened them to the Fates of Greek mythology or the witches of Macbeth.

What Can Oedipus Rex Teach You?

The ancient Greeks would easily relate to how an intelligent, aggressive options trader—with a strong market position—ends up taking a massive, net loss. The Greeks coined a word for what often happens to otherwise skillful traders. It was "hubris," the common definition of which is simply "overbearing pride." You will talk to a trader about the risk of his or her position only to get a response like—"Don't worry about me. I KNOW where the market is going!"

You'll often find three witches accompanying hubris. They are hope, fear, and greed. We personally believe this foursome has brought more people, who could have been successful in the market, to their financial knees than just about anything else.

How Do You Control Them?

The answer may also be hidden in the past. Just as the Ancients offered an ox or a goat to the gods, you must make sacrifices. We often refer to it as "swallowing one's pride." One way of doing this is being brutally honest with yourself in your diary.

Let's say your system flashes a sell signal for a long position when an area of resistance is reached. You override it, only to watch your profits evaporate as prices head to the next lower area of support. In your diary—if it is to be of any real value to you—you must state how you violated your system. Your journal must force discipline upon your trading. If it does only this, it will be well worth all the time and trouble it takes to maintain.

Sacrifices must be made to the witches as well. Let's take greed as an example. You must prove to the market that you have "conquered" or at least can manage greed.

How can you do this? You do it by never letting a profitable position become a losing position. Let's say you bought an in-the-money silver call. Your expectations were to make 10 cents per ounce profit before expiration which was six weeks away when you placed the trade. Silver unexpectedly moved 25 cents higher almost immediately after you are filled. What do you do?

(a) Take your unexpected profit?
(b) Wait for it to go up farther?
(c) Place a close stop to protect profits?

If you selected "b," you're testing the gods, and the gods and the markets punish mere mortals who challenge their authority. If you chose "a," you pocket $1,250 (less transaction costs) and the gods are pleased you accepted their gift.

Those of you who selected "c" are still fighting greed. But you have shown at least some management. You're still in the market. You still have a profit, at least on paper. If the gods smile on you, you'll eventually be stopped out with your profit. If not, the market will limit through your stop and plunge lower until you see the evil of your ways.

If you trade multiple positions, you can demonstrate your mastery of greed to the gods by closing out part of your position when it becomes profitable. For example, let's say to trade in three lots. You are holding three calls. The market moves up to one-half to two-thirds of your "final" objective. You close out one position at this point. Then close your second when your objective is hit and speculate with the third using a trailing stop. This approach should please you and the deities that watch over these matters.

"Hope Springs Disaster!"

Eternal hope can put you in the poor house. You may survive on hope in your personal life, but it can be extremely damaging in the markets. The usual scenario evolves around a position that is moving against all your best judgments. Just about everything indicates you are wrong—but you keep hoping the market will turn in your favor.

Hope's witches brew is addictive, numbing your discipline. Open your diary and write down why you are staying in this market. If you're frank with yourself and write "because I hope it will go my way tomorrow," you're in trouble. Cut your losses short. If you still think the market will turn, place a stop reversal order in the market. But do it only after re-evaluating the situation and entering it as a complete new trade that meets all your criteria for a new trade.

The last witch is fear. It's one we face daily in the markets. Fear of losing money. Fear of making a stupid error. Fear of looking foolish in the eyes of our peers or broker. Fear, fear, fear.

Probably the most effective way of controlling fear is by sacrificing a portion of our profit. The old adage—bears win, bulls win, hogs lose—evolves from those that have learned to deal with fear. For example, you can limit some market fear by not trying to pick tops or bottoms. If you are riding a bull market to seventh heaven, get off at the sixth cloud. Take your profits and bank them.

Another suggestion is to continually take excess profits out of your account. Then, when you do have a drawdown, it is not as crushing. You still have profits to show. You don't feel as threatened and fear doesn't overwhelm you.

New traders often disregard fear, until they have their first serious setback. This can occur even when they make money overall on a trade. For example, a trade makes a spectacular move generating a profit of $10,000. Before it can be offset, the market reverses and the trader gives $5,000 back to the market. It happens so fast, the trader has problems adjusting. For the first time, this person realizes money can be lost just as fast or faster than it can be made. "The market giveth and the market taketh away." You must be psychologically prepared to deal with the fear of being financially burned at some point in your trading career.

Chapter 7

What a Difference the Computer Chip Has Made

"To err is human but to really foul things up requires a computer."
Farmers' Almanac for 1978 (1977)

Key Concepts

◆ Reasons for Using a Computer

◆ Danger of Relying on Computers

◆ Basic Types of Trading Programs

◆ How to Buy Software

◆ The Impact of the Chip on Market Trends

◆ See Appendix for Information on Specific Software Programs

Trading Software

There are some very compelling reasons to consider making the computer a part of your trading system. Here are just a few:

1. *Discipline.* A good computerized trading system helps you tame your impulses. Successful traders, in our experience, rely on their system and follow its rules. They are controlled and systematic, not wild and unrestrained. Software is no substitute for a stable personality, but at times it can slow down someone who is overly emotional.

2.*Education.* Many of the software packages do an excellent job of teaching traders how the market reacted to past events, providing insight into what could happen in the future.

3. *System Testing.* If you have an idea how you'd like to trade a market, you can simulate past markets and evaluate or fine-tune your approach.

4. *Saving Time/Speed.* Properly managed and structured, a computerized system can reduce, for example, the time it takes to update 40 markets each day from hours to minutes. Another good example is the calculation and recalculation of complex equations, like the Black-Scholes Formula for theoretical option prices.

5. *Historical Perspective.* With a few key strokes on many systems, you can view a long-term or short-term chart of a specific market. This can often be done simultaneously with multiple windows on a single screen.

6. *Ease of Analysis.* Sometimes it is just easier to do certain types of analysis on computer. Examples would be drawing Gann lines and squares, or calling up the meaning of Japanese candlesticks formations.

7. *Second Guessing.* Some traders review various computerized studies to make sure they aren't missing an important signal.

8. *Paranoia.* Technical analysis can be a self-fulfilling prophecy. A quick review of various technical studies gives you an idea into what others in the market are likely to do.

9. *Error Prevention.* Simple tasks, like inputting prices, or calculations can be accomplished without human error.

This is not a complete list of the advantages. But we do hope it gives you an idea of the edge computerized technical analysis can provide.

Computers, like anything else, are nowhere near perfect. You must guard against the false feeling of security they can give you. Never forget what we discussed earlier about price changes being random in nature. Computer analysis often creates the allusion that extremely reliable trends can be uncovered. This often occurs when you are testing or reviewing a trading system using historical data.

Let's say someone is trying to sell you a computer program that analyzes one of the entities underlying an options market, like the futures or stock markets. The seller purports it will alert you to long-term trends and pinpoint prices at which you should enter and exit trades. Running this program using historical data exhibits superior results.

Since the program is using actual price data, what possibly could be wrong? Why couldn't you use the program to spot long-term trends and then buy options to profit from those trends?

When testing or evaluating computer programs using historical data, traders often make some assumptions that are not necessarily reliable when they try to replicate the success in actual trading. Here are some of those hypotheses:

1. *Good fills*—most systems assume you will get good fills. They often mechanically calculate the midrange between when the buy or sell signals are generated. In real life, the fills are not usually as good.

2. *All trades are filled*—systems devised by inexperienced traders neglect limit up or down days, when no trading takes place, or days that are illiquid and fills are not as good as they are on high volume days.

3. *Slippage overlooked*—slippage is the difference between the price you expect when you place an order and your actual fill. The market, for example, continues

to move while you decide (a) whether or not to take a signal the program gives; (b) the time it takes to call your broker; (c) the time it takes him to relay your order to the floor; (d) the floor clerk's time needed to relay your order to a floor broker; and (e) his time to read, record, and enter your order. A lot can happen during those five steps and most computer systems make no allowance for any lost time. They get a signal and enter it in the historical trading session. No wonder they get such good fills, so consistently.

4. *Unrealistic commission*—it is not uncommon to review programs that totally neglect the impact of commissions and fees. This can substantially change the hypothetical track record of a system that otherwise looks pretty good.

5. *Human error*—the pressure of trading—making or losing real money, your money—causes errors. We've seen even experienced traders become excited and buy a put when they wanted a call or order the wrong strike price, month, etc.

6. *Use of favorable data*—when someone decides to test a system, they can select whatever data they wish to use in the simulation. If you're evaluating a trend following system, why not choose a period of time markets trended? The problem is that when you decide to actually trade, the markets may not move as they did during the simulated trading sessions.

These problems are so serious that the Commodity Futures Trading Commission (CFTC) requires the following statement to accompany any hypothetical track records used to promote professional traders, called CTAs (commodity trading advisors):

> "Hypothetical or simulated performance results have certain inherent limitations. Unlike an actual performance record, simulated results do not represent actual trading. Also, since the trades have not actually been executed, the results may have under-or-over compensated for the impact, if any, of certain market factors, such as lack of liquidity. Simulated trading programs in general are also subject to the fact that they are designed with the benefit of hindsight. No representation is being made that any account will or is likely to achieve profits or losses similar to those shown."

The Securities and Exchange Commission requires a similar statement adjacent to hypothetical performance records of stock portfolio managers used to solicit new accounts.

We are by no means debunking the use of a computer in options trading. On the contrary, we are strong advocates. The Wasendorf Trading System (WTS), which we use daily, is completely computerized. Each day, after the markets are closed, the WTS is updated and our trading signals are recalculated. Our point is simply that you must not get caught up in someone else's enthusiasm for a system or software program. If a computerized system could produce superior results (like a marketing system that "always" produces a profit), would it be for sale at any price? Personally from the success we have seen by some individual traders over the years, there may be some superior programs or systems out there but we haven't seen any of them for sale.

This takes us back to step one. If prices are random and there isn't any perfect software, why bother? Our answers are the same as before—discipline, organization, consistency, etc. Much of market analysis is very tedious number crunching and record searching. Why not ask your computer to do it for you? Then there is fact finding—primarily prices, statistics, and news. All of these tasks are well-suited for telecommunication via computers. If all this isn't enough, what about information retrieval? The use of CD-ROM technology will take market analysis for individual traders to new levels of intensity in the next few years.

Which Software/Hardware Is Right for You?

Before you can select the hardware (CPU, modem, CRT, memory, printer, mouse, etc.), you must know what software you will be using. For example, if you choose a trading system that runs on a DOS operating system, you may not be able to run the program on a UNIX or Macintosh operating platform. Equally important are the attributes—such as speed, memory size, and screen quality of the system you select. Many of the complex trading programs are memory hogs. They demand a lot of random access memory (RAM) and read only memory (ROM). Or, a high resolution, color monitor might be a requirement to distinguish between the many lines, such as Gann squares or angles, used in the analysis process.

Before you purchase any software, you must decide how you are going to make your trading decisions. How does computerization fit into your trading system? Does it drive your trading or will you use some software as an auxiliary tool? To aid you in this process, we'll now discuss what we consider the major classes of software. See the appendix for a description of some programs developed specifically for option traders.

Black versus White Box

The first way we classify trading software is whether it is black or white box. Black box programs are not fully disclosed. They perform a specific function(s), but that's all you know. Additionally, you cannot make any adjustments. You acquire these programs to satisfy a specific need or answer specific questions— you can make little or no changes.

It's common for this type of program to be trendy. They get "hot"—work for a while and then fade into obscurity. We think the reason is that they handle one type of market, such as a trending one. Once that changes, the program no longer works. It cannot adjust or be adjusted by the user.

Another problem we have with these black box specials is that it is very difficult for someone to design a program that's exactly right for someone else. Therefore, many people buy them only to find them unusable for their system, trading tactics, or personality. Also, certain trading approaches work for one commodity or stock classification, but not all. Which ones are right for a particular software package?

From time to time, we have found a use for certain programs. You might want to find one that complements your basic trading system. It could provide you confirmation of what your system tells you. Let's say your analysis alerts you to a buying opportunity in soybeans. You also have a program that analyzes options. It determines which ones are currently over or under priced. Additionally, it figures the risk-reward ratio of a variety of strategies (spreads, straddles, etc.) and ranks them based on profitability.

Or you may have a program that predicts seasonal patterns. You double check it to make sure you are not bucking a seasonal trend before you place a trade or you use this program to alert you to upcoming seasonal opportunities.

White box programs, on the other hand, provide in-depth explanations of the analysis, how it works, often including formulas, and instructions on adjusting or modifying the output. They are flexible—allowing you to adjust to changing markets and your trading style. You drive the software, rather than the software driving you. But these programs require much more of your time.

Naturally, there is much middle ground, the "gray" programs. These permit minor changes and adjustments. We found that one of the keys we use to distinguish between black and white is the amount of instruction you get from the program and documentation. The more you learn, the whiter is the box. If you get nothing from the program but an answer, it's a black box for sure.

Neither is necessarily right or wrong. It's your needs that count. In some cases, all we want is a reliable answer. In other cases, we want to learn all there is to know about an analytical technique. Then we want to be able to customize it for our own use.

Single versus Multiple Programs

Computer programs can do a single function or they can take the tool box approach by providing many technical studies. This applies to either black or white box type applications.

A typical black tool box program might, for example, provide price charts. On these charts, you could overlay moving averages, relative strength indexes, Gann lines, etc., by pushing a few keys. You would have a very limited ability to make any modifications to what is available. Some of these services can be very extensive in the studies they provide. They are like supermarkets where you pick and choose whatever you need depending on the situation. This is the type of service that is often available from services that provide live (actual time) quotes.

The quintessential white tool box program, in our opinion, is CompuTrac. As Figure 7.1 shows, it includes over 65 programs ranging from relatively simple open interest studies to very complex ones, like Williams %R or his "Ultimate" Oscillator. The documentation alone could be considered a definitive study on technical analysis.

Figure 7.1 Computrac's Programs

Advance-Decline
Alpha-Beta Trend Channel
Andrews Pitchfork
Arms Ease of Movement
Average True Range
Black-Scholes Option Analysis
  Module
Bollinger Bands
Bolton-Tremblay
Commodity Channel Index
Commodity Selection Index
Compression of Data
Crocker Charts
Cutler RSI
Cycle Finder
Demand Aggregate
Demand Index
Detrend
Directional Movement
Envelopes
Fibonacci Fanlines, Arcs and
  Time Zones
Fourier Analysis
Gann Lines
Gann Square of Nine
HAL Momentum
Haurlan Index
Herrick Payoff Index
Linear Regression
Moving Average Convergence/
  Divergence (MACD)
McClellan Oscillator
Median Price
Momentum

Moving Average
Normalization
Norton High/Low Indicator
Notis %V
Oil Crack Spread
Open Interest
Oscillator
Parabolic (SAR)
Percent RetracementPoints
  and Figure
Planets Module
Quadrant Level Lines
Rate of Change
Ratio
Relative Strength Index (RSI)
Schultz A/T
Shift
Soybean Crush Margin
Spread
Standard Deviation
Stochastic (%K, %D)
Stoller STARC Bands
Swing Index
Tirone Level Lines
TRIX
Trading Index
Trend Lines
Volatility
Volume
Volume Accumulator
Wave
Weighted Close
Williams %R
Williams "Ultimate" Oscillator

Our last classification includes programs designed to assist you in developing your own trading system. They fall into two basic types. The first is what is known as an expert system, which attempts to mimic a master. You feed your trading rules and experience into the system. It then takes the data and does the analysis. You constantly fine tune the operation and it even "learns" on its own by combining the rules or lessons of the expert. These are very sophisticated programs.

A variation of this approach is the neutral network. These programs manipulate data with the knowledge of the desired output in hopes of finding the rules or patterns. They require much patience, time, and experience.

Neither the expert or neutral network approach, in our opinion, can totally compensate for the randomness of price activity. The rules and patterns governing price activity are constantly in flux. It is doubtful these systems can do more than help you predict the odds on any given trade. But this may be all you are looking for from a system. For a detailed discussion of trading systems, read *The Business ONE Irwin Guide to Trading Systems* by Bruce Babcock, Jr. (See Appendix 2.)

Which approach suits your needs? Only you can answer that one.

So far we have discussed why you should consider computerizing your trading and the general classes of software available. Now we'll explore a method of selecting the software that suits your needs.

The Ideal System

There is an approach to problem solving that also works well for selecting software. It's called the "Ideal System." What you do is let your imagination run wild. You ask yourself: How could I ideally solve this problem? If I had no financial, internal, political, or personal restraints, what would I do? You then write down the ideal solution to your problem.

Once you have brainstormed the situation and outlined the best of all possible approaches, you begin to compromise with reality. What can you afford to do? What can you live without? What do you have time to do? What restraints are real and which are imaginary? How can you circumvent some of the limitations? What's left?

The rationale for this approach is that this exercise often opens new avenues of thought. You find unique and valuable approaches you may have previously overlooked. It's not uncommon that some of these new insights will substantially improve the solution you eventually reach.

To apply the Ideal System concept to the selection of software, you prepare a list of all the features you ideally would like to have as part of the software you want. This becomes your checklist as you evaluate potential packages. To keep you in touch with reality, you can mark those that you feel are an absolute necessity. Here's an example:

Software Features Absolutely Necessary: (X)
Live Price Quotations   ( )
Chart Formations   ( )
   (Trendlines, Channels, etc.)
Basic Studies   ( )
   (RSI, Moving Averages, etc.)
Advanced Studies   ( )
   (Black-Scholes Option Price Calculator)
Unlimited Studies   ( )
   (100+ basic & advanced)

Artificial Intelligence	( )
(Expert System)	
Neutral Network	( )
Historical Testing Capability & Data	( )
Portfolio Analysis	( )
Risk-Reward Ratio Calculator	( )
Spread Sheet	( )
News	( )
Weather	( )
Fact Database	( )
Order Placement	( )

There isn't room here, but you could make a shopping list of the hundred plus individual studies, programs, functions, and accessories currently available. Then check the ones you feel fit into your trading system or style of trading.

Your objective is to clarify your thinking. How are you going to select trades? Entry, exit points? What tools do you absolutely need to make these decisions? How much information do you need? How automated are you going to be? Will you input price quotations live, daily, or manually? Are you going to look to your system for money management assistance, as well as trading? Will you maintain your trading diary on computer as well? Can you communicate your orders to your broker electronically?

Once you ascertain what you want or need, reality sets in as you price out your selections. A quote system providing online price ticks with a decent variety of studies runs $300 to $500 per month. Additionally, you may have to add something to cover the transmission of the signal (cable, satellite dish, dedicated telephone line, FM antenna, etc.), depending on where you are geographically located. A white tool box type of program, like CompuTrac 3.21, costs between $695 and $1,895, depending on which modules you acquire. A single study program, like "OptionVue," goes for $895.00.

If you would like to have price quotes but can live with a 10 or 15 minute delay, there are reasonable priced (under $50.00 per month) alternatives, like DTN and Broadcast Partners' FarmDayTa. The delay allows you to get the quotations without having to pay each exchange a fee, varying from $30.00 to $50.00 per month per exchange. Four futures exchanges could cost you $120.00 to $200.00 in exchange fees alone each month.

Research Your Choice

Let's say you narrow the field to a half dozen programs that meet your needs. What do you do next?

The first thing we recommend is to visit, if possible, someone who is using the system in a way like you plan to use it. Does it really work the way the promoters claim? Can it provide the information you vitally need to trade successfully?

Next, find out if the software has been battle tested. Who has traded stock, index, and/or commodity options using the software? Make sure you distinguish between real time action, as opposed to simulated or hypothetical trading. For a variety of reasons, most importantly our human emotional responses to pressure, it is not uncommon for historical simulation to look great, while live action falls flat. Some trading approaches appear to be automatic, but in real life trading require a flow of decisions.

Get a tight fix on two critical inputs—your time and money. Many programs require daily highs, lows, opens, and closes. Some may additionally ask for volume and open interest. How is this data to be entered into your computer? If the answer is electronically, what computer format(s) does the program support? If you have an online quote system, will the software accept the data directly or is conversion necessary? If so, is it expensive or even available? The last thing you need is a program you can't update easily or inexpensively.

Always research the user friendliness of the program and customer support supplied by the vendor. The easiest-to-use programs today provide pull down menus and support a mouse. Also, check the hours customer support is available compared to when you will normally be using the program.

We always like to have an insight into how many times the program has had major upgrades. This is usually a whole number change in the version, version 1.0 versus version 2.0. Minor changes often are recorded by a decimal change, version 3.5 versus version 3.6. Beware of version 1.0, it may still have some bugs to be found and corrected. Check to see if you get free upgrades when the software is improved.

Always try to get a demonstration diskette. Preferably one that runs the program on some limited basis, as opposed to a one that creates a computerized slide show. The actual running demos provide a much better insight into what the program does and "how it feels" to you.

Caveat Emptor

"Let the buyer beware!" If it sounds too good to be true, it probably is. Therefore, don't order anything that doesn't have a good guarantee. Also, use your credit card, so if you don't like what you get, you can send it back and refuse to pay the charge.

There really are some excellent, well-written programs available. It takes time and research to find them.

There are other positive-negative aspects to the influence of the computer chip on the markets we trade, particularly for the underlying markets. For example, the futures markets and the options-on-futures can be extremely volatile. At times, they can be characterized as nervous. This characteristic makes them very responsive to news and herd psychology.

In B.C.C. (before computer chips) times, someone physically close to the markets would become aware of market-making news and trade it. The word would spread out from the pits. On day two, brokers would be telling their customers about it. By day three, it would be on radio and television.

The closer you were to the floor, the sooner you got in the market on the right side to take advantage of the impact of news. The farther from the epicenter, the more of the move you missed. In these times, professional traders had a strategic advantage. The periodontist in Peoria got the word too late—just in time to get creamed by the blow-off top.

The good news is that a trader in Jackson Hole now has cable, a satellite dish, and a personal computer (PC) with a modem—he's wired to the world! These traders get the word just as fast, often faster, than the boys in the pits. The playing field has leveled somewhat. More important are the studies and analysis that can be done by those with the computer horsepower, even the lowly PC.

The trading edge has shifted from the floor traders to the professional traders. The former chairman of the Chicago Board of Trade, William F. O'Connor, described this phenomenon this way in the Chicago Tribune: "Exchange members used to have a time and place advantage. But the edge is no longer. Simply put, the information advantage has gone upstairs." The one with the biggest advantage now appears to be those trading massive portfolios for institutions or funds. What's happening in the futures markets mirrors the impact of program trading that took hold of the stock market over the last decade.

The more chip power you can put behind your order tickets, the more responsive your trading can be. Or, at least that's the current theory. The ultimate, for the moment, seems to be the Market Information Machine (MIM) created by Logical Information Machine, Inc. of Austin, Texas. It's nothing more than a massive database of the stock and futures markets. What makes it unique is what is known as declarative programming paradigms. This allows the trader to instantly access all the data in the database, which is all stored in the computer main memory. Normally, data is housed on disks. When presented with a query, the computer searches disk after disk, or drive after drive, to find the answer. It can take from minutes, to hours, to days. MIM queries go straight to the main memory and the answers come "instantaneously," regardless of the complexity of the question.

It is particularly usefully for traders seeking correlations between two or more market events. You might ask MIM what to expect from the S & P 500 when the Consumer Price Index is down 5% over the last six months and S & P 500's price-earning ratio is down an equal amount. You could ask for a weekly price chart for the 10 trading days following each time this event occurred. MIM delivers these charts in seconds.

But don't get your hopes up, since the cost is prohibitive for most individual traders. You'd need a $15,000.00 computer work station and approximately $3,000.00 a month to access the data. You may find a brokerage firm that has one though.

Computer analysis has also changed the way the markets perform. Or, at least that's our perception. We believe we have seen, over the last decade, more and more of what we characterize as false technical signals or false breakouts in the futures markets. We attribute this to the ever growing number of traders relying on computerized trend-following systems. These traders all get a signal at or about the same time. Their collective responses make the signal a self-fulfilling prophecy. But few of these analysts are truly committed to the trade. After it moves a little bit in their favor, they get cold feet and exit the trade. Their exit produces a reversal signal and the phenomenon repeats itself.

This brings up another important insight into the markets you should be aware of. It's called the "Pot Never Boils When You Watch It Syndrome." For example, if a market move takes a long time to occur and the whole trading world is waiting for a trendline to be broken, the break usually becomes a non-event. In other words, closely watched and well-publicized technical formations usually fizzle out. We remember a well-publicized head and shoulder in the corn market, written about in at least six advisory newsletters that we used to read—it never reached its potential. Too much expectation was built into the market. If you know something is going to happen and you know everyone else also knows, you can't become really committed to it.

If, on the other hand, you think you know a secret, something that is going to cause a stock to make a mega move, and you're the "only" one with that information, you are more likely to stick with the trade. The less press, the less explanation available about an upcoming move, the more likely it will be a big trade.

The computer chip, which makes communications faster and analysis of large amounts of data easier for larger numbers of traders, has forever changed the way markets move. But there are still plenty of opportunities. Actually, there are more for small traders than ever before.

Chapter 8

Selecting the Broker That Is Right for You

"Because I don't trust him, we are friends."
Bertolt Brecht (*Mother Courage*, 1939)

Key Concepts

◆ Understanding the Basic Conflicts of Interests

◆ Matching Your Needs to Your Broker's Resources

◆ The Art of Managing Your Broker

◆ Choosing Between a Full Service and Discount Brokerage Firm

The last chapter ended with a warning to buyers to be wary. This one begins with another one. As you read this chapter, please keep in mind that the authors are brokers, proud of our profession and our staff.

Nonetheless, there is a basic conflict of interest between buyers and sellers. Your stock or commodity broker is the seller; you, naturally, are the buyer.

This conflict of interest is not unique to the investment industry. Brokers are middlemen. Their function is to bring buyers and sellers together. Rarely do they get paid by both parties or an uninterested third party. Normally, the seller pays the sales commission. This means the broker works for the seller and has the seller's interest utmost in his mind.

For example, when you buy a home or a car, doesn't the real estate agent or the salesman receive a portion of what you pay as his or her compensation? Yet we all buy homes, cars, insurance, and hundreds of other things sold to us by some sort of intermediary.

Let's carry this one step farther. Most brokers in the investment arena work on straight commissions, or mostly commissions. This means that if they do not sell you anything, they do not get paid. Even brokers on salary, a new wrinkle among discounters, must make sales to keep their jobs and receive raises.

These are serious conflicts of interest you need to be aware of—but they are nothing unusual, nor should they be disturbing. You just need to be sensitive to them. We tell our brokers that while your direct interest may be somewhat different than your customers, your goals can be the same. Most of our clients have the objective of making money. Our brokers know if they help their clients make money, they will make money. Setting mutual goals helps deal with some of these situations.

As you read this chapter, you should review the preceding chapters. A successful broker-client relation is a partnership. Each party contributes substantially to the success of the trading. You seek a broker who complements your specific need for market knowledge, experience, background, trading expertise, equipment, research, etc. Therefore, as you work your way through the broker selection process, you create a list of what you want from a broker.

Let's very quickly review what we've covered so far. We'll just run through each chapter and list some of what you might ask yourself to define what the "ideal" broker for you would be.

Chapter 1
    What do you need from a broker in the way of basic knowledge
        and background?
    About trading options?
    About markets?

Chapter 2
    What help do you need regarding understanding and selecting
        strategies?

Chapter 3
    How will you reach an opinion of market direction and strength?
    Fundamental or technical analysis?
    What research, facts, information, etc., will you seek from your broker?

Chapter 4
    Will you expect volatility estimates and insights from your broker?

Chapter 5
    How does your broker fit into your trading plan?

Chapter 6
    What help do you need putting your trading system together?

Chapter 7
    Will you be looking to your broker for price quotations, theoretical
        prices, implied volatility, or other computer generated trading
        signals?

Another area many of our customers look to their brokers for is feedback from the trading pits. Is it important for your broker to know what's going on in Chicago, New York, wherever? Should your broker have actual experience on the trading floor? You may, for example, be approached by a broker who has traded for his own account in a pit. He'll tell you this is extremely valuable to you. Is it so?

One way to approach this question is to compare on-floor with off-floor trading. Let's talk first about the on-floor trader. There are basically two types. The first are "locals" trading their own account; the second are brokers filling other people's orders. Additionally, some exchanges allow brokers to dual trade, for their own account and off-floor customers.

Probably the most prominent characteristic of on-floor, local traders is their short-term view of the markets. Rarely do these type of traders hold positions overnight. These guys are often scalpers, trying to shave a cent, or even a fraction of a cent, profit on the contracts they trade. Being members of the exchange, their per transaction costs are extremely low, while their volume is extremely high.

Scalpers provide a very important function—they are the price police and market makers. Their attention is constantly directed at the bid-ask range, looking for anything that's over or under priced. If they spot anything out of line, they jump on it and hold it until it is fairly priced again. They make their profits on the correction. The market benefit is that bid and ask prices are kept in fair ranges.

Their activity also adds liquidity to the markets. This is critical to off-floor traders for two reasons. First, it allows you to enter or exit a market promptly. Secondly, the range between the bid and the ask price is tighter, which usually means you get better fills.

Liquidity is a particularly important issue in the options market because it is often lacking in some strike prices—particularly those out-of-the-money. Secondly in some of these illiquid markets, brokers are "not held" for all their orders. This means that, if an option order is entered in the market within the bid-ask range, it still may not be filled, if another broker doesn't have an offsetting order for it. In other words, the brokers do not have to "make a market" for all strike prices.

Last of all, when an order comes into the pits at the upper limit or even outside the bid-ask range, the market may take that order as the new bid or ask price. In other words, the range stretches in these illiquid markets to capture any order it can. This sometimes results in a bad fill for the retail (off-floor) customer. Before your (off-floor) broker places an order for you, he may want to call the pit to get a feel for the current liquidity.

The other type of floor broker is one working for a broker-dealer or a futures commission merchant (FCM) filling orders for their customers. These traders learn the internal workings of the exchange, but may not be as shortsighted as the scalper.

The importance to you of knowing how the pits really work—and the reason good brokers cultivate friendships with floor personnel—is that this knowledge can help get better fills. Or the floor brokers can help recommend where to place stops. The people on the floor are constantly talking to each other. Ex-floor traders can read interday pivot points better, due to their understanding of the day trader's mentality. They want to know who's behind a bid or ask order. Is it a giant institutional trader or a small speculator? You can't tell no matter how hard or how long you stare at a price quote screen.

The floor people also know who is holding orders and at what price. Are there some stop orders at a certain price that will stop or slow down an up or downtrend? Information like this can only come from the floor.

Therefore, it is not so important that your broker has actually braved the cruel world of the pits. It is critical that he/she, or the firm you trade through, have contacts to get reliable information fast. As a matter of fact, if a prospective broker tells you he traded as a local, this doesn't guarantee he's a better broker. Floor traders, particularly scalpers, usually trade only a few markets. They may not be well-rounded in all the stocks and/or commodities you wish to trade.

When trading that single market, they are not looking at the medium to long term. Not even the short term—a few days—as most off-floor traders classify it. Overcoming this perspective can be very difficult. Ex-scalpers may encourage customers to take profits too soon. They can leave a lot of money in the pits. Also, since they traded only a few markets they may lack an understanding of the importance of diversifying your portfolio.

Our point is simply this—information from the pits can be very important at certain times. Your broker needs the capability of delivering it to you when necessary. A good broker is one that satisfies your needs; it doesn't matter if he/she ever stepped foot in a trading pit. Your needs are the critical issue.

How Do You Spot a "Good" Broker?

First off, the key word is "good." It means good for you, your trading style, your personality, and your needs. Do you need assistance in selecting trades, tracking them, money management, technical and fundamental information, order placement, exchange floor reports, etc.?

One of the best places to develop a list of what you want from a broker is to develop a list of your limitations. Your broker should become your partner; you make money together. Your broker must earn his or her commissions.

There are at least four common limitations most individual traders must overcome. The first is time—time to follow the markets and to sort out the important information from the false rumors that clutter the pits. The second is the flow and cost of information available about the markets. As fast moving as the futures markets are, you often need tick-by-tick price quotation equipment. At times, the stock market is equally fluid. Additionally, you need immediate access to the wire services and other forms of news. Therefore, you require some expensive and sophisticated equipment, which most individuals cannot justify as part-time traders.

Next is the experience that only comes from trading the markets day after day, year after year, facing bull markets and bear rallies, spotting the major moves early, and avoiding getting whipsawed by false breakouts.

Last of all, there is just an enormous amount of background information you need at your fingertips to trade and avoid making expensive errors. You need to know all the specifications of the options you're trading, the hours the markets are open, what days they are closed, if they are closing early for some reason, how to place orders, when important government reports that will impact markets are to be released, what rumors are sweeping the exchanges—and it goes on and on.

Therefore, develop your list of what you are going to look for in a broker before you begin to interview (usually by telephone) broker candidates. And, we do mean candidates. Use all the skills you learned over the years in hiring employees or vendors, selecting schools for yourself or your children, and other critical buying decisions. Make a "T" list on all candidates after you talk with them. Refer to Figure 8.1. If you do this for each broker you interview, the selection process becomes much easier.

Our experience with working with and training hundreds of brokers over the years has shown us the following are some characteristics common to "good" brokers:

◆ *Availability*—Good brokers are available to their customer whenever they are needed. This often equates to long hours from covering the early grain markets to the evening Treasury Bond sessions, or tracking and trading the stock markets from New York to the Pacific Coast to Japan to Europe and back. When they aren't personally available, they see to it that an assistant or associate is. You're never out of touch. Ask prospective brokers about how "reachable" they are. Then, when you open an account, test them (call them at 8:00 a.m. and again at 8:00 p.m.) before a market emergency occurs. Do they offer you their home phone number?

◆ *Responsiveness*—You need a broker who'll help you overcome your limitations and satisfy your needs. Therefore, this person must be responsive. In the interview process, ask him or her to send you some obscure piece of information such as, "When is the Federal Reserve releasing the next beige book?". Find out in advance how the broker performs. Ask how fast you'll get fills? Try to discern how hard s/he'll push to respond to your needs.

◆ *Honesty*—Naturally, you must trust and have confidence in your broker. You can often learn a lot about sincerity when you ask about the risk of futures trading or a specific stock trade. If the broker evades or glosses over the high risk involved, beware. You should receive a serious, no holds barred discussion from prospective brokers regarding the buying of options—the risk is limited to the cost of the option (premium) and the transaction costs (brokerage commission and fee)—but, you can lose 100% of this amount. Most options expire worthless. Few traders make money in options. If he tells you this is a serious investment with high risks, it's a big plus.

◆ *Dealing with Losses*—Under the stress of losing other people's money and the pressures of trading, many brokers come apart. The first sign is often a lack of communications with the losing client. This is almost impossible to detect in the early interview stage of the selection process; but when you start to trade, you should become sensitive to it. If possible, ask for some reference of past customers you can call. Ask them how the broker performed when the account was in a drawdown? The best brokers don't let it bother them because losing money is a large part of options trading. Don't get us wrong. They take it seriously, but they can manage it and go on.

Figure 8.1 Broker Interview "T" List

Broker's Name: _____

Firm: _____

Phone Number: (_____)_____

My Need and/or Limitations *Pro/Con*

My Need and/or Limitations	Pro	Con
1. Is he a stock (commodity) options broker?	*Commodity*	
2. Is he an experienced options trader?	*3 years*	
3. Appears knowledgeable about my futures markets (stocks)?		*No, but other ones*
4. Live Quotes	*Yes*	
5. Black-Scholes Model available	*Yes*	
6. Sounds like he has good trading system		*Not sure?*
7. How does firm sound?	*Okay*	
8. Commission rates?		*$125 (all up front)*
9. Good floor contacts?	*Yes*	

My overall impression is:

_____

_____

_____

_____

◆ *Trading*—Find out how they trade. What system do they use? Are they fundamentalists, technicians, or a combination? Have them "sell you a trade." Just ask them what their current trade recommendation is? You want to learn how well they present an opportunity to you. Is it well thought out? Convincing? Have they done their homework?

◆ *Discipline*—Good traders and brokers are very disciplined. They spend hours studying the market and refining their system. Weaker brokers will try to emotionally sell you the "hot trade of the day." Probe to get a feel for the daily routine of brokers you are interviewing. Do they keep a trading diary? What do they do each day that assures that your positions will be reviewed?

◆ *Experience, Knowledge, Track Record*—If you know more or have traded more than a prospective broker, who's going to help whom? Find out what they have done, what they know, and how that's going to make you more successful.

The question of a trading track record is tricky. Most brokers do not have one. If they do not take total discretion in an account (Power of Attorney that permits them to actually trade the account as if it were their own), the customer must approve each trade. Therefore, the broker is merely a consultant and the customer is the trader. The broker cannot use these accounts to create a track record of his/her own.

Next, there are some very stringent regulations imposed by the Securities and Exchange (SEC) and the Commodity Futures Trading Commission (CFTC) regarding track records. These regulations make it difficult and expensive for a broker to prepare a track record. This is another reason most brokers do not have one. Personally, if a broker shows or offers a track record that is not part of a full blown disclosure document that has been reviewed by the federal regulators, you should be very suspicious.

These are just a few of the areas to which you must be sensitive as you select and work with a broker. Always remember that it is your money that's being invested in the market; you're the one who is financially responsible.

As you interview prospects, you'll find two basic types—discounters and full service brokers. You'll also find some who claim to provide full service at discount prices. All too often, new traders make their decision based on the prices of the service, as opposed to their needs. Before you talk to any broker prepare a written list of what you want—need—from your broker. Don't get sucked into the least expensive service if it can't deliver what it takes to make your trading successful.

Let's talk dollars for a moment. The per trade cost at a discounter ranges between $20 and $35 for futures. Stocks depend on volume, usually with a minimum of $35 to $40 for the first trade. In most cases, the trader places toll-free telephone calls to the order desk at the discounter headquarters. An order clerk takes the order and relays it to the order desk at the appropriate exchange.

To utilize this type of service, you need a lot of experience. The order clerk is not in a position to assist you in choosing or evaluating a trade. Their function is strictly to execute orders. In most cases, they will not even provide current price quotes or other information—like highs, lows, trading ranges, trends, market news, volatility, etc.—you may want at the time you are placing your order. Discount costs match the services, as a general rule. Discounters serve full-time traders, who have the time and money to generate all the information they need for their trading system.

The latest innovation in discounting is direct access to the futures or stock markets via personal computers. Most firms limit stock options to covered options. There are two routes you can take. One is through public database services, such as CompuServe or Prodigy, and the other is to connect to the main frame computer of the brokerage firm. Direct access earns an additional 10% discount in most cases. The main advantage is being able to trade whenever the spirit inspires you.

Full-service firms are set up to work in tandem with both experienced and inexperienced traders who need assistance in gathering and interpreting information. You would expect a full-service broker to assist with your understanding of the market, supply information (news, price quotes, theoretical option prices, volatility estimates, etc.) and research. You look to these firms for ideas, advice, and experience. Hopefully, you'll find a firm that can truly become your partner.

The cost per trade for full service is naturally higher. It ranges from $50 to over $100 per trade for futures. For stocks, options are usually sold in dollar packages. The broker will offer you "X" number of options on a certain stock for $2,500 with the commission built into this figure. Another consideration is whether the brokerage firm charges commissions on options on a half-in, half-out basis. Or, half the commission when you place the trade and half when (and if) you offset. Many options expire worthless. Therefore, if you let an option expire, you would not be charged the half-out side of the commission.

There is an old saying in the industry—"If the client is making money, the commission rate isn't an issue." There is a lot of truth to this axiom. Your objective should be to make a profit on your investment. If you don't get what you need from your broker, it doesn't matter what you pay.

Chapter 9

Knowing a Little About Federal Regulations Can Sometimes Smooth Rough Waters

"Money doesn't talk, it swears."

Bob Dylan (1941-)

Key Concepts

◆ Licensing of Stock and Futures Brokers

◆ Understanding Exactly What the Account Documents Are Telling You

◆ Learn Your Rights as an Investor

◆ What Is and What Isn't a Legitimate Complaint Against a Broker

◆ Reading Daily and Monthly Brokerage Statements

◆ Type of Trading Discretion You Can Give Your Broker

People selling investments and services may be licensed or unlicensed. These licenses are granted on state and/or federal levels. Knowing the supervisory structure under which your options broker is licensed provides you with some insights into your recourse if you ever feel you have been unfairly treated.

Let's start with the option brokers who are not required to be licensed. They usually sell what are known as dealer options, normally gold or silver bullion. They sell options to buy on the cash metals markets. Here you are buying the actual metal, when and if you exercise your option. The prices of these options and the brokerage commissions traditionally cost more than options on futures or stocks, but these options may be for longer periods of time.

Since these brokers are unlicensed, there is no regulatory association or commission to appeal to if you have an unresolved complaint with your broker or his/her firm. Your recourse would be to the Better Business Bureau, your state's attorney general, the FBI, Fraud Division of the United States Postal Service, or local police authorities. While all of these organizations do a fine job, none specialize in the particular problem of dealer options. Unless the problem is widespread, you may not get the attention you deserve. Of course, you can always bring a civil or criminal suit directly via your attorney. This can be expensive and is not a reasonable alternative unless a large sum of money is in question.

Is the problem of customer complaints dealt with any better when the broker is licensed? First, the licensing process can be on the state or federal level. Doctors, lawyers, and real estate agents are supervised and licensed on a state by state basis. In most cases, there is no reciprocity between states. For example, if you are registered in one state, you must go through the registration process required by each state in which you wish to conduct business. This usually requires passing a competency test. In some cases, registration is available only to residents of that state.

When it comes to selling exchange traded options, licensing is done nationally. Option brokers are required to pass a national exam, and there are two of these, one for stock brokers and a second for futures brokers. Stock brokers must additionally register in each state they do business. As was mentioned when we were discussing the differences between options on stock and futures, these different types of options are generally traded on different exchanges, stock exchanges for stock options and futures exchanges for options-on-futures.

The key for broker licensing is the exchange. To accept orders for a futures exchange, you must be a licensed futures broker. This requires passing the National Commodities Futures Exam, known as the Series 3 exam. Conversely, to take orders from customers for stock options, you must be a registered stock broker. This requires passing the General Securities Exam, known as the Series 7 Exam. Series 3 and 7 are just part of the overall licensing possibilities for someone to sell various investment products. For example, to just sell mutual funds, one would need to pass the Series 6 Exam, and the Series 62 to sell corporate securities. The possibilities go on and on. There is no prohibition against a broker being registered as both a series 3 and 7, but it is somewhat unusual. It's even more unusual, as we discussed previously, for a broker to trade both stock and futures options. The problem is being able to stay on top of these two very diverse markets.

Conducting business with individual brokers and brokerage firms requiring registration means there are regulators who understand options trading, monitoring sales, and trading activities. This is not a guarantee regulated investments will be a better investment than a nonregulated one. Profitability is a function of savvy investing, not regulations. Regulators do not always concern themselves with the profitability of specific investments or trades. Their *raison d'être* is to enforce the rules.

If regulation doesn't protect you against losses, what does it do? First, every person registered to sell exchange traded options passes either the Series 3 or 7 exam. Therefore, you know you are talking to someone who at least knows the basics.

Secondly, the regulatory organizations, the National Security Dealers Association (NASD) for stock brokers and National Futures Association (NFA) for options-on-futures, monitors the activities of the members. This is done by investigation of any customer complaints they receive and by periodic visits to member's offices. At these visits, the regulators audit the member firms for compliance

with all their regulations. These regulations cover back office (accounting practices, order placement, customer reporting) operations, as well as sales practices.

One of the important areas that NASD and NFA compliance auditors check
are the account papers you will be required to fill out in order to open an option
trading account. Account papers are the basic agreement between yourself and
the brokerage firm (FCM).

You need to read them carefully because they detail:

1. The risk you face trading options.
2. Your responsibilities.
3. Your rights (and the rights you waive) as a customer of a specific
   brokerage firm.
4. The services you'll receive.
5. The cost of the brokerage services.
6. The rights the brokerage firm assumes when you sign the account
   papers.

Think about account papers from three points of view. First of all, these
forms are written by attorneys working for the brokerage firms. Therefore, it is
only common sense to assume much of the language and stipulations will be for
the protection of the brokerage firms. For example, by signing account papers
you give your broker the right to close out your positions, without prior notice, if
you account does not have the proper funds in it.

In its self-interest and for its self-preservation, brokerage firms will do all in
their power to collect what is due them. If a client owes margin money to a
brokerage firm, the firm must put that money up to cover the trade or the exchange on which it is trading will take action. The exchange and its clearing
corporation will not allow a brokerage firm to hold positions that are not properly margined. The integrity of the market must be preserved, so the trader on the
other side of your trade can immediately act. It is for this reason that the entire
industry is so concerned about every trade being properly financed.

If you receive a margin call or a call for more funds, you may have to wire
them within 24 hours or lose your position(s). This is another condition you agree
to when you sign the account papers.

Another point-of-view that comes out loud and clear in the account forms is
that of the regulators. The Security and Exchange Commission (SEC) and the
Commodity Futures Trading Commission (CFTC) oversee the NASD and the
NFA respectively. The SEC and CFTC receive their authority from Congress.
Figure 9.1 ranks the various regulators.

These two regulators want to be sure you understand the risks and that you
are qualified to trade. The risks of loss of all your trading equity is spelled out in
frank terms. After reading it, we sometimes wonder why anyone trades—but the
glimmer of superior returns to equity seems to prevail. Also, as many S & L
shareholders and commercial real estate developers of the early 1980s will attest,
there are no foolproof investments—no matter how much regulation exists!

Figure 9.1 Oversight Hierarchy

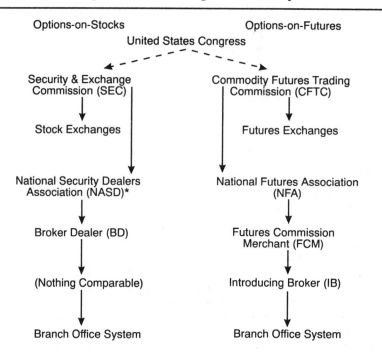

Options-on-Stocks   Options-on-Futures
                 United States Congress

Security & Exchange   Commodity Futures Trading
Commission (SEC)   Commission (CFTC)

Stock Exchanges   Futures Exchanges

National Security Dealers   National Futures Association
Association (NASD)*   (NFA)

Broker Dealer (BD)   Futures Commission
                             Merchant (FCM)

(Nothing Comparable)   Introducing Broker (IB)

Branch Office System   Branch Office System

*Stock brokers must also register in each state in which they do business.

The federal regulatory procedures require stock or commodity futures brokers to pass competency exams. Additionally, the business practices of the brokers and their firms are supervised to assure ethical standards are maintained. The NASD and NFA also provide a formal customer complaint procedure.

To determine your suitability to trade options and to satisfy the regulators dictum that brokers must know their customers, the account papers include a series of questions you are required to answer. Specifically, you will be asked:

Your true name and address.
Your principal occupation.
Your current estimated annual income and net worth.
Your age.
Your previous investing experience.

If for some reason, you prefer not to answer one or more of these questions, say the one on net worth, you'll be asked to put your reasons in writing. And, you may be asked to acknowledge you have a net worth equivalent to at least the minimum acceptable to the brokerage firm. That might be something like

$100,000.00, for example. If your reasons for not answering a question was acceptable, your account may be opened. On the other hand, brokerage firms do not open every account presented to them by their brokers.

The third point of view to consider as you study the account papers is your own. Do you understand and are you prepared to live up to all the conditions? For example, if you were to write an uncovered option or exercise an option for a position in the futures market, you now have "unlimited" risk of loss. You can lose more than what you have invested in the original position and are subject to "on demand" margin calls. This is completely different than buying an option with its predefined risk.

Account papers are not written to protect the investor. They do let you know exactly what your risks and rights are—if you read them!

There is one particular form that is part of all account papers that isn't always explained in as much detail as it probably should. It is the "Predispute Arbitration Agreement." It binds you and your brokerage firm, including all its employees and owners, to final arbitration. This agreement usually includes the following additional stipulations:

◆ Both parties waive their rights to seek remedies in a court of law. In other words, you can't sue your broker.

◆ The discovery or investigative portion of the hearings are more limited. You don't have to spend a lot of time and money digging up information.

◆ The arbitrator's awards or decisions are not required to include factual findings or legal reasoning. This means the individual or panel judging the case do not have to stick strictly to the letter of the law. If they think someone has been wronged, but no law has been violated, they can still find for the complainant.

◆ The avenues available to seek modifications of rulings is limited. In other words, you waive some of your rights to appeal. You agree to binding arbitration.

◆ The panel of arbitrators normally will be composed of mostly people affiliated with the futures or security industries. The reason this occurs is that it is often difficult to find unbiased arbitrators who also have a solid understanding of options. This is not necessarily negative to the individual bringing the complaint. Industry insiders are often very stern with their compatriots, if they believe their actions are hurting the industry. But in most cases, you can request a "mixed" panel of industry and non-industry people.

The specific arbitrators or arbitration panels depend on whether the complaint is against a stock or commodity brokerage firm. Stock companies tend to use arbitrators from the exchange on which the trade took place, the NASD or the American Arbitration Association. With futures firms, the National Futures Association handles all arbitration.

Geography also can come into play. The complainant isn't expected to travel long distance. If you had a complaint about a trade on the New York Stock Exchange and you lived in Sandusky, Ohio, you wouldn't be expected to travel to New York City. Other arrangements would be made. Occasionally, the arbitration takes place by phone, for example, or the nearest major city.

The objective is to obtain fast, inexpensive, and fair resolutions to disputes. You don't need a lawyer, nor do you need to be well-versed in rules of evidence. It often comes down to your word against your broker's.

The $64 question is: Should you sign the "Pre-dispute Arbitration Agreement"? By not signing it, you do not give up the right to ask for arbitration. Additionally, the NASD and the NFA can compel members to respond to the request for arbitration of clients. If you are a small trader with a small account, it is probably to your advantage in our opinion to sign it. Some firms, like the discount stock brokers, have a pre-dispute clause built into their customer agreement.

When or if you have a complaint with your broker or his/her firm, you contact the NASD for stock problems and the NFA for futures. The NASD gives you the name of a staff person who guides you through the process. The first thing this person asks for is a written summation. After reviewing this, the staff member will assist you.

For disputes with futures brokers, you contact the NFA. They'll first attempt to arbitrate it. If this doesn't resolve it, you file a formal complaint and a hearing is set. You might want to call the NFA for a copy of their booklet, "A Guide to Arbitration of Customer Disputes." Or, you can file a complaint with the CFTC. If you are considering this approach, contact them for a copy of their free booklet "Questions & Answers About How You Can Resolve a Commodity Market-Related Dispute." They have basically three reparation procedures:

◆ Voluntary

◆ Summary

◆ Formal

The voluntary procedure is used for claims under $10,000. It is administered by judgment officers appointed by the CFTC. Both parties have an opportunity to uncover facts ("discovery") and present their arguments in writing. There is no oral hearing. Decisions are final, and no appeal is permitted. A non-refundable $25 fee is required.

The summary procedure is similar to the voluntary, but it allows for both a limited oral presentation and a written presentation, which takes place in Washington, DC. Further, you can appeal the decision to the CFTC and to a court of law if you are still not satisfied. It handles complaints of $10,000 and less and requires a $50 non-refundable filing fee.

The formal procedure is designed to handle major complaints, over $10,000. A court-like hearing is conducted in one of 20 locations throughout the United States before an administrative judge. You can be represented by an attorney if you wish. Appeals to the CFTC and the courts are possible. A $200 non-refundable fee is required to file.

Besides the NFA and the CFTC, you can take a complaint to the American Arbitration Association or file a civil suit. If you think your broker or his firm has committed a criminal offense, you can contact the Federal Bureau of Investigation (FBI), or if the U.S. mail was involved, the Chief Postal Inspector of the United States Postal Service.

If you are invested in a limited partnership or a fund, you may be able to appeal to your local state attorney general or the Security and Exchange Commission. Other places with which you may check are the Better Business Bureau and the Federal Trade Commission.

For help deciding your most effective alternative, you should probably sit down and discuss it with your attorney. Please keep in mind two very critical considerations:

1. Your most effective protection results from systematically conducting due diligence research when selecting a broker. Act with reason—don't get caught up in an emotional response to the potential the stock or futures markets may offer.

2. In our opinion, sticking to investments that are federally regulated usually give you a better dispute resolution process than unregulated investments.

Over the many years we have been in this business, the most beneficial arbitration has been done, in our opinion, between brokers and clients. Once it goes beyond this stage, the costs and complications seem to outweigh the results. Our advice is to work hard at this level to keep the lines of communication open. Efforts in this area pay dividends in better trading, fewer errors, and more enjoyable trading.

You may be wondering what can be considered as grounds for a legitimate complaint. Losing money? Bad advice? A trade gone sour? An honest error? None of the above. All these should be expected. Anyone who has ever traded options, or just about anything else for that matter, will attest that losing money on some trades is a way of life. Bad advice simply means your broker, or his/her company's research, cannot foretell the future accurately. Nobody can. This shouldn't be a surprise either. Nor should an occasional error upset you, especially when you consider the enormous trading volume that takes place.

The following are some of the grounds for a formal complaint:

◆ Being high-pressured into opening an account or taking a recommended trade.

◆ Receiving unreasonable promises, like—"You can't lose money trading options!"

◆ Any fraudulent or deceitful communications made to you by your broker or his/her firm.

◆ Excessive trading in an account that a third party is directing for you.

◆ Trading your account without your permission or direction.

◆ Uncorrected errors made in your account.

In just about all of these situations, the broker is being untruthful. To high-pressure you into a trade, for example, he may exaggerate the profit potential or the urgency with which you act.

The last three describe problems you can monitor, if you pay close attention to the statements you receive from your broker. Each transaction you make—a trade, deposit, withdrawal, exercise of an option, etc.—generates a statement. Additionally, each month you'll receive a monthly summation of the month's activities.

Because these written reports arrive two to three days after a trade has taken place, all too many option traders don't pay any attention to them. You need to study these statements as closely as you balance your checkbook, maybe even closer. Ask yourself:

◆ Are the commissions and fees correct?

◆ Do I remember making all these trades? (Always keep at least a log of trades, if not a diary.)

◆ Are the entry and exit prices the same as the fills my broker gave me?

◆ Am I on the correct (put or call) side of each trade?

◆ Have proper debits and credits been made?

◆ Is the extension from a per unit to a full contract price correct?

◆ Is my name, address, and account number correct?

If you question anything at all, call your broker promptly. Don't wait. The longer you put it off the harder it is for your broker to reconstruct the situation and make sense out of it. Good brokers are extremely busy, but always ready to help you. Figure 9.2 shows an example of a statement.

Discretionary Accounts

Some brokers are so helpful, they'll even trade for you. This is called "taking trading discretion" in an account and there are varying degrees of discretion.

On the lowest level, you give your broker either time or price discretion. This means you have decided which stock or commodity option you wish to buy or sell, the side of the market (put or call) and the quantity. You give your broker instructions to act at a certain time or when a price is hit.

The next notch up on the discretionary ladder is the guided account. Here a professional trader suggest specific trades. Your only choice is either to accept or

Figure 9.2 Combined Commodity Statement

PFG Peregrine Financial Group, Inc.
802 Main Street • Cedar Falls • Iowa • 50613
(319) 277- 1306 • FAX (319) 277-0880

Introduced by Wasendorf & Son Company

COMBINED COMMODITY STATEMENT

	DATE
	MAY 11, 1993
	ACCOUNT NUMBER
	227-12345

MR. I. M. WELLOFF
1600 FAIRVIEW BLVD.
PROSPEROUS, PA 19013

DATE	BOUGHT LONG	SOLD SHORT	COMMODITY/OPTION DESCRIPTION	PRICE	AMOUNT DEBIT	CREDIT
		SEGREGATED FUNDS				
05/11/93	ACCOUNT BALANCE		SEGREGATED FUNDS			5,100.90
			----------CONFIRMATION----------			
WE HAVE MADE THIS DAY THE FOLLOWING TRADES FOR YOUR ACCOUNT AND RISK						
	1		DEC 93 CORN C 250	.10	500.00	
			PREMIUM PAID		500.00	
		1*	OPTION EXPIRATION 11/20/93	COMM	75.00	
				FEE	4.25	
			TOTAL COMMISSIONS & FEES		79.25	
			NET PROFIT OR LOSS FROM FUTURES			00
			NET PREMIUMS PAID/RECEIVED FOR OPTIONS		500.00	
CURRENT ACCOUNT BALANCE			SEGREGATED FUNDS			4,521.65
			----------OPEN POSITIONS----------			
03/10/93	2		JUL 93 COMEX SILVER C 600	.25		3,000.00
			PREMIUM VALUE			3,000.00
			SETTLEMENT PRICE	.30		
	1		SEPT 93 SOYBEAN P 500	.12		500.00
			PREMIUM VALUE			500.00
			SETTLEMENT PRICE	.10		
	1		DEC 93 CORN C 250	.10		400.00
			PREMIUM VALUE			400.00
			SETTLEMENT PRICE	.08		
			TOTAL OPEN TRADE EQUITY		.00	
			TOTAL EQUITY			4,521.65
			TOTAL LONG OPTION MARKET VALUE			3,900.00
			TOTAL SHORT OPTION MARKET VALUE		.00	
			NET LIQUIDATING VALUE			8,421.65
			----------SECURITIES ON DEPOSIT----------		VALUE	
06/07/93		10,000	US TREASURY BILL			9,000.00
				TOTAL		9,000.00

Grains in 000's   Retain for Tax Records.   Terms and Conditions on Reverse Side.

You'll receive a statement each time some activity occurs in your trading account. This could be an addition, withdrawal or trade. Monthly you receive a statement that summarizes the month's activity. Always carefully check your statements for accuracy.

reject the trades. If you accept, the trade is executed. Unlike the normal relationship with a broker, there is no discussion or meeting of the minds. Either you accept or pass on the recommendations.

With the next level of discretion, you sign a limited power of attorney giving your broker authority to trade your account as he/she sees fit. If the person actually trading the account is someone other than your broker, called a third party advisor, the advisor may be required to supply you with a disclosure document. This is called a managed account. A disclosure document is basically a prospectus explaining all the details of the advisor's past trading, risk factors, strategies, and personal history. The general exceptions to the disclosure document requirement is an immediate family member of yours, an advisor who does not solicit accounts and manages only a few accounts each year, and a properly licensed broker with two years experience as a broker.

Another possibility is a fund, pool, or limited partnership. These could be public or private. In either case, you receive a formal placement memo or prospectus, which provides all the details. It would be rare for a fund or a pool to only trade options. Most trade stocks or commodities primarily, with the right to trade options when special opportunities present themselves.

Chapter 10

The Single Biggest Mistake New Traders Make—Plus a "Few Other Common Ones!" (And, of Course, How to Avoid Them)

"Too smart is dumb."

Old German Proverb

Key Concepts

◆ "Well-packaged research is NOT truth!"

◆ There's no free lunch.

◆ Getting caught up in a fury of excitement.

◆ Falling for a scam.

◆ Options are risk free.

◆ Trying to run first.

◆ Forgetting to negotiate commissions.

◆ Not looking over your shoulder.

◆ Managing your broker.

"Soaring Sugar Prices Could Mean Stunning Profits For Speculators"

This is an actual headline from a publication put out by a now defunct, but what was at one time a very large and very profitable options brokerage firm. The subhead read: "A move of this magnitude could allow you to multiply your initial investment many times over."

How would you react if you receive a call from a very pleasant person who seemed extremely interested in your financial well-being. In the course of the conversation, this person asks what your financial aspirations are. Your dreams?

What you would do if you could add another $10,000 or $100,000 to your annual income? Here's what the conversation might sound like.

Salesperson: "Living in Coral Gables must be very pleasant with the beaches...the oceans and the endless sunshine. Sure beats winter's snow and slush. Do you take advantage of the ocean at your door step?"

Prospect: "Well, we do occasionally. The beaches are great. I'd like to do more fishing."

Salesperson: "What kind of boat do you have?"

Prospect: "We don't have one at the moment."

Salesperson: "If you could own any boat you wanted...if money was no object...what kind of boat would you buy?"

Prospect: "Gee...I don't know. There are so many great ones down here. I guess I'd go for one of those fishing yachts. You know what I mean...half pleasure boat, but rigged for deep sea fishing."

Salesperson: "I know exactly what you mean. It would be my choice too. I think I'd like something around 30-foot. How about you?"

Prospect: "That's a good size, but a new one would be very expensive."

Salesperson: "Let's not worry about cost yet. What all would you want on it? How many bunks? What type of galley? How about radar and fish finders?"

Prospect: "It's sounding better and better. I'd want plush furnishings and a couple of big diesel engines...and, of course, lots of fishing gear."

Salesperson: "Now we're cooking. I saw a rig like that not too long ago in a magazine. The price tag was just under $100,000.00. If I could show you how to turn a couple of thousand into over a hundred thousand for that yacht—would you be interested?"

Prospect: "Of course, but how risky is it?"

Salesperson: "With the investment I'm talking about, the risk is very limited BUT THE PROFIT IS UNLIMITED! Is that the type of investment you're looking for?"

Prospect: "Tell me more ..."

It doesn't take any imagination to see where this sales conversation is headed. The salesperson probes the prospect to learn how much cash is available, then begins selling the story on the potential of sugar options. The salesperson closes this conversation by promising to overnight all the details on the sugar trade.

What is wrong with this scenario? Was the headline a complete fabrication? Did it have any basis in fact? What about the telephone sales presentation? Was it all just a fish story?

The headline and accompanying story was well-researched and had bases in fact. Sugar can be an extremely volatile market. It often makes spectacular moves, as anyone who remembers the world-class move it made in 1974. That year started with some bullish fundamentals. The year-end (1973-1974) stock/consumption ratio was low—20%. The sugar beet crop in Europe was faced with some adverse growing conditions. Fundamentals might account for 20 or 30-cent sugar, but it eventually more than doubled to over 65 cents. There was even talk of dollar per pound sugar. In the final months of this wild bull rally, futures prices shot up 36 cents/lb. in two months. Thirty-six cents is three times higher than the prior post World War II high! Then sugar came down faster than it went up, leveling in the 15 to 20 cent range. A similar market "panic" occurred in 1980. It was not as severe, but sugar rallied to 45 cents that time.

The sugar story called for 20-cent per pound sugar. At the time, sugar was trading around the 14-cent level. An increase to 20 cents would have been a six cents times 112,000 pounds per contract or $6720.00 for an option that was in-the-money when the move began. The story did fairly state: "If the sugar market fails to move or moves against you, you could lose all or part of your purchase price. But your risk is strictly limited to the total purchase price of your options—a fraction of the underlying futures contract's actual market value." The fact that this company's commissions were large by industry standards and included in "total purchase price" was not spelled out.

On the follow-up call, the salesperson ties it all together—the dream boat, the volatile sugar market, and outstanding fundamental reasons why a 6-cent move is well within expectations. Account papers were in the overnight packet with the sugar article. Also included was a return overnight envelope. The salesperson matched an appropriate number of options to the maximum cash available and had the prospect overnight everything back, including a cashier's check.

What did the prospect buy? In our opinion, nothing but a dream. The year being discussed was 1989 and sugar traded in the 14 to 15-cent range. All the options would have expired worthless.

In our opinion, buying a dream—rather than working hard to make a well-balanced, diversified investment in options—is the biggest single mistake the majority of novice options traders make. All too often, options trading is presented as being a simple, limited risk investment.

Think about all we said so far in this book about the Law of Probability, the distribution of winning and losing trades, the random nature of price activity, the need to survive losing trades to be in the right market, on the right side, at the right time. These are the realities of options trading! For someone to think they can select a single trade and buy a dozen or so options that will net them $100,000.00 the first time they trade is not credible.

Options trading is a complex, highly speculative investment. Spectacular returns are possible, but they don't normally come easily. Professional traders, who make the above average returns you have heard about, earn them.

The second biggest reason new traders lose, in our opinion, is they become overwhelmed by the research provided to them. Well substantiated—and well presented—projections based on historical patterns take on the aura of inevitability. Analysts take great pains drawing parallels to past moves they hope will be mirrored again. For example, the 1989 sugar situation was compared to 1974 and 1980. It seemed inconceivable that anything but a major bull move would occur.

Traders, even very experienced ones, get caught up in the excitement. Once the "facts" get circulated, everyone is talking about them. Herd psychology prevails. For awhile, expectations often become self-fulfilling prophecies. Susceptibility to this phenomenon is another reason traders lose.

How Vulnerable Are You to Mass Hysteria?

We often think of ourselves as being too logical or level-headed to be turned around by some bizarre social reality. We never bought a hoola hoop. We know Elvis is truly dead.

We all are vulnerable to some extent and we all have our Achilles' heels. If you understand how these phenomena of herd psychology work, you'll be better prepared to deal with them.

And, as an options trader, you must be able to see reality for what it is in order to profitably trade reality. Let's start with a few examples to illustrate the point.

In London in 1524, the city awaited its doom. Numerous astrologers and fortune tellers had foretold a massive flood. The great Thames, one of the world's best behaved rivers, was to jump its bank and engulf the entire city on February 1. Doom and gloom was predicted by just about anybody anyone would listen to. Over 20,000 citizens, nearly the entire population, moved to higher ground.

On February 1st nothing happened. But the charlatans had an answer. A minor miscalculation had occurred. The flood was coming in 1624. Londoners were safe at least for awhile. Sound like any economic forecasters you know?

If you think these things only happened in the middle ages and that only the "poor dumb masses" are caught up, think again. The "red bating" frenzy of McCarthyism even caught up the ACLU. That is a group who considers themselves above emotionalism. The fact is they too were swept along in the 1950s and refused to defend suspected communists.

This type of behavior occurs in options trading regularly. Traders get caught in the power of mass delusion—"Prices are going through the ceiling!" "There's no end to this bull move!"—that causes them to lose control of their trading.

Let's take a quick look at how these fantasies develop. Our personal and collective body of beliefs can be roughly divided into two distinctly different types. The first is deeply rooted in physical fact. If we touch something very hot with our bare hand, we get burned. It is extremely difficult for anyone to get us to change our minds regarding these beliefs.

When we get into very complicated areas in which we have strong feelings, yet our understanding is somewhat vague, we tend to rely on others that we consider to be authorities. In the case of religion, it is ministers or priests. In politics, it is politicians. In finance, it is bankers, advisors, etc.

Options trading is no different. It certainly can be complex and vague. We look to professional traders, journalists, brokers, newsletter writers, etc. When they get caught up in the image of what "everyone" thinks is happening, they whip traders into a wild frenzy. This pulls the average investor in off the street. Everyone thinks the market will never stop. Novice option traders get burnt!

You need the discipline that comes with an understanding of the mass psychology that can overcome even the best traders' common sense. Add to this the courage to stand up to anyone trying to bully you or dazzle you into a trade. As we discussed earlier, successful traders control their emotions.

Another pitfall traders can encounter is old-fashioned fraud. This can involve classic Ponzi schemes, falsified research, or a creative presentation of research. For example, a dishonest broker locates 50 or so prospects who will listen to his pitch. He tells them he is backed by an excellent market analyst who has an incredible system for anticipating the direction of the S & P 500 Index. To demonstrate just how accurate it is, this pitch man offers to share the research with each of the 50 prospects for the next four weeks. With each weekly call, the prospects are told whether the system is calling for higher or lower prices. Half of the group are told higher and the other half lower.

Despite what happens in the S & P, at the end of four weeks, there are at least six people who have seen four perfect market projections. These six are convinced and could be taken advantage of.

This is only one of the many, many scams perpetrated against would be investors. There tends to be a common thread among these types of sales presentations, and that is an unbalanced presentation between the possibility of loss compared to the easy gains that can be made.

If you are solicited by a stock or futures broker who is using some type of promotion that delivers an unbalanced presentation of the enormous profits to be made from the market with little or no mention of risk, you'll know at least two important facts. First, the material is in violation of federal regulations. Secondly, beware of whoever is presenting the materials. If their initial overture is so out of tune, the rest of their song will probably be as well. The next refrain most likely will be a high-pressure sales presentation, consisting of overnight movement of account papers and checks. Consider yourself forewarned and keep your distance.

Advertising, which is balanced and informative, can be very helpful to you both in deciding if you are suited for options trading and if you want to learn more. As you absorb these type of messages, you'll learn how much risk you'll be accepting and have a more complete picture of profit opportunities.

You'll often see a big difference between the ethical broker and one who plays fast and loose. The former will spend time with you, send you information, such as newsletters, and be sincerely interested in learning about your investment needs. The wheeler-dealer's objective is to raise the prospects' greed level to such a fever pitch that you buy "the dream," rather than reality. This is high-pressure sales. There's no time for thought and reflection. You'll hear lines like this:

◆ "An opportunity this good only comes by once in a blue moon!"

◆ "If you don't get $2,000.00 to me by noon tomorrow, you'll miss your chance to turn it into $10,000.00 in the next two weeks!"

◆ "Gold is going sky high—starting tomorrow!"

From ethical brokers, you'll hear descriptions of opportunities won and opportunities lost. The legitimate sales representative will tell you that sooner or later another good, solid trading opportunity will appear. You'll also be provided with a balanced presentation of the risk, something you won't hear from "deal-peddlers." Remember the old adage: "An option trade that sounds too good to be true probably is."

In their booklet, *Before You Say Yes*, the NFA lists 15 questions that can help you distinguish qualified investment sales people from swindlers. The following is a paraphrased version of those questions:

1. What is the commission rate? Other costs?
2. What are the risks?
3. Can you send me a written explanation of the risk involved?
4. Can you send me copies of your sales literature?
5. Are you selling an investment sold on a regulated exchange?
6. Which governmental or industry regulator supervises your firm?
7. Specifically, where would my money be held?
8. When and where can we meet in person?
9. How and when can I liquidate my investment if I so desire?
10. Will you send me your entire proposal in the mail?
11. If a dispute arises, what are the means available to resolve it?
12. Where did you get my name?
13. Would you mind explaining your proposal to my lawyer?
14. Would you give me the names of your principals and officers?
15. Can you provide references?

Experience has shown that the dishonest sales people usually resist or are not prepared for this type of interrogation. Their "marks" are impulsive buyers who make entirely emotional decisions. The answers you get are vague and evasive. For example,

Question: How much are commissions?
Response: They're never a problem.

Question: If I have a complaint, what can I do?
Response: Don't even worry about that, I'll take care of you personally.

By gathering a lot of information and taking some time making your decision, you can protect yourself from the majority of swindlers—but not all. The very best mimic legitimate sales operations, but most can be uncovered if you do your homework and control your emotions.

Another simple procedure you can do to avoid scam artists is call the NASD or the NFA Information Centers and ask these questions:

1. Give the name of the person you've talked with and ask if s/he is registered.

2. With which firm?
3. How long has s/he been registered?
4. Has the NASD or NFA taken any public disciplinary action against her/him?
5. Has s/he been registered with any firm that has been cited for compliance problems?
6. Is there anything else you can tell me about her/him, since I'm considering investing with her/him?

Once you decide who you think the right broker is, you make your selection by completing the account papers, which we've already reviewed in Chapter 9. Your broker should ask you to read them carefully and fill them out in your own handwriting. The reason for you to do it in your own hand is so the broker is assured that you saw them and had the opportunity to read them. The broker will ask you if you understand them and have any questions. The account papers describe the risks you are assuming. You have no one to blame but yourself if you ignore them or sign them without reading them carefully.

If the broker offers to fill them out for you ("I'll just get them typed up for you"), consider this a warning signal. The easier the broker makes it for you to fill out the account papers, the less likely you are to study them. They are worth the time and effort it takes to understand what you are signing because they define the risk you face in great detail.

Poor communications is another miscue that often occurs between clients and their brokers. It's important that you and your broker set up some guidelines. Here are some to use to sidestep this problem. Be sure to cover them all before trading begins.

1. Time of day you are most easily accessible.
2. Whether you are to call in or whether your broker will call you.
3. What steps will be taken if you can't be contacted, i.e., should your broker put stops in the market, close out positions after 4, 8, 12, or 24 hours of not being in contact, etc.
4. What steps will be taken if the account goes into debit? Do you plan to wire money into the account? Transfer from another account? Overnight a check?
5. How trading emergencies will be handled.
6. What hours you are available and who to contact when you are not available.
7. Normal office hours, plus any evening hours your broker is available.
8. You may need to provide your broker with your home or office phone number, if that's the only way for him to stay in touch with you.
9. Your broker needs to know who to contact if you are not always near a phone. This person should be able to reach you quickly. For example, farm wives are often in radio contact with their husbands during planting and harvesting. Many business people carry cellular phones when out of their offices.

10. You need to make provisions for unusual situations, such as when you are traveling or taking a vacation.

The point is simply this: It is easy to avoid the mistake of losing contact with your broker. If a situation arises where you are going to be out of touch, either put stops in the market, close out the positions or even your account. Do not risk trading when you cannot be reached quickly, if the market situation warrants it. If your broker doesn't mention this, be sure you do.

Another common misfire made by new option traders is jumping the gun. Many traders come to the conclusion there is no reason to hesitate since the risk of buying a put or a call can be predetermined. They reason: "The option only costs $900, or $1,000 including fees and commissions. I can afford that. Go ahead and buy it."

First, if the option expires worthless, you lose 100% of your investment. Think of it in those terms, rather than a dollar amount you can stand to lose.

When you think of it as 100%, you start trying to figure how to salvage some of it. What about cutting the loss to 50%? Or 20%? It's this kind of thinking that leads to the use of placing trailing stops behind your positions.

The opposite—waiting too long to trade—can be equally debilitating. Some people wait until they learn everything there is to know about options trading before they place their first trade. Of course, this never happens.

On the other hand, if you have the gut feeling that options may not be for you, don't fight it. You don't have to trade. Trading stock and futures options is highly speculative, not suited for every investor. Never let a broker or "friend" bully or dare you into trading. Hang up on any broker who challenges like this:

"If you don't have the guts for this trade,
you better get a testosterone check!"

"If you have to ask your husband for permission
to trade, you're not a 1990s woman!"

Your motivation for placing an options trade should be profit based on a sound, unemotional evaluation of the strategy, the market, and the trades risk-to-reward ratio.

A variation of these last scenarios is the purchasing of an option at the wrong strike price or month because you don't have enough money in your account to buy the right one. For example, let's say you are considering buying a December crude oil call. The futures price is $20.54 per barrel and you're looking at the $20.00 strike price. It's at $0.74 or $740.00 (1000 bbl × $0.74). Since you only have $500.00 in trading equity, you settle on a $21.00 per barrel strike price. It's at $0.16 or $160.00 plus commission and fees.

This is a big change, from approximately 50 cents in-the-money to 50 cents out. The in-the-money call had $500.00 of intrinsic value and the rest was for time to expiration. Since the out-of-the-money option has less time value than the in ($160.00 vs. $240.00), the market is telling you time is not valuable. But the key error is comprising your strategy to accommodate your wallet. Also, you must resist the suggestion of your broker to down trade in these circumstances. Brokers normally work on commissions and are continuously looking for ways to sell a trade.

You're usually better off searching for a new trade that meets all your criteria and also is affordable—or standing aside the market. Standing aside is a totally acceptable stance. Inexperienced traders often make the mistake of over-trading, feeling they should always have something going in order to be successful. The pros often sit on the bench when the game is not going their way or they are not sure which way it is headed. This leads to the next subject, which is the proper way to get into the markets in the first place.

Chapter 11

Getting Started, or the Secrets of Successful Options Trading

"What we call the beginning is often the end. And to make an end is to make a beginning. The end is where we start from."

T. S. Eliot (*Little Gidding*, 1942)

Key Concepts

◆ The Secret Behind the Secret

◆ Master Trader, Journeyman, Loser—Which Will You Be?

◆ Option Traders Checklist

◆ Getting Started the Right Way

When we're approached by a reporter for an interview, the first thing that comes to mind is are they going to pull that old iron out of the fire and ask: "Well, Mr. Wasendorf, what's your secret for successful options trading?" If editors thought about how dumb that question is, they would instruct all their reporters never to broach the subject.

Just the word "secret" should tell them something. If we do have a secret, could we tell them and still have one? There is also the concept of greed. All options traders have it to one degree or another. It helps us overcome the fear of loss, allowing us to enter the markets. Since we do have a healthy dose of it, would any successful trader share a secret that could open the door to untold wealth? For free? Especially if sharing the secret could very well reduce or destroy the effectiveness of it? Keep these thoughts in mind when you read books or articles offering trading "secrets."

The secret to options trading is the same as the secret of success in any field. There are two basic aspects—one evolves nature, the other nurture. For good measure, you can throw in some good old-fashioned luck.

What Does The Successful Fashion Designer or NFL Linebacker Have in Common?

First of all, you'll say they are very good at what they do. The designer has attended some outstanding schools, worked for years under a well-known "rabbi" and got a big "break"—catapulting him/her to the top. The linebacker sweated out 10 to 12 seasons on a variety of levels to become an NFL rookie.

After two or three years in the pros without a career-ending injury (luck), he's at the Pro or Super Bowl.

In both cases, years were spent in study, learning the rules. But it took more than that. To become superstars, they had to have a special knack for knowing what excites the fashion world or which way a misdirection play is really headed. Without this special ability, this sixth sense, these two individuals could have very nice careers in their chosen fields, but on more modest levels. Also, without some luck, they may have drifted to other fields in which they may not be as well-suited.

This analysis additionally needs to take into consideration accidents of nature. If the potential designer was born color blind, how would this diminish chances for success? Or what if the football player had a club foot? They might have the hearts of lions, but certain physical and mental faculties are usually necessary for them to compete successfully. For the option trader math skills and a good memory are a must. If you can't do simple math quickly and accurately in your head, you'll find yourself at a distinct disadvantage. You're constantly finding yourself having to figure the value of a spread or converting a 40-point move in sugar to dollars and cents ($448.00).

To make all the spur of the moment mathematical calculations, you need to be able to immediately recall hundreds of facts and figures. Additionally, we have met few successful traders who were not able to recollect past price patterns and moves. History repeats itself daily in the pits. Your mind must become an encyclopedia of trivia about the markets you trade. This is another reason we often caution new traders to concentrate on only a few stock issues or commodity markets in the beginning.

The secret of success also entails performing the hard work needed to learn the rules others have found necessary. We shared many of these with you in an earlier chapter, but we can't teach you the discipline to follow them. This is part of the nurturing aspect of learning to trade.

Let's jump to the natural or intuitive part of trading. How do you know if you have it? What's the test? If you don't have "it," is there any hope?

As with any profession, there at least two levels of proficiency—the masters and the journeymen. In this industry, the masters are called market wizards. You should read Jack Schwager's book "Market Wizards," for inspiration and information. It's a series of interviews with a group of recognized trading masters.

If you're not a master, do you want to be a journeyman? When you seriously consider it, it is not all that bad. A journeyman options trader follows the rules, trades when the risk-to-reward is well in his/her favor, and primarily stays with the more conservative strategies (spreads, for example). The journeyman's profit objective, by option trading standards, is also modest. Usually in the 25% to 50% return to equity per annum. By other investment standards, it isn't modest.

Can any trader become a journeyman? Unfortunately...no! There is one other class of individuals also present in all other vocations or avocations. We are referring to the losers.

How Do You Know If You Are Likely
to Be a Loser in Options Trading?

No one, of course, knows for sure, but there are some telltale characteristics. The losers often know in their hearts before they trade. A negative personality rarely earns profits consistently. They are usually attracted to options for the wrong reasons—to make a lot of money fast without exerting much effort. Therefore, they don't spend the time required to learn some of the more complicated strategies that are more conservative by comparison.

This lack of patience also reflects in the inability to wait for a trade with an above average risk-to-reward ratio. Losers are impatient and act very impulsively. They usually refuse to keep trading journals and rarely learn from their mistakes. Brokers can strongly influence them by offering quick fixes to lagging winnings, which usually compounds the problem. Loss of independence in the option game often equates to loss of capital.

Success requires focus, patience, and the ability to act fast and decisively without losing control of your emotions, trade too many markets, or refuse to wait for strategies to succeed. Quite frankly, options trading can sometimes be tiresome. When you buy an option, you buy time. Time for the market to move as you anticipate. And, that can take awhile. For example, trades may stay open two or three months. During the first 30 to 60 days, there may be an insignificant change in your position. You must be prepared and patient.

While waiting for something to happen, you can lose faith, both in yourself and your trades. Persistence of purpose is another virtue of the successful.

One clue that you have the potential to be a master, or at least an upper level journeyman, is your gut feeling. As you read this book, do you hear yourself saying: "I can do that!" Or, do you keep hearing the refrain—"This is too risky. This is too risky. Do I really want to tackle something this speculative?"

There is nothing wrong with either reaction. If in your soul you're not comfortable with all you've learned so far—give it up! Thank your lucky stars you didn't pay $500, $1,000 or $10,000 for the same lesson, as others have. Take a philosophic approach to the experience. You bought a book, you learned a lot about a unique type of investment, and you got your money's worth.

On the other hand, if you're chomping at the bit to fill out account papers and attack the markets at this stage, take a cold shower. Then write down the answers to these questions:

1. Describe why you are psychologically and financially suited to trade options.
2. What are your goals? Are they realistic? Specific?
3. How do you want and plan to use options to reach your objectives?
4. What are your limitations, and how do you plan to manage them?
5. Will you trade stocks or futures options?
6. Which stock or futures markets do you plan to trade? Describe your prospective portfolio.

Figure 11.1 The Trading Process

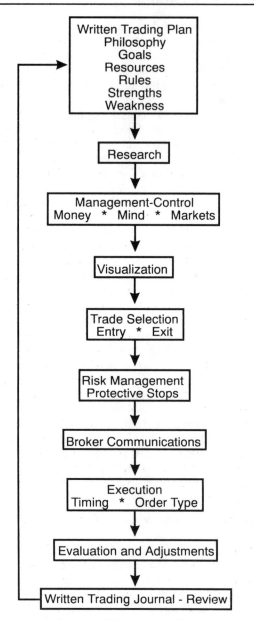

Trading is called a process because it is on-going. It never stops, just as the markets are continuously in flux.

7. How will you analyze the markets? Will you trade for the long, medium or short term?

8. What system will you use to select trades, entry-exit price points, trailing protective stops, trading volume, number (size) of positions, type of orders, software, price quotation source or equipment, etc.?

9. Do you have a clear understanding of money management? Do you have a written set of rules? Do you fully understand the concept of survivability as it pertains to options trading?

10. What do you need or want from a broker and his/her firm?

11. Are you comfortable with all the nitty-gritty that goes along with options trading, like understanding the account papers, your rights and responsibilities, daily and monthly statements, etc.?

Once you have answers to these questions—again, we strongly recommend putting them in writing because it clarifies thinking—you're ready to begin the broker selection process.

As you are searching for a good broker, we'd recommend one additional exercise before you fund an actual trading account. Consider doing some practice or paper trading.

There are some computer programs that simulate options trading you might want to check into. One is available from COMEX at a cost of $69. It's called "The Game." You start with $10,000 in equity and trade COMEX gold and silver options.

Before you invest in "The Game," you might want to call the Coffee, Sugar, and Cocoa Exchange for a free copy of their program called "SOFTSware." It's divided into three parts.

The first part, "About Options," provides a brief overview of options terminology and strategy. It includes the contract specifications for coffee, sugar, and cocoa options and sources for more information.

The second and third sections will be the ones most useful to you. For example, "Choose Strategy," which is part two, prompts you to pick a commodity to trade. Naturally, your choices are coffee, sugar, or cocoa. Next you select a market opinion: bullish, bearish, or neutral. With the next screen, you pick a strategy appropriate to that type of market. You are presented with several different strategies to test. If your market opinion choice was neutral, for example, you could try any one of the following strategies:

◆ "A" Butterfly

◆ "V" Butterfly

◆ "A" Condor

◆ "V" Condor

◆ Long Straddle

◆ Short Straddle

◆ Long Strangle

◆ Short Strangle

◆ Conversion

◆ Box

◆ Call Ratio Write

You have similarly appropriate selections for bullish or bearish market sentiments.

Once a strategy is chosen, the next screen provides an explanation and example of the trade. You then have four more information screens. One gives you details of the profit and loss of the trade, at expiration, based on a wide variety of prices for the underlying commodity. The next screen graphs the trade. This is a valuable picture of the profit and loss potential for each of the many strategies illustrated. A Time-Volatility screen lets you change the time to expiration, volatility rate, and/or interest rate. You can see the impact of changes in volatility in dollars and cents. If you're not pleased with your strategy selection, you can switch to a new one and compare profitability.

The last part of "SOFTSware" gives you the opportunity to build your own strategy. You can combine up to four different options into a strategy after selecting the commodity and market direction. You fill in the following blanks:

1. Long or short
2. Call, put, or futures
3. Strike or futures price
4. Number of contracts
5. Option premium

The program then calculates the four screens previously described for the "Choose Strategy" section. You can then make refinements (change, volatility, etc.) at will. This portion is a great way to test yourself to make sure you understand how and when to use a bull spread, condor, butterfly, etc.

This program is designed to promote the Coffee, Sugar, and Cocoa Exchange. These are exciting markets to trade, but sometimes liquidity is not as high as one would wish for when trading the first time. Always be cautious of thin markets, no matter what exchange.

What Else Should You Do to Prepare?

Consider investing in a seminar or two. Most of the exchanges, stock and futures, offer courses on a variety of educational levels. Contact those nearby or the ones you think you'll utilize in your trading. If you plan to trade options-on-futures, contact the Chicago Merc or the CBOT. If you're into stock options, contact the appropriate stock exchange nearest to you. (See reference section for addresses and telephone numbers.)

We'd also recommend a subscription to "Futures Magazine" and to one or more of the newsletters in the field. We'd be happy to send you a free trial to ours. As you'll see when you review the Appendix, there are also many excellent books on options trading.

One, rather two, final admonitions. There is only one way to really understand options trading and that is by doing it. You can spend the rest of your days studying it, but until you place your first trade, you'll never experience what all the excitement is about.

Last of all, never forget the simple fact that you, and everyone else trading options, are attempting to anticipate what will happen five minutes, five weeks, or five months from the time you place a trade. No one knows the future. Therefore, you must never marry a position and you should take what the market gives you.

Appendix 1
Glossary of Terms

Actuals The physical or cash commodity, as distinguished from commodity futures contracts.

Administrative Law Judge (ALJ) A CFTC official authorized to conduct a proceeding and render a decision in a formal complaint procedure.

Aggregation The policy under which all futures positions owned or controlled by one trader or a group of traders are combined to determine reporting status and speculative limit compliance.

All Or None (AON) An order which must be filled in its entirety or not at all.

American Type Option An option which may be exercised at any time prior to expiration.

Arbitrage The simultaneous purchase of one commodity against the sale of another in order to profit from distortions from usual price relationships. *See also* Spread, Straddle.

Arbitration A forum for the fair and impartial settlement of disputes that the parties involved are unable to resolve between themselves. NFA's arbitration program provides a forum for resolving futures-related disputes. NASD handles stock-related complaints.

Assignment Notice to an option writer that an option has been exercised by the option holder. This can happen at any time during the life of an option with American type options and only at or near expiration for European style options.

Associated Person (AP) An individual who solicits orders, customers, or customer funds on behalf of a Futures Commission Merchant, an Introducing Broker, a Commodity Trading Advisor, or a Commodity Pool Operator and who is registered with the Commodity Futures Trading Commission (CFTC) or the National Futures Association (NFA).

At-the-Money An option whose strike price is equal to the market value of the underlying futures contract. Can also refer to an order to buy a futures contract at the current bid-ask price (*See* Market Order).

155

Automatic Exercise The exercise by the clearing house of an in-the-money option at expiration, unless the holder of the option submits specific instructions to the contrary.

Award *See* Reparations Award.

Back Spread A spread in which more options are purchased than sold, and where all options have the same underlying entity and expire at the same time. Back spreads are usually delta neutral.

Backwardation A futures market where the more distant delivery months for a commodity trade at a discount to the near-term delivery months.

Basis The difference between the cash or spot price and the price of the nearby futures contract.

Bear market (bear/bearish) A market in which prices are declining; a market participant who believes prices will move lower is called a "bear". A news item is considered bearish if it is expected to produce lower prices.

Bear Spread Any spread in which a decline in the price of the underlying entity will increase the value of the spread.

Beta Measure of how the options market correlates to the movement of the underlying futures market.

Bid An offer to buy a specific quantity of a commodity at a stated price.

Board of Trade Any exchange or association of persons who are engaged in the business of buying or selling any commodity or receiving the same for sale on consignment. Usually means an exchange where commodity futures and/or options are traded. *See also* Contract Market or Exchange.

Box A long call and short put at one exercise price, and a short call and a long put at a different exercise price. All four options must have the same underlying entity and expire at the same time.

Break A rapid and sharp price decline.

Broker A person paid a fee or commission for acting as an agent in making contracts or sales; floor broker in commodities futures trading, a person who actually executes orders on the trading floor of an exchange; account executive (associated person) the person who deals with customers and their orders in commission house offices. *See* Registered Commodity Representative or Registered Representative (stock broker).

Brokerage A fee charged by a broker for execution of a transaction, an amount per transaction or a percentage of the total value of the transaction; usually referred to as a commission fee.

Bucket, Bucketing Illegal practice of accepting orders to buy or sell without executing such orders; and the illegal use of the customer's margin deposit without disclosing the fact of such use.

Bull Market (bull/bullish) A market in which prices are rising. A participant in futures who believes prices will move higher is called a "bull". A news item is considered bullish if it is expected to bring on higher prices.

Bull Spread Any spread in which a rise in the price of the underlying entity will theoretically increase the value of the spread.

Butterfly The sale (purchase) of two identical options, together with the purchase (sale) of one option with an immediately higher exercise price, and one option with an immediately lower exercise price. All options must be of the same type, for the same underlying entity, and expire at the same time.

Buy or Sell on Close or Opening To buy or sell at the end or the beginning of the trading session.

Buyer The purchaser of an option, either a call option or a put option. Also referred to as the option holder. An option purchase may be in connection with either an opening or a closing transaction.

Buy/Write The purchase of an underlying contract and the simultaneous sale of a call.

Buying Hedge (or Long Hedge) Buying futures contracts to protect against possible increased cost of commodities which will be needed in the future. *See* Hedging.

Calendar Spread Another name for a time spread.

Call (option) The buyer of a call option acquires the right but not the obligation to purchase a particular futures contract at a stated price on or before a particular date. Buyers of call options generally hope to profit from an increase in the futures price of the underlying commodity.

Car(s) This is a colloquialism for futures contract(s). Came into common use when a railroad car or hopper of corn, wheat, etc. equaled the amount of a commodity in a futures contract. *See* Contract.

Carrying Broker A member of a commodity exchange, usually a clearinghouse member, through whom another broker or customer, chooses to clear all or some trades.

Carrying Charges Costs incurred in warehousing the physical commodity, generally including interest, insurance, and storage.

Carryover That part of the current supply of a commodity consisting of stocks from previous production/marketing seasons.

Cash Commodity Actual stocks of a commodity, as distinguished from futures contracts; goods available for immediate delivery or delivery within a specified period following sale; or a commodity bought or sold with an agreement for delivery at a specified future date. *See* Actuals and Forward Contracting.

Cash Forward Sale *See* Forward Contracting.

Certificated Stock Stocks of a commodity that have been inspected and found to be of a quality deliverable against futures contracts, stored at the delivery points designated as regular or acceptable for delivery by the commodity exchange.

Charting The use of graphs and charts in the technical analysis of futures markets to plot trends of price movements, average movements of price volume, and open interest. *See* Technical Analysis.

Christmas Tree A type of ratio vertical spread where options are sold at two or more different exercise prices.

Churning Excessive trading of the customer's account by a broker, who has control over the trading decisions for that account, to make more commissions while disregarding the best interests of the customer.

Class of Options All call options—or all put options—on the same underlying stock or futures contracts.

Clearing The procedure through which trades are checked for accuracy after which the clearinghouse or association becomes the buyer to each seller of a futures contract, and the seller to each buyer.

Clearing Member A member of the clearinghouse or association. All trades of a nonclearing member must be registered and eventually settled through a clearing member.

Clearinghouse or Clearing Corporation An agency connected with exchanges through which all futures and option contracts are made, offset, or fulfilled through delivery of the actual commodity and through which financial settlement is made; often, is a fully chartered separate corporation rather than a division of the exchange proper. Once a trade has been cleared, the clearing corporation becomes the buyer to every seller and the seller to every buyer.

Clearing Price *See* Settlement Price.

Close (the) The period at the end of the trading session, officially designated by the exchange, during which all transactions are considered made "at the close."

Closing Purchase Transaction An exchange transaction in which the purchaser is reducing or eliminating the short position in the option series involved in the transaction.

Closing Range A range of closely related prices at which transactions took place at the closing of the market; buy and sell orders at the closing might have been filled at any point within such a range.

Closing Sale Transaction An exchange transaction in which the seller is reducing or eliminating the long position in the option series involved in the transaction.

Combination A trading strategy. Combinations involved buying or selling both a put and a call on the same stock or futures. A position created either by purchasing both a put and a call or by writing both a put and a call on the same underlying entity.

Commission 1) A fee charged by a broker to a customer for performance of a specific duty, such as the buying or selling of futures contracts or stock issued. 2) Sometimes used to refer to the Commodity Futures Trading Commission (CFTC).

Commodity An entity of trade or commerce, services, or rights in which contracts for future delivery may be traded. Some of the contracts currently traded are wheat, corn, cotton, livestock, copper, gold, silver, oil, propane, plywood, currencies, Treasury bills, bonds, and notes.

Commodity Exchange Act The federal act that provides for federal regulation of futures trading.

Commodity Futures Trading Commission (CFTC) A commission set up by Congress to administer the Commodity Exchange Act, which regulates trading on commodity exchanges.

Commodity Pool An enterprise in which funds contributed by a number of persons are combined for the purpose of trading futures contracts and/or options on futures. Not the same as a joint account.

Commodity Pool Operator (CPO) An individual or organization which operates or solicits funds for a commodity pool. Generally required to be registered with the Commodity Futures Trading Commission.

Commodity Trading Advisor (CTA) Individuals or firms that, for a fee, issue analysis or reports concerning commodities, advise others on the value or the advisability of trading in commodity futures, options, or leverage contracts.

Condor The sale (purchase) of two options with consecutive exercise prices, together with the purchase (sale) of one option with an immediately lower exercise price and one option with an immediately higher exercise price. All options must be of the same type, have the same underlying entity, and expire at the same time.

Confirmation Statement A statement sent by a commission house or broker dealer to a customer when a futures, options, or stock position has been initiated or some other transaction has taken place. The statement shows the number of contracts (stock shares) bought or sold and the prices at which the contracts were bought or sold. It might also show any funds moved in or out of the account. Sometimes combined with a Purchase and Sale Statement.

Complainant The individual who files a complaint seeking a reparations awarded against another individual or firm.

Consolidation A pause in trading activity in which price moves sideways, setting the stage for the next move. Traders evaluate their positions during periods of consolidation.

Contango A futures market where the more distant delivery months for a commodity trade are at a premium to the near-term delivery months.

Contingency Order An order which becomes effective only upon the fulfillment of some condition in the marketplace.

Contract A term of reference describing a unit of trading for a commodity.

Contract Grades Standards or grades of commodities listed in the rules of the exchanges which must be met when delivering cash commodities against futures contracts. Grades are often accompanied by a schedule of discounts and premiums allowable for delivery of commodities of lesser or greater quality than the contract grade.

Contract Market A board of trade designated by the Commodity Futures Trading Commission to trade futures or option contracts on a particular commodity. Commonly used to mean any exchange on which futures are traded. *See also* Board of Trade and Exchange.

Contract Month The month in which delivery is to be made in accordance with a futures or options contract.

Controlled Account *See* Discretionary Account.

Corner To secure control of a commodity so that its price can be manipulated.

Correction A price reaction against the prevailing trend of the market. Common corrections often amount to 33%, 50%, or 66% of the most recent trend movement. Sometimes referred to as a retracement.

Cost of Recovery Administrative costs or expenses incurred in obtaining money due the complainant. Included are such costs as administrative fees, hearing room fees, charge for clerical services, travel expenses to attend the hearing, attorney's fees, filing costs, etc.

Cover To offset a previous futures transaction with an equal and opposite transaction. Short covering is a purchase of futures contracts to cover an earlier sale of an equal number of the same delivery month; liquidation is the sale of futures contracts to offset the obligation to take delivery on an equal number of futures contracts of the same delivery month purchased earlier.

Covered Option An option that is written against an opposite position in the underlying stock, futures contract, or commodity at the time of execution or placement of the order.

Covered Writer The seller of a covered option, put, or call.

Credit Money received from the sale of options.

Current Delivery (Month) The futures or options contract which will come to maturity and become deliverable during the current month; also called "spot month."

Customer Account An account established by the clearing member solely for the purpose of clearing exchange transactions by the clearing member on behalf of its customers other than those transactions of a floor trader.

Customer Segregated Funds *See* Segregated Account.

Day Order An order that, if not executed, expires automatically at the end of the trading session on the day it was entered.

Day Traders Traders who take positions and then liquidate them prior to the close of the trading day.

Dealer Option A put or call on a physical commodity, not originating on or subject to the rules of an exchange, written by a firm which deals in the underlying cash commodity.

Debit Money paid for the purchase of options.

Debit Balance Accounting condition where the trading losses in a customer's account exceed the amount of equity in the customer's account.

Deck All of the unexecuted orders in a floor broker's possession.

Deep-out-of-the-Money Options Definitions vary by exchange. These are options with strike prices that are not close to the strike price nearest the current price of the underlying entity. A typical definition would be two strike prices, plus the number of calendar months remaining until the option expires, away from the strike price closest to the current value of the underlying stock issue or futures contract.

Default 1) In the futures market, the failure to perform on a futures contract as required by exchange rules, such as a failure to meet a margin call or to make or take delivery. 2) In reference to the federal farm loan program, the decision on the part of a producer of commodities not to repay the government loan, but instead to surrender his or her crops. This usually floods the market driving prices lower.

Deferred Delivery The distant delivery months in which futures trading is taking place, as distinguished from the nearby futures delivery month.

Delivery The tender and receipt of an actual commodity or warehouse receipt or other negotiable instrument covering such commodity, in settlement of a futures contract.

Deliverable Grades *See* Contract Grades.

Delivery Month A calendar month during which a futures contract matures and becomes deliverable. Options are also assigned to delivery months.

Delivery Notice Notice from the clearinghouse of a seller's intention to deliver the physical commodity against a short futures position; precedes and is distinct from the warehouse receipt or shipping certificate, which is the instrument of transfer of ownership.

Delivery Points Those locations designated by commodity exchanges at which stocks of a commodity represented by a futures contract may be delivered in fulfillment of the contract.

Delivery Price The official settlement price of the trading session during which the buyer of futures contracts receives through the clearinghouse a notice of the seller's intention to deliver, and the price at which the buyer must pay for the commodities represented by the futures contract.

Delta The sensitivity of an option's theoretical value to a change in the price of the underlying entity.

Delta Neutral Spread A spread where the total delta position on the long side and the total delta position on the short side add up to approximately zero.

Diagonal Spread A 2-sided spread consisting of options at different exercise prices and with different expiration dates. All options must be of the same type and have the same underlying entity.

Discount 1) A downward adjustment in price allowed for delivery of a quantity of a commodity of lesser than deliverable grade against a futures contract. 2) Sometimes used to refer to the price difference between futures or options of different delivery months, as in the phrase "July at a discount to May," indicating that the price of the July is lower than that of the May.

Discovery The process which allows one party to obtain information and documents relating to the dispute from the other party(ies) in the dispute.

Discretionary Account An arrangement by which the holder of the account gives written power of attorney to another, often a broker, to make buying and selling decisions without notification to the holder; often referred to as a managed account or controlled account.

Elasticity A characteristic of commodities which describes the interaction of the supply, demand, and price of a commodity. A commodity is said to be elastic in demand when a price change creates an increase or decrease in *consumption*. The supply of a commodity is said to be elastic when a change in price creates change in the *production* of the commodity. Inelasticity of supply or demand exists when either supply or demand is relatively unresponsive to changes in price.

Equity The dollar value of an account.

European Option An option which may only be exercised on the expiration date.

Exchange An association of persons engaged in the business of buying and selling commodity futures, stocks, and options. *See also* Board of Trade and Contract Market.

Exercise Exercising an option means the holder elects to accept the underlying stock or futures contract at the option's strike price.

Exercise Price The price at which the buyer of a call (put) option may choose to exercise his right to purchase (sell) the underlying stock or futures contract. Also called strike price.

Expiration Date Generally the last date on which an option may be exercised.

Extrinsic Value The price of an option less its intrinsic value. The entire premium of an out-of-the-money option consists of extrinsic value. Also referred to as time value.

F.O.B. Free on board; indicates that all delivery, inspection, and elevation or loading costs involved in putting commodities on board a carrier have been paid.

Fair Value Another name for theoretical value.

Feed Ratios The variable relationships of the cost of feeding animals to market weight sales prices, expressed in ratios, such as the hog/corn ratio. These serve as indicators of the profit return or lack of it in feeding animals to market weight.

Fence A long (short) underlying position, together with a long (short) out-of-the-money put and a short (long) out-of-the-money call. All options must expire at the same time. When the fence includes a long (short) underlying position, it is sometimes known as a risk conversion (reversal).

Fibonacci Number or Sequence of Numbers The sequence of numbers (0,1,1,2,3,5,8,13,21,34,55,89,144,233...), discovered by the Italian mathematician Leonardo de Pise in the 13th century and the mathematical basis of the Elliott Wave Theory, where the first two terms of the sequence are 0 and 1 and each successive number is the sum of the previous two numbers.

Fiduciary Duty Responsibility imposed by operation of law (from congressional policies underlying the Commodity Exchange Act or the Security Act) which requires that the broker act with special care in the handling of a customer's account.

Fill Or Kill (FOK) An order which must be filled immediately, and in its entirety. Failing this, the order will be canceled.

First Notice Day First day on which notices of intention to deliver cash commodities against futures contracts can be presented by sellers and received by buyers through the exchange clearinghouse.

Floor Broker An individual who executes orders on the trading floor of an exchange for any other person.

Floor Trader Members of an exchange who are personally present, on the trading floors of exchanges, to make trades for themselves and their customers. Sometimes called scalpers or locals.

Forwarding Contracting A cash transaction common in many industries, including commodities, in which the buyer and seller agree upon delivery of a specified quality and quantity of goods at a specified future date. Specific price may be agreed upon in advance or there may be agreements that the price will be determined at the time of delivery on the basis of either the prevailing local cash price or a futures price.

Free Supply Stocks of a commodity which are available from commercial sale, as distinguished from government-owned or controlled stocks.

Free Trade An option spread initiated by purchasing a close to in-the-money put or call and later completed by selling a further out-of-the-money put or call of the same expiration period at the same premium. When completed, it requires no margin or equity.

Front Spread Another name for a ratio vertical spread.

Fully Disclosed An account carried by the Futures Commission Merchant in the name of the individual customer; opposite of an omnibus account.

Fundamental Analysis An approach to analysis of price trends which examine the underlying factors which will affect the supply and demand equation and thus the price of a stock or futures contract. (*See also* Technical Analysis.)

Futures Commission Merchant (FCM) An individual or organization which solicits or accepts orders to buy or sell futures contracts or commodity options and accepts money or other assets from customers in connection with such orders. Must be registered with the Commodity Futures Trading Commission or the National Futures Association.

Futures Contract A standardized binding agreement to buy or sell a specified quantity or grade of a commodity at a later date, i.e., during a specified month. Futures contracts are freely transferable and can be traded only by public auction on designated exchanges.

Futures Industry Association (FIA) The national trade association for the futures industry.

Futures Type Settlement Accounts are settled daily, mark-to-the-market. Excess cash can be withdrawn by owner.

Gamma The sensitivity of an option's delta to a change in the price of the underlying entity.

Gap A trading day during which the daily price range is completely above or below the previous day's range causing a gap between them to be formed. Some traders then look for a retracement to "fill the gap."

Good Til Canceled (GTC) An order to be held by a broker until it can be filled or canceled.

Grantor A person who sells an option and assumes the obligation but not the right, to sell (in the case of a call) or buy (in the case of a put) the underlying stock,. futures contract or commodity at the exercise price. Also referred to as Writer.

Gross Processing Margin (GPM) Refers to the difference between the cost of soybeans and the combined sales income of the soybean oil and meal which results from processing soybeans.

Guided Account An account that is part of a program directed by a Commodity Trading Advisor (CTA) or Futures Commission Merchant (FCM). The CTA or FCM plans the trading strategies. The customer is advised to enter and/or liquidate specific trading positions. However, approval to enter the order must be given by the customer. These programs usually require a minimum initial investment and may include a trading strategy that will utilize only a part of the investment at any given time.

Hedging The sale of futures contracts or options in anticipation of future sales of cash commodities as a protection against possible price declines, or the purchase of futures contracts or options in anticipation of future purchases of cash commoditiy or stock as a protection against increasing costs. *See also* Buying Hedge, Selling Hedge.

Holder Reference Buyer

Horizontal Spread Another name for a time spread.

Inelasticity A characteristic that describes the interdependence of the supply, demand and price of an entity. A commodity is inelastic when a price change does. not create an increase or decrease in consumption; inelasticity exists when supply and demand are relatively unresponsive to changes in price. *See also* Elasticity.

Intermarket Spread A spread consisting of opposing positions in instruments with two different underlying markets.

Initial Margin Customers' funds required at the time a futures position is established, or an option is sold, to assure performance of the customer's obligations. Margin in commodities is not a down payment, as it is in securities. *See also* Margin.

In-the-Money An option having intrinsic value. A call is in-the-money if its strike price is below the current price of the underlying stock or futures contract. A put is in-the-money if its strike price is above the current price of the underlying stock or futures contract.

Intrinsic Value The absolute value of the in-the-money amount; that is, the amount that would be realized if an in-the-money option were exercised.

Introducing Broker (IB) A firm or individual that solicits and accepts commodity futures orders from customers but does not accept money, securities, or property from the customer. An IB must be registered with the National Futures Association and must carry all of its accounts through an FCM on a fully disclosed basis.

Inverted Market Market in which the nearer months are selling at premiums over the more distant months; characteristically, a market in which supplies are currently in shortage.

Invisible Supply Uncounted stocks of a commodity in the hands of wholesalers, manufacturers, and producers which cannot be identified accurately; stocks outside commercial channels but theoretically available to the market.

Kappa Another name for vega.

Last Trading Day Day on which trading ceases for the maturing (current) delivery month.

Leg One side of a spread position.

Leverage Essentially allows an investor to establish a position in the marketplace by depositing funds that are less than the value of the contract

Leverage Contract A standardized agreement calling for the delivery of a commodity with payments against the total cost spread out over a period of time. Principal characteristics include: Standard units and quality of a commodity and of terms and conditions of the contract; payment and maintenance of margin; close out by offset or delivery (after payment in full); and no right to or interest in a specific lot of the commodity. Leverage contracts are not traded on exchanges.

Leverage Transaction Merchant (LTM) The firm or individual through whom leverage contracts are entered. LTMs must be registered with the Commodity Futures Trading Commission.

Life of Contract Period between the beginning of trading and the expiration of trading.

Limit See position limit, price limit, variable limit, and reporting limit.

Limit Move A price that has advanced or declined the limit permitted during one trading session as fixed by the rules of a contract market.

Limit Order An order in which the customer sets a limit on either price or time of execution, as contrasted with a market order, which implies that the order should be filled at the most favorable price as soon as possible.

Liquidation Offsetting positions by acquiring exactly opposite positions.

Liquidity (or liquid market) A broadly traded market where buying and selling can be accomplished with small price changes and bid and offer price spreads are narrow.

Liquid Market A market where selling and buying can be accomplished easily due to the presence of many interested buyers and sellers.

Loan Program Primary means of government agricultural price support operations, in which the government lends money to farmers at announced rates, with crops used as collateral. Default on these loans is the primary method by which the government acquires stocks of agricultural commodities.

Long One who has bought a cash commodity or stock or a commodity futures contract or option, in contrast to a short, who has sold a cash entity, stock, futures or option.

Long Hedge Buying futures or option contracts to protect against possible increased prices of stocks or commodities. *See also* Hedging.

Maintenance Margin The amount of money that must be maintained on deposit while a futures position is open. If the equity in a customer's account drops under the maintenance margin level, the broker must issue a call for money that will restore the customer's equity in the account to required initial levels. *See also* Margin.

Margin In the futures industry, it is an amount of money deposited by both buyers and sellers of futures contracts to ensure performance against the contract. It is not a down payment.

Margin Call A call from a brokerage firm to a customer to bring margin deposits back up to minimum levels required by exchange regulations; similarly, a request by the clearing house to a clearing member firm to make additional deposits to bring clearing margins back to minimum levels required by clearinghouse rules.

Market Order An order to buy or sell a stock, futures, or options contract which is to be filled at the best possible price and as soon as possible. In contrast to a limit order, which may specify requirements for price or time of execution. *See also* Limit Order.

Mark-to-the-Market Futures and options contracts in an account are extended daily using the settlement price and the profit or loss is calculated.

Maturity Period within which a futures contract can be settled by delivery of the actual commodity; the period between the first notice day and the last trading day of a commodity futures contract.

Maximum Price Fluctuation *See* Limit Move.

Minimum Price Fluctuation *See* Point.

Misrepresentation An untrue or misleading statement concerning a material fact relied upon by a customer when making his/her decision about an investment.

Momentum Indicator A line that is plotted to represent the difference between today's price and the price of a fixed number of days ago. Momentum can be measured as the difference between today's price and the current value of a moving average. Often referred to as momentum oscillators.

Moving Average A mathematical procedure to smooth or eliminate the fluctuations in data. Moving averages emphasize the direction of a trend, confirm trend reversals and smooth out price and volume fluctuations or "noise" that can confuse interpretation of the market.

Naked Writing Writing a call or a put on a stock or futures contract in which the writer has no opposite cash or futures market position. This is also known as uncovered writing.

National Association of Futures Trading Advisors (NAFTA) The national trade association of Commodity Pool Operators (CPOs), Commodity Trading Advisors (CTAs) and related industry participants.

National Futures Association (NFA) The industry-wide self-regulatory organization of the futures industry.

National Securities Dealers Association The industry-wide self-regulatory organization of the securities industries.

Nearby Delivery (Month) The futures contract closest to maturity.

Nearbys The nearest delivery months of a futures and options contracts.

Net Asset Value The value of each unit of a trading pool. Basically, a calculation of assets minus liabilities plus or minus the value of open positions (marked-to-the-market) divided by the number of units.

Net Performance An increase or decrease in net asset value exclusive of additions, withdrawals and redemptions.

Net Position The difference between the open long (buy) contracts and the open short (sell) contracts held by any one person in any one futures contract month or in all months combined.

Neutral Spread Another name for a delta neutral spread. Spreads may also be lot neutral, where the total number of long contracts and the total number of short contracts of the same type are approximately equal.

Nominal Price Declared price for a futures or options contract, sometimes used in place of a closing price when no recent trading has taken place in that particular delivery month; usually an average of the bid and asked prices.

Nondisclosure Failure to disclose a material fact needed by the customer to make a decision regarding an investment.

Normalizing An adjustment to data, such as a price series, to put it within normal or more standard range. A technique used to develop a trading system.

Not Held An order submitted to a broker, and over which the broker has discretion as to the prices and time at which the order will be executed, *if at all*.

Notice Day *See* First Notice day.

Notice of Delivery *See* Delivery Notice.

Offer An indication of willingness to sell at a given price; opposite of bid.

Offset The liquidation of a position in the stock or futures markets by taking an equal, but opposite, position. All specifications must be the same.

Omnibus Account An account carried by one futures commission merchant with another in which the transactions of two or more persons are combined, rather than designated separately, and the identity of the individual accounts is not disclosed.

Open The period at the beginning of the trading session officially designated by the exchange during which all transactions are considered made "at the open."

Open Interest The total number of futures contracts of a given commodity which have not yet been offset by opposite futures transactions nor fulfilled by delivery of the actual commodity; the total number of open transactions, with each transaction having a buyer and a seller.

Open Outcry Method of public auction for making bids and offers in the trading pits or rings of exchanges.

Open Trade Equity The unrealized gain or loss on open positions.

Opening Range Range of closely related prices at which transactions took place at the opening of a market session; buying and selling orders at the opening might be filled at any point within such a range.

Opening Transaction A purchase or sale which establishes a new position.

Option Class All option contracts of the same type, covering the same underlying futures contract, commodity, or security.

Option Contract A unilateral contract which gives the buyer the right, but not the obligation, to buy or sell a specified quantity of stocks or futures contracts at a specific price within a specified period of time, regardless of the current market price. The seller of the option has. the obligation to sell the stock or futures contract or buy it from the option buyer at the exercise price, if the option is exercised. *See also* Call (Option) and Put (Option).

Option Premium The money, securities, or property the buyer pays to the writer (grantor) for granting an option contract.

Option Seller *See* Grantor.

Order Execution Handling of a customer order by a broker—includes receiving the order verbally or in writing from the customer, transmitting it to the trading floor of the exchange where the transaction takes place, and returning confirmation (fill price) of the completed order to the customer.

Orders *See* Market Order, Stop Order.

Original Margin Term applied to the initial deposit of margin money required of clearing member firms by clearinghouse rules; parallels the initial margin deposit required of customers.

Out-of-the-Money A call option with a strike price higher or a put option with a strike price lower than the current market value of the underlying asset.

Out Trade A trade made on an exchange which cannot be processed due to conflicting terms reported by the two parties involved in the trade.

Overbought A technical opinion that the market price has risen too steeply and too fast in relation to underlying technical or fundamental factors.

Oversold A technical opinion that the market price has declined too steeply and too fast in relation to underlying technical or fundamental factors.

P & S Statement *See* Purchase and Sale Statement.

Par A particular price, 100 percent of principal value.

Parity A theoretically equal relationship between farm product prices and all other prices. In farm program legislation, parity is defined in such a manner that the purchasing power of a unit of an agricultural commodity is maintained at its level during an earlier historical base period.

Pit A specially constructed arena on the trading floor of some exchanges where trading in stocks, futures or options contracts are conducted by open outcry. On some exchanges, the term "ring" designates the trading area.

Point The minimum fluctuation in futures prices or options premiums.

Point Balance A statement prepared by Futures Commission Merchants to show profit or loss on all open contracts by computing them to an official closing or settlement price.

Pool Investments of more than one individual grouped together. *See* Commodity Pool.

Position A market commitment.

Position Limit The maximum number of futures contracts in certain regulated commodities that one can hold, according to the provisions of the CFTC. Reference Reporting Limits.

Position Trader A trader who either buys or sells contracts and holds them for an extended period of time, as distinguished from the day trader, who will normally initiate and liquidate a position within a single trading session.

Premium 1) The additional payment allowed by exchange regulations for delivery or higher-than-required standards or grades of a commodity against a futures contract. 2) In speaking of price relationships between different delivery months of a given commodity, one is said to be trading at a premium over another when its price is greater than that of the other. 3) Also can mean the amount paid a grantor or writer of an option by the buyer.

Price Limit Maximum price advance or decline from the previous day settlement price permitted for a futures or option cos contract in one trading session by the rules of the exchange.

Primary Markets The principal market for the purchase and sale of a cash commodity.

Principal Refers to a person that is a principal of a particular brokerage company or entity; 1) Any person including, but not limited to, a sole proprietor, general partner, officer or director, or person occupying a similar status or performing similar functions, having the power, directly or indirectly, through agreement or otherwise, to exercise a controlling influence over the activities of the entity; 2) Any holder or any beneficial owner of 10 percent or more of the outstanding shares of any class of stock of the entity; 3) Any person who has contributed 10 percent or more of the capital of the entity.

Private Wires Wires leased by various firms and news agencies for the transmission of information to branch offices and subscriber clients.

Proceeding Clerk The member of the commission's staff in the Office of Proceedings who maintains the Commission's reparations docket, assigns reparation cases to an appropriate CFTC official, and acts as custodian of the records of proceedings.

Producer A person or entity that produces (grows, mines, etc.) a commodity.

Public Elevators Grain storage facilities, licensed and regulated by state and federal agencies, in which space is rented out to whomever is willing to pay for it; some are also approved by the commodity exchanges for delivery of commodities against futures contracts.

Purchase Price The total actual cost paid by a person for entering into a commodity option transaction, including premium, commission or any other direct or indirect charges.

Purchase and Sale Statement (P&S) A statement sent by a. commission house to a customer when a futures or options position has been liquidated or offset. The statement shows the number of contracts bought or sold, the gross profit or loss, the commission charges, and the net profit or loss on the transaction. Sometimes combined with a confirmation statement.

Put (option) An option that gives the option buyer the right but not the obligation to sell the underlying asset at a particular price on or before a particular date.

Pyramiding The use of profits on existing positions as margins to increase the size of the overall position, normally in successively smaller increments; such as the use of profits on the purchase of five futures contracts as margin to purchase an additional four contracts, whose profits will in turn be used to margin an additional three contracts.

Quotation The actual price or the bid or ask price of either cash commodities or futures, stocks or options contract at a particular time. Often called quote.

Rally An upward movement of prices. *See also* Recovery.

Rally Top The point where a rally stalls. A bull move will usually make several rally tops over its life.

Range The difference between the high and low price of a commodity during a given period, usually a single trading session.

Ratio Spread any spread where the number of long market contracts and the number of short market contracts are unequal.

Ratio Vertical Spread A spread where more contracts are sold than are purchased, with all contracts having the same underlying entity and expiration date. Ratio vertical spreads are usually delta neutral.

Ratio Writing A strategy used by options writers. It involves writing a covered call option as well as one or more uncovered call options. One of its objectives is to reduce some of the risk of writing uncovered call options, since the covered call does provide some degree of protection.

Reaction A short-term counter trend movement of prices.

Recovery An upward movement of prices following a decline.

Registered Commodity Representative (RCR) *See* Broker or Associated Person (AP).

Registered Representative A stock broker. Stock brokers are registered with the NASD and by the state(s) in which they conduct business.

Regulations (CFTC) The regulations adopted and enforced by the federal overseer of futures markets, the Commodity Futures Trading Commission, in order to administer the Commodity Exchange Act.

Reparations Compensation payable to a wronged party in a futures or options transaction. The term is used in conjunction with the Commodity Futures Trading Commission's customer claims procedure to recover civil damages.

Reparations Award The amount of monetary damages a respondent may be ordered to pay to a complainant.

Reporting Limit Sizes of positions set by the exchange and/or by the CFTC at or above which commodity traders must make daily reports to the exchange and/or the CFTC as to the size of the position by commodity, by delivery month, and according to the purpose of trading, i.e., speculative or hedging.

Resistance The price level where a trend stalls. Opposite of a support level. Prices must build momentum to move through resistance.

Respondents The individuals or firms against which the complaint is filed and a reparations award is sought.

Retender The right of holders of futures contracts who have been tendered a delivery notice through the clearinghouse to offer the notice for sale on the open market, liquidating their obligation to take delivery under the contract; applicable only to certain commodities and only within a specified period of time.

Retracement A price movement in the opposite direction of the prevailing trend. *See* Correction.

Reverse Conversion (Reversal) A short underlying position, together with a long call and short put, where both options have the same exercise price and expiration date. A reverse conversion is a short underlying position offset by a long synthetic underlying position.

Rho The sensitivity of an option's theoretical value to a change in interest rates.

Ring A circular area on the trading floor of an exchange where traders and brokers stand while executing futures or options trades. Some exchanges use pits rather than rings.

Round Lot A quantity of a commodity equal in size to the corresponding futures contract for the commodity, as distinguished from a job lot, which may be larger or smaller than the contract. In stocks, a 100 share trade.

Round Turn The combination of an initiating purchase or sale of a futures contract and offsetting sale or purchase of an equal number of futures contracts to the same delivery month. Commission fees for commodity transactions cover the round turn.

Rules (NFA or NASD) The standards and requirements to which participants who are required to be Members of National Futures Association or National Association of Security Dealers must subscribe and conform.

Sample Grade In commodities, usually the lowest quality acceptable for delivery in satisfaction of futures contracts. *See* Contract Grades.

Scalper A speculator on the trading floor of an exchange who buys and sells rapidly, with small profits or losses, holding positions for only a short time during a trading session. Typically, a scalper will stand ready to buy at a fraction below the last transaction price and to sell at a fraction above, thus creating market liquidity.

Security Deposit *See* Margin.

Segregated Account A special account used to hold and separate customer's assets from those of the broker or firm.

Selling Hedge Selling futures or option contracts to protect against possible decreased prices of commodities or stocks which will be sold in the future. *See* Hedging and/or Short Hedge.

Serial Expiration Options on the same futures contract or stock which expire in more than one month.

Series All options of the same class having the same exercise price and expiration date.

Settlement Price The closing price, or a price within the range of closing prices, which is used as the official price in determining net gains or losses at the close of each trading session.

Short One who is expecting prices to decline. For example, a trader who has sold a cash commodity or a commodity futures contract or bought a put, in contrast to a long, who has bought a cash commodity or futures contract or a call.

Short Hedge Selling futures or options to protect against possible decreasing prices of commodities or stocks. *See also* Hedging.

Speculator One who attempts to anticipate price changes and make profits through the sale and/or purchase of stocks, commodity futures or option contracts.

Spot Market for the immediate delivery of the product and immediate payment. May also refer to the nearest delivery month of a futures or options contract.

Spot Commodity *See* Cash Commodity.

Spread (or Straddle) The purchase of one futures or option delivery month against the sale of another. For example, the purchase of one delivery month of one option against the sale of the same delivery month of a different option. *See also* Arbitrage.

Stop Loss A risk management technique used to close out a losing position at a given point. *See* Stop Order.

Stop Order An order that becomes a market order when a particular price level is reached. A sell stop is placed below the market, a buy stop is placed above the market. Sometimes referred to as a stop loss order.

Straddle A trading strategy. A straddle involves writing a put as well as a call on the same stock or futures. Both options also carry the same strike price and the same expiration date.

Stock Type Settlement A settlement procedure in which the purchase of a contract requires immediate and full payment by the buyer to the seller. In stock type settlement the actual cash profit or loss from a trade is not realized. until the position is liquidated.

Strike Price *See* Exercise Price.

Support A price level at which a declining market has stopped falling. Opposite of a resistance price range. Once this level is reached, the market usually trades sideways for a period of time.

Switch Liquidation of a position in one delivery month of a commodity and simultaneous initiation of a similar position in another delivery month of the same commodity. When used by hedgers, this tactic is referred to as "rolling forward" the hedge.

Synthetic Call A long (short) underlying position together with a long (short) put.

Synthetic Put A short (long) underlying position together with a long (short) call.

Synthetic Underlying A long (short) call together with a short (long) put where both options have the same underlying exercise price, and expiration date.

Technical Analysis An approach to analysis of stock and futures markets. Technicians normally examine such indicators as price charts patterns, rates of price changes, and changes in volume of trading and open interest.

Tender The act on the part of the seller of futures contracts of giving notice to the clearinghouse that he or she intends to deliver the physical commodity in satisfaction of the futures contract. The clearinghouse in turn passes along the notice to oldest buyer of record in that delivery month of the commodity. *See also* Retender.

Theoretical Value An option value generated by a mathematical model given certain prior assumptions about the terms of the option, the characteristics of the underlying entity, and prevailing interest rates. The most commonly used formula is known as the Black-Scholes.

Theta The sensitivity of an option's theoretical value to a change in the amount of time to expiration.

Tick Refers to a change in price up or down. *See also* Point.

Ticker Tape A continuous paper tape transmission of commodity or security prices, volume, and other trading and market information which operates on private or lease wires by the exchanges, available to their member firms and other interested parties on a subscription basis. Nowadays, it has been replaced by more efficient electronic transmission media.

Time Spread The purchase and sale of options with the same exercise price on the same stock or futures contract, but with different expiration dates. Also known as calendar and horizontal spreads.

Time Value Any amount by which an option premium exceeds the option's intrinsic value. Sometimes called extrinsic value or time-premium.

To-Arrive Contract A type of deferred shipment in which the price is based on delivery at the destination point and the seller pays the freight in shipping it to that point.

Traders 1) People who trade for their own account; 2) Employees of dealers or institutions who trade for their employer's account.

Trading Range An established set of price boundaries with a high price and a low price that a market will spend a marked period of time within.

Transferable Notice *See* Retender.

Trendline A line drawn that connects either a series of highs or lows in a trend. The trendline can represent either support, as in an uptrend line, or resistance as in a downtrend line. Consolidations are marked by horizontal trendlines.

Unauthorized Trading Purchase or sale of stocks, commodity futures or options for a customer's account without the customer's permission.

Underlying Futures Contract The specific futures contract that the option conveys the right to buy (in the case of a call) or sell (in the case of a put).

Underlying Security The security underlying an option. It would be purchased or sold were the option exercised.

Variable Limit A price system that allows price movements for larger than normally allowed price movements under certain conditions. In periods of extreme volatility, some exchanges permit trading and price levels to exceed regular daily limits. At such times, margins may be automatically increased.

Variation Margin Call A mid-season call by the clearinghouse on a clearing member requiring the deposit of additional funds to bring clearing margin monies up to minimum levels in relation to changing prices and the clearing member's net position.

Vega The sensitivity of an option's theoretical value to a change in volatility.

Vertical Spread A spread in which one option is bought and one option is sold, where both options are of the same type, have the same underlying entity, and expire at the same time. The options differ only by their exercise prices.

Volatility A measure of a the tendency of an asset's (stock, option, etc.) price to move up and down in price, based on its daily price history over a period of time.

Volume of Trade The number of contracts traded during a specified period of time.

Warehouse Receipt Document guaranteeing the existence and availability of a given quantity and quality of a commodity in storage; commonly used as the instrument of transfer of ownership in both cash and futures transactions.

Wirehouse *See* Futures Commission Merchant (FCM).

Write or Writer *See* Grantor.

Writing The sale of an option in an opening transaction.

Note: This glossary is included to assist the reader. It is not a set of legal definitions, nor a guide to interpreting the Commodity or Security Exchange Acts or any other legal instrument. For all legal assistance, contact your personal attorney.

Appendix 2
Sources of More Information

Books

Babcock, Bruce, Jr., *The Business One Irwin Guide to Trading Systems,* (1989) Business One Irwin, Homewood, IL 60430.

Bernstein, Jake, *Facts on Futures: Insights and Strategies for Winning in the Futures Markets,* (1987) Probus Publishing Company, 1925 North Clybourn Avenue, Chicago, IL 60614.

Bookstaber, Richard M., *Option Pricing and Investment Strategies,* 3rd Edition (1991) Probus Publishing Company, Chicago, IL.

Caplan, David L., *The Options Advantage: Gaining A Trading Edge Over the Markets,* (1991) Probus Publishing Company, Chicago, IL.

Chance, Dom M., *An Introduction to Options and Futures,* (1989) The Dryden Press, Chicago, IL.

Derosa, David F., *Options on Foreign Exchange,* (1992) Probus Publishing Company, Chicago, IL.

Elliot, R.N., *The Wave Principle,* (1938) Elliott, New York, NY.

The Encyclopedia of Historical Charts, Commodity Perspective, Chicago, IL.

Futures and Options Fact Book, (1992) Futures Industry Institute, Washington, D.C.

Gann, William D., *How to Make Profits in Commodities,* (1951) Lambert-Gann, Pomeroy, WA.

Gann, William D., *Truth of the Stock Tape,* (1932) Financial Guardian, New York, NY.

Labuszewski, John W. and Sinquefield, Jeanne Cairns, *Inside The Commodity Option Markets,* (1985) John Wiley & Sons, Inc., New York, NY.

Mehrabian, Albert, Ph.D., *Your Inner Path to Investment Success: Insights into the Psychology of Investing,* (1991) Probus Publishing Company, Chicago, IL.

Natenberg, Sheldon, *Option Volatility and Pricing Strategies: Advanced Trading Techniques for Professionals,* (1988) Probus Publishing Company, Chicago, IL.

Petzel, Todd E., *Financial Futures and Options: A Guide to Markets, Applications, and Strategies,* (1989) Quorum Books, New York, NY.

Schwager, Jack D., *A Complete Guide to the Futures Markets: Fundamental Analysis, Technical Analysis, Trading, Spreads, and Options,* (1984) John Wiley & Sons Inc., New York, NY.

Schwager, Jack D., *Market Wizards: Interviews with Top Traders,* (1989) Simon & Schuster, New York, NY.

Schwager, Jack D., *The New Market Wizards: Conversations with America's Top Traders,* (1992) Harper Business, New York, NY.

Newsletters & Magazines

Cycles, Foundation for the Study of Cycles, 2600 Michelson Drive, Suite 1570, Irvine, CA 92715

Futures Magazine: Commodities, Options & Derivatives, 219 Parkade, Cedar Falls, IA 50613

Futures and Options Factors Newsletter, Wasendorf & Son Company, 802 Main Street, Cedar Falls, IA 50613

Opportunities in Options Newsletter, P. O. Box 2126, Malibu, CA 90265

Pocket Charts: Commodity Price Charting Service, Wasendorf & Son Company, P. O. Box 849, Cedar Falls, IA 50613

Technical Analysis of Stocks and Commodities, 9131 California Avenue SW, Seattle, WA 98136

Agencies

Alliance Against Fraud Telemarketing
c/o National Consumers League
815 15th St. NW, Suite 516
Washington, DC 20005

American Association of Individual Investors
612 North Michigan Avenue
Chicago, IL 60611
312/280-0170

Commodity Futures Trading Commission
2033 K Street NW
Washington, DC 20581
202/254-6387

Council of Better Business Bureaus
1515 Wilson Boulevard
Arlington, VA 22209
703/276-0100

Federal Bureau of Investigation
Justice Department
9th St. & Pennsylvania Ave., NW
Washington, DC 20580
202/326-3650

Federal Trade Commission
6th St. & Pennsylvania Ave., NW
Washington, DC 20580
202/326-3650

National Association of Securities Dealers
1735 K Street, NW
Washington, DC 20006
202/728-8044

National Consumers League
815 15th St., NW
Suite 516
Washington, DC 20006
202/639-8140

National Futures Association
200 W. Madison, Suite 1600
Chicago, IL 60606
Toll-free: 800/621-3570
In IL: 800/621-3570

National Association of Securities Dealers, Inc.
1735 K Street NW
Washington, DC 20006-1506
202/728-8000

North American Securities Administration Association
2930 SW Wanamaker Drive
Suite 5
Topeka, KS 66614
913/273-2600

The Options Industry Council
440 S. LaSalle Street
Suite 2400
Chicago, IL 60605

Securities and Exchange Commission
450 Fifth St., NW
Washington, DC 20006
202/728-8233

United States Postal Service
Chief Postal Inspector
Room 3021
Washington, DC 20260-2100
202/268-4267

Trading Schools (Also contact exchanges)

Commodity Educational Institute
219 Parkade
Cedar Falls, IA 50613
319/277-6341

International Trading Institute
440 S. LaSalle Street
Suite 3112
Chicago, IL 60605
312/663-8999

Appendix 3

Long-Term Volatility Charts for Selected Stocks and Commodities

Charts courtesy of OptionVue Systems International, Inc.,
175 E. Hawthorn Parkway, Suite 180, Vernon Hills, IL 60061
(708)816-6610.

U.S. Treas Bonds (CBT) Volatilities

Soybeans (CBT) Volatilities

Gold (CEC) Volatilities

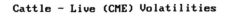

Cattle - Live (CME) Volatilities

Orange Juice (CTN) Volatilities

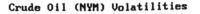

OPTIONVUE IV

Crude Oil (NYM) Volatilities

OPTIONVUE IV

Telefonos De Mexico Volatilities

20-Day Statistical   — — — Implied

OPTIONVUE IV

Hewlett-Packard Volatilities

20-Day Statistical   — — — Implied

OPTIONVUE IV

Japan Index Volatilities

OPTIONVUE IV

S&P 100 Index Volatilities

OPTIONVUE IV

Orange Juice (CTN) Volatilities

Japanese Yen (Phil) Volatilities

U.S. Treas Bonds (CBT) Volatilities

OPTIONVUE IV

Crude Oil (NYM) Volatilities

OPTIONVUE IV

Gold (CEC) Volatilities

20-Day Statistical   – – – Implied

OPTIONVUE III

NYSE (cash) Volatilities

20-Day Statistical   – – – Implied

OPTIONVUE IV

Eurodollar (IMM) Volatilities

OPTIONVUE IV

Borland Volatilities

OPTIONVUE IV

Merck & Co. Volatilities

Costco Wholesale Volatilities

Appendix 4
Exchanges and Options Offered

All exchanges have public information, public relations, marketing, or sales departments, which prepare and distribute a wide variety of instructional material. Most of them conduct seminars to teach investors how to trade the options listed on their exchange. They are an excellent source to obtain additional information.

Stock Options (Since there are so many options offered, you need to contact one of the exchanges below for the 76-page *Directory of Exchange Listed Options*.)

AMERICAN STOCK EXCHANGE
Derivative Securities
86 Trinity Place
New York, NY 10006 USA
1-800-THE-AMEX

OR 2, London Wall Buildings
London Wall
London EC2M 5SY ENGLAND
44-71-628-5982

CHICAGO BOARD OPTIONS EXCHANGE
LaSalle at Van Buren
Chicago, IL 60605 USA
1-800-OPTIONS
(312)786-5600

NEW YORK STOCK EXCHANGE
Options and Index Products
11 Wall Street
New York, NY 10005 USA
1-800-692-6973
(212)656-8533

THE OPTIONS CLEARING CORPORATION
440 South LaSalle Street
Suite 2400
Chicago, IL 60605 USA
1-800-537-4258
(312)322-6 0

PACIFIC STOCK EXCHANGE
Options Marketing
115 Sansome Street, 7th Floor
San Francisco, CA 94104 USA
1-800-TALK-PSE
(415)393-4028

PHILADELPHIA STOCK EXCHANGE
Philadelphia Board of Trade
(Foreign Currency Options)
1900 Market Street
Philadelphia, PA 19103 USA
1-800-THE-PHLX
(215)496-5404

OR PHLX European Office
39 King Street
London EC2V 8DQ ENGLAND
44-71-606-2348

Options-on-Futures Exchanges

CHICAGO BOARD OF TRADE
141 West Jackson Boulevard
Chicago, IL 60604
(312)435-3500

CHICAGO MERCANTILE EXCHANGE
Index & Option Market
International Monetary Market
30 South Wacker Drive
Chicago, IL 60606
(312)930-8200

COFFEE, SUGAR & COCOA EXCHANGE
Four World Trade Center
New York, NY 10048
(212)938-2800

COMMODITY EXCHANGE INC.
Four World Trade Center
New York, NY 10048
(212)938-2900

KANSAS CITY BOARD OF TRADE
4800 Main Street
Kansas City, MO 64112
(816)753-7500

MidAmerica COMMODITY EXCHANGE
141 West Jackson boulevard
Chicago, IL 60604
(312)341-3000

MINNEAPOLIS GRAIN EXCHANGE
150 Grain Exchange Building
Minneapolis, MN 55415
(612)338-6212

NEW YORK COTTON EXCHANGE
Four World Trade Center
New York, NY 10048
(212)938-2650

NEW YORK FUTURES EXCHANGE
30 Broad Street
New York, NY 10004
(212)623-4949

NEW YORK MERCANTILE EXCHANGE
Four World Trade Center
New York, NY 10048
(212)938-2222

Specifications for Exchange Traded Option-on-Futures for U.S. Markets

COMMODITY	EXCH.	TRADING HRS Central Time	DELIVERY MONTHS	CONTRACT SIZE	TICK SIZE	DAILY LIMITS	STRIKE PRICE INCREMENTS
Australian Dollar	IMM	7:20-2:00	F,H,J,M,N,U,V,Z	100,000 AD	1pt = $10.00	150 pts	Every 50 pts (i.e. 7350, 7400, 7450)
British Pound	IMM	7:20-2:00	H,M,U,Z	62,500 BP	02¢/£ = $12.50	400 pts	Every 02¢/£ (i.e. 170, 172, 174)
Canadian Dollar	IMM	7:20-2:00	H,M,U,Z	100,000 CD	1pt = $10.00	100 pts	Every 1/2¢ (i.e. 7300, 7350)
Cattle,Fdr	CME	8:45-1:00	F,H,J,K,Q,U,V,X	50,000 lbs	2 ½¢/cwt = $12.50	None	2¢ increments (i.e. .64¢, .66¢, .68¢)
Cattle,Live	CME	8:45-1:00	G,J,M,Q,V,Z	40,000 lbs	2 ½¢/cwt = $10.00	None	2¢ increments (i.e. .64¢, .66¢, .68¢) back months
Cocoa (Metric)	NYCSCE	8:30-1:10	H,K,N,U,Z	10M ton (22,046)	1pt=$10.00	None	$50 increments for prices below $1500 / $100 increments for prices between $1500 & $3600 / $200 increments for prices above $3600
Coffee	NYCSCE	8:15-12:58	H,K,N,U,Z	37,500 lbs	1¢/lb = $375	None	.025 increments for prices below $1.00 / .05 increments for prices between $1.00 and $2.00 / .10 increments for prices above $2.00
Copper,High Grade	COMEX	8:25-1:00	F,H,K,N,U,Z	25,000 lbs	5pt=$12.50	None	1¢/lb increments for prices below 40¢ / 2¢/lb increments for prices between 40¢ and $1.00 / 5¢/lb increments for prices above $1.00
Corn (2)	CBOT	8:30-1:45	H,K,N,U,Z	5,000 bu	1/8¢=$6.25	10¢=$500(4)	Every 10¢ per bushel (i.e. $2.80, $2.90, $3.00)
Corn	MA	8:30-1:45	H,K,N,U,Z	1,000 bu	1/8¢=$1.25	10¢=$100(4)	Every 10¢ per bushel (i.e. $2.80, $2.90, $3.00)
Cotton	NYCTE	9:30-1:40	H,K,N,V,Z	50,000 lbs	1¢/cwt =$5.00	None	1¢ increments for prices 74¢ and below / 2¢ increments for prices 76¢ and above
CRB Index	NYFE	8:45-1:45	H,K,N,U,Z	500xCRB Index	5pts = $25.00	None	Less than $300.00 - $5.00 increments / Above $300.00 - $10.00 increments
Crude Oil	NYME	8:45-2:10	All Months	1,000 barrels	1pt = $10.00	None	100 point intervals
Deutschemark	IMM	7:20-2:00	H,M,U,Z	125,000 DM	1pt = $12.50	150 pts	Every 50 points (i.e. 5500, 5550, 5600)
Eurodollar	IMM	7:20-2:00	H,M,U,Z	$1,000,000	01 index pt = $25.00	None	25 point increments
Gasoline,Unleaded	NYME	8:50-2:10	All Months	42,000 gal	1pt =$4.20	None	200 point intervals
Gold	COMEX	7:20-1:30	G,J,M,Q,V,Z	100 troy oz	10¢/oz =$10.00 (option quote price in $/oz)	None	$10 increments for prices below $500 / $20 increments for prices between $501 and $1000 / $50 increments for prices above $1000
Gold	MA	7:20-1:40	F,H,J,M,N,U,V,Z	33.2 troy oz	10¢/oz =$3.32	None	$10 increments for prices below $400 / $20 increments for prices between $400 and $600 / $30 increments for prices between $600 and $900 / $40 increments for prices above $900
Heating Oil	NYME	8:50-2:10	All Months	42,000 gal	1pt=$4.20	None	200 point intervals
Hogs	CME	8:45-1:00	G,J,M,N,Q,V,Z	40,000 lbs	2.5¢ cwt =$10.00	None	2¢ increments (i.e. .48¢, .50¢, .52¢)
Japanese Yen (1)	IMM	7:20-2:00	H,M,U,Z	12,500,000 JY	1pt = $12.50	150 pts	Every 50 points (i.e. 7400, 7450, 7500)
Lumber	CME	9:00-1:05	F,H,K,N,U,Z	160,000 bd ft	10¢ =$1.60	None	$5.00 increments
M M I Index	CBOT	8:15-3:15	All Months	500xMMI	5pts = $25.00	15 index points	5 index points
Municipal Bonds (2)	CBOT	7:20-2:00	H,M,U,Z	$1000 x BB Index	1/64 = $15.63	96/32 = $3000	1 point intervals (i.e. 8800, 6900, 9000)
Nikkie Index	CME	8:00-3:15	H,M,U,Z	$5.00 x Index	5pts = $25.00	None	Every 500 pts (i.e. 275.00, 280.00, 285.00)
NYSE Index	NYFE	8:30-3:15	H,M,U,Z	500 x Index	5pts = $25.00	None	Every 200 points (i.e. 94, 96, 98)

Oats (2)	CBOT	9:30-1:15	H.K.N.U.Z	5,000 bu	1/8¢=$6.25	10¢=$500	Every 10¢ per bushel
Oats	MA	9:30-1:45	H.K.N.U.Z	1,000 bu	1/8¢ $1.25	10¢=$100	Every 10¢ per bushel (i.e. 200, 230, 240)
Orange Juice	NYCTE	9:15-1:15	F.H.K.N.U.X	15,000 lbs	5pts=$7.50	None	Every 250 pts (i.e. 122.50, 125.00, 127.50)
Platinum	NYME	7:20-1:30	F.J.N.V	50 troy oz	$0.10=$5.00	None	$20.00 per troy oz
Pork Bellies	CME	8:45-1:00	G.H.K.N.Q	40,000 lbs	0.0025¢/lb=$10.00	None	2¢ per pound intervals (i.e. 64¢, 66¢, 68¢)
S&P 500 Index	IOM	8:30-3:15	H.M.U.Z	500x S&P Index	5pts = $25.00	None	Every 500 points (1000 pts in 3rd and 4th nearest month in quarterly cycle.)
Silver	COMEX	7:25-1:25	F.H.K.N.U.Z	5,000 troy oz	0.01¢/oz = $25.00	None	20¢ increments for prices below $8.00 / 50¢ increments for prices between $8.00 and $15.00 / $1.00 increments for prices $15.00 and above
Silver New (2)	CBOT	7:25-1:25	G.J.M.Q.V.Z	1,000 troy oz	0.01¢/oz = $1.00	$1.00=$1000(3)	25¢/oz increments for prices below $8 / 50¢/oz increments for prices from $8 to $20 / $1.00/oz increments for prices above $20
Soybean Meal	CBOT	8:30-1:15	F.H.K.N.Q.U.V.Z	100 tons	5¢/ton = $5.00	$10/1000pts(4)	$5 if less than $200 $10 if more than $200
Soybean Oil (2)	CBOT	8:30-1:15	F.H.K.N.Q.U.V.Z	60,000 lbs	1pt=$6.00	1¢/100pts(4)	Less than 2500 pts 50 pt increments / More than 2500 pts 100 pt increments
Soybeans	CBOT	8:30-1:15	F.H.K.N.Q.U.X	5,000 bu	1/8¢=$6.25	30¢=$1500(4)	Every 25¢ per bushel (i.e. $7, $7.25, $7.50)
Soybeans	MA	8:30-1:15	F.H.K.N.Q.U.X	1,000 bu	1/8¢=$1.25	30¢=$300	Every 25¢ per bushel (i.e. $7, $7.25, $7.50)
Sugar	NYCSCE	9:00-12:50	H.K.N.U.V	112,000 lbs	0.01¢ = $11.20	None	1/2¢ increments for prices below 10¢ / 1¢ increments for prices between 11¢ and 40¢ / 2¢ increments for prices 42¢ and over
Swiss Franc (1)	IMM	7:20-2:00	H.M.U.Z	125,000 SF	0.01¢/SF = $12.50	150 pts	Every 50 points (i.e. 7750, 7800, 7850)
T-Bills 90-Days (1)	CME	7:20-2:00	H.M.U.Z	$1,000,000	1pt = $25.00	None	25 point increments
T-Notes 5yr	CBOT	7:20-2:00	H.M.U.Z	$100,000	1/64¢ = $15.63	96/32 = $3000(4)	1/2 point ($500) (i.e. 93.00, 93.50, 94.00)
Treasury Bonds	MA	7:20-3:15	H.M.U.Z	$50,000	1/64¢ = $7.81	96/32 = $1500	Every 2 full points (i.e. 64, 66, 68)
Treasury Notes	CBOT	7:20am-2:00pm / 6:00pm-9:30 'm	H.M.U.Z	$100,000	1/64¢ = $15.63	96/32 = $3000 (4)	Every 1 full point (i.e. 77, 78, 79)
U.S. Dollar Index	NYCTE	7:20-2:00	H.M.U.Z	500 x index	1pt = $10.00	None	Every 2¢ (i.e. 100, 102, 104)
Wheat	CBOT	8:30-1:15	H.K.N.U.Z	5,000 bu	1/8¢=$6.25	20¢=$1000(4)	Every 10¢ per bushel (i.e. $3.50, $3.60, $3.70)
Wheat	KCBT	8:30-1:15	H.K.N.U.Z	5,000 bu	1/8¢=$6.25	25¢=$1250	Every 10¢ per bushel (i.e. $3.50, $3.60, $3.70)
Wheat	MPLS	8:30-1:45	H.K.N.U.Z	5,000 bu	1/8¢=$6.25	25¢=$1250	Every 10¢ per bushel (i.e. $3.50, $3.60, $3.70)
Wheat	MA	8:30-1:45	H.K.N.U.Z	1,000 bu	1/8¢=$1.25	20¢=$200	Every 10¢ per bushel (i.e. $3.50, $3.60, $3.70)

Exchanges:

CBOT =Chicago Board of Trade
CME =Chicago Mercantile Exchange
COMEX =Commodity Exchange, Inc (NY)
IMM=International Monetary Market, Div of CME
IOM=Index and Options Market, Div of CME
KCBT =Kansas City Board of Trade
MA =Mid America Commodity Exchange
MPLS =Minneapolis Board of Trade
NYCSCE =New York Coffee, Sugar and Cocoa Exchange
NYCTE =New York Cotton Exchange
NYFE =New York Futures Exchange
NYME =New York Mercantile Exchange

Footnotes:

(1) Trades on GLOBEX Electronic Trading Hours, CBOT Options 10:30 pm - 6:00 am, CME - 6:00 pm - 6:00 am (CST).
(2) On last trading day, all CBOT options expire at noon (CST).
(3) No limit 2 days prior to delivery month.
(4) No limit last trading day.

Abbreviations for Months

Month	Current Year	Following Year
JAN	F	D
FEB	G	E
MAR	H	I
APR	J	L
MAY	K	O
JUN	M	P
JUL	N	T
AUG	Q	R
SEP	U	B
OCT	V	C
NOV	X	W
DEC	Z	Y

The information contained in this table is from sources believed to be reliable, but we cannot be held responsible for either its accuracy or completeness   All contract specifications are subject to change by action of the respective commodity exchange   Therefore, the specifications can be changed, sometimes without notice.   You need to be in touch with your broker before entering any trade   Limits are subject to change and to variable limit rules of the repective exchange

Appendix 5
Description of Option Trading Software

Editor's Note: Prices are always subject to change without notice.

Training Programs (Market Simulators)

SOFTSware
Coffee, Sugar & Cocoa Exchange, Inc.
4 World Trade Center
New York, NY 10048
1-800-HEDGE IT
(212) 938-2966
Price: FREE

Here's an excellent tutorial to bring you up to speed on options quickly. In one mode, it suggests the best strategies based on given market conditions. In the next mode, it lets you build the strategy you think will be most profitable. In both situations you see the profit and loss results at expiration for a range of prices. We particularly find the graphs useful in helping new traders visualize the P/L relationships. Includes contract specifications for coffee, sugar and cocoa options.

"The Game"
COMEX
Commodity Exchange, Inc.
Publications Department
Four World Trade Center
New York, NY 10048
1-800-THE-NYFE
(212)938-2900
Price: $69.00

This program simulates the trading of gold and silver options on COMEX. You trade $10,000 of equity as if it were your own ... selecting strategies, deciding on quantity, entering and exiting the markets. Find out if you have what it takes—without risking real money in the markets!

Trading Programs

A I Q Incorporated
P. O. Drawer 7530
Incline Village, NV 89452-9934
1-800-332-2999
Price: $898.00

A I Q (Stock) Option Expert analyzes daily stock prices and volume data for all the stocks in your database and recommends which ones to consider for trading. The system then evaluates the options for each stock you have selected and recommends the best strategy or positions to take. It also recommends when to offset positions. Being an expert system, it calculates more than 30 technical indicators and then evaluates this price analysis against 160 rules to generate buy-sell recommendations. Needless to say, AIQ is a very sophisticated system. Additionally, it can identify leading/lagging groups of stocks, equity, and index option opportunities. The Profit Manager module is designed to protect your principal and profits. The graphics are extensive and impressive.

COMPUTRAC
CompuTrac Software, Inc.
1017 Pleasant Street
New Orleans, LA 70115
800-274-4028
(504)895-1474
$695.00 to $1,895.00

"The first is still the best" is their slogan. This software takes a very large toolbox approach to technical trading. It provides just about all the major studies with excellent documentation. It's for the very serious technician. The list of studies available can be found in Chapter 7.

Harloff Inc.
26106 Tallwood Drive
North Olmsted, OH 44070
(216)734-7271
Price: $199.00

Call/Put Options software utilizes a proprietary formula for option evaluation of American style options. The valuations are valid at any time in the life of the option, including expiration. Computes hedge ratios and break even hedge stock prices. It will also determine optimum times to buy and sell puts and calls. A stock option product. Also available for Apple computers.

Options-80
15 Stow Street
P. O. Box 471
Concord, MA 01742
(508)369-1589
Price: $150.00

Options-80 is for listed stock options. Program analyzes calls, puts, and spreads, does Black-Scholes modeling, and calculates market-implied volatility. It plots annualized return on investment against expiration price of underlying stock, guiding the user to optimum investment. Unique algorithms account for future payments, as well as buying and selling costs and time value of money. Presents tables and charts for choosing transactions to give highest yield for price action user thinks most likely. It is good for investigating "what if" scenarios. Prints out, stores to disk, and can be backed up. Comes with a comprehensive indexed Manual. Also available for Macintosh computers.

International Advanced Modes Inc.
P. O. Box 1019
Oak Brook, IL 60522
(708)369-8461
Price: $124.50

OptionExpert - The Strategist analyzes stocks and stock index option. Utilizes the Black-Scholes model. Contains provisions for taking commissions and dividends into account. Online data retrieval is not required. Calculates deltas and volatilities, which can be adjusted and analyzed. Calculates and ranks strategies, based on risk and potential reward. Program is menu-driven, requiring no memorization of commands.

Optionomics Corporation
2835 East 3300 South
Suite 200
Salt Lake City, UT 84109
(801)466-2111
(800)255-3374
Price: $350.00 - $995.00 per month

Optionomics Systems, includes Portfoliomic and Strategist, analyzes options in real-time alerting traders to the impact of changes in implied volatility, deltas, gammas, vegas, and thetas. It also generates and evaluates strategies and allows operator to ask a wide variety of "what if" questions. Portfoliomics manages, evaluates, and tracks diversified option portfolios. Very strong in risk management.

Montgomery Investment Group
P. O. Box 508
Wayne, PA 19087-0508
(215)688-2508
Prices: $395.00 to $995.00

If you are a spreadsheet analyst, you'll love Montgomery's product line. They are add-ons to Excel and Lotus 1-2-3, not templates. Functions are added to these spreadsheet programs to calculate fair market value using seven of the most commonly used formulas, plus implied and historical volatility, deltas, gammas, thetas, and vegas. Evaluates options on stocks, bonds, foreign exchanges, commodities, futures, indices, derivatives, real estate, scores, and warrants. Additionally, it can link to a variety of price quotation services for updates.

Discount Corporation of New York Futures
Madison Plaza
200 West Madison, 2nd Floor
Chicago, IL 60606
(312)368-2200
Price: $1,495.00

Opposition Position Manager tests strategies, evaluates portfolios under various scenarios by changing futures prices, volatility, and time to expiration. Displays risk/reward potential in tabular form, two and three dimensional graphs on screen or paper. Calculates theoretical prices, deltas, gammas, zetas (vegas), and theta over a range of prices and time intervals. Uses either average volatility of markets or the individual option. Tracks open trade quantity, average trade price, settlement price, implied volatility for each option, unrealized gains (losses), and commissions.

OPA Software
P. O. Box 90658
Los Angeles, CA 90009
(213)545-3716
(800)321-4100
Prices: $195.00 - $750.00

Option Pricing Software is a reasonably priced package that claims the ability (expert system) of not only calculating fair market value of stocks, indexes, and futures option contracts, but to select the best option and strategy. Additionally, OPS analyzes straddles, combinations, and spreads. It generates maximum profits-losses, margin requirements, deltas, and omegas. No limitation is placed on the type of strategy to be studied. It's set up to run repeated "what if" scenarios.

OptionVue Systems International, Inc.
175 E. Hawthorn Parkway, Suite 180
Vernon Hills, IL 60061
(708)816-6610
(800)733-6610
Price: $895.00

OptionVue IV software is designed for the sophisticated stock option trader interested in stocks, stock indexes, cash-carry commodities, convertible securities,
warrants, and arbitrage. The program utilizes a dividend adjusted Black-Scholes
Formula. The uniqueness of the program is its ability to calculate "what if" runs
on its own. This function generates "all" the possible opportunities (outright
positions, spreads, etc.) and ranks them as to potential return and risk. Includes a
communications module to update price information automatically and 1 1/2
years of volatility history on each optioned asset in the United States, so traders
can study volatility patterns. An add-on module accommodates futures options
and real-time price quotations.

Terco Computer Systems
P. O. Box 1803
Lombard, IL 60148
(708)347-9182
Price: $95.00

OptionMaster calculates the fair market premium and deltas for stocks, futures,
bonds, and physical commodities for put and call contracts. Uses Black-Scholes
and Cox-Ross-Rubenstein (binomial) formulas. Ideal for determining implied
volatility or fair market value arrays to spot over or under valued options.

Revenge Software, Inc.
P. O. Box 1073
Huntington, NY 11743
Price: $145.00

Option Valuator - Option Writer software has been written for the stock option
trader. It provides the capability of calculating the information needed to evaluate options, primarily option value and volatility. The Option Writer part of the
program enables the investor to evaluate and track a covered stock option writing
program.

$ Dollar/Soft
P. O. Box 822
Newark, CA 94560-0822
(415)656-5649
(800)678-4664
Prices: $99.00 - $199.00

Option Trader classifies itself as "an expert system for the put and call options trader." For pricing of calls, it utilizes Black-Scholes formula for stock and indexes. For calls in the futures markets, it uses Fisher Black formula. Puts are calculated by the Academic or Conversion Models. The program handles a variety of spreads (Bull/Bear, Butterfly, Ratio, Horizontal, Diagonal, etc.), as well as net long-short strategies. Includes calculations for writer's margin and return.

Institute for Options Research, Inc.
P. O. Box 6586
Lake Tahoe, NV 89449
(800)334-0854, Ext 840
(702)588-3590
Price: $89.95

Option Master is an affordable program for the novice option trader. This program allows you to calculate the volatility of the stock, futures, or index options you are considering. Once you do this, you can calculate the fair market value (FMV) for one or all of the options' strike prices. By comparing the FMV with the ask price, you locate options that appear to be over or under priced. The Institute sells a complete line of books, audio/video tapes, and software programs. Call for a catalog.

Townsend Analytics, Ltd.
100 South Wacker Drive, Suite 1506
Chicago, IL 60606
(312)621-0141
(800)827-0141
Price: $2,000.00

Option Risk Management TM evaluates risk to return of option portfolios of large traders (stocks, futures, stock indexes, debt instruments). Risk and return are measured by thetas, vegas, gammas, deltas, option valuations, and profit-loss. Require Microsoft(R) Windows (TM) 3.0. Townsend also sells a data service to link Option Risk Management to live quotation services.

INDEX

A

Abbot, Bud, 1,3
Account papers, 131
ACLU, 146
American Arbitration Association, 131
American style option, 12
Astrological analysis, 64

B

Bar charts, 53-59
"Before You Say Yes", 142
Berlin Wall, viii
Better Business Bureau, 127
Billings, Jack, 21
Black, Fischer, 68
Black-Scholes, 68, 70, 75
Bond, James, 91
Breakeven analysis, 24, 28
Brecht, Bertolt, 119
Broadcast Partners' Farm DayTa, 114
Broker selection, 119-135
Bulls, 26
Butterfly spread, 38, 151
Bureau of Economic Analysis, 49
Business cycles, 49
Buyers, 3

C

Call, 1
Carrying charges, 68
Character-of-Market, 63
Chart formations, 55-59
Chicago Board of Options Exchange
    (CBOE), 82

Chicago Board of Trade (CBOT), 2, 3, 5,
    7, 116, 152
Chicago Mercantile Exchange (CME), 5,
    16
Churchill, Winston, 47
Coffee, Sugar & Cocoa Exchange (CSC),
    5, 152
Coin flipping, 70
Commodity Futures Exam, 128
Commodity Exchange, 5
Commodity Futures Trading Commission
    (CFTC), 40, 109, 125, 128, 130
Computers, 107-118
CompuServ, 126
CompuTrac, 111-112
Contrary opinion, 65
Correlation analysis, 64
Costello, Lou, 1, 3
Covered option writer, 41-42
CTA, 52
Currencies, 18
Customer complaints, 127-30
Cycles, 62, 96

D

Daytimer, 102
Deep-out-of-the-money options, 3, 15
Delivery months, 17
Delta, 11
Department of Commerce, 49-50
Depreciation, Great, viii
Desert Storm, viii
Discipline, 101
Discount broker, 119
Discretion, 134
Diversification, 89
DOS, 110

Dow Averages, 48, 50
Dow, Charles, 48
DTN, 114
Dylan, Bob, 127

E

Elliot, T.S., 147
Elliot Wave, 62, 98
Exercise Price, 2, 68
European style option, 12

F

Farmers' Almanac, 107
Fear, 105
Federal Bureau of Investigation (FBI), 127
Fibonacci numberical progression analysis, 64
Frost, Robert, 67
Full service broker, 119
Fundamental analysis, 25, 47-51
Futures Commission Merchant (FCM), 121
"Futures Magazine", 153

G

Gambling, x
Gamma, 15
Gann, 63, 98, 110
General Securities Exam (Series 7), 128
Globex, 5
Goals, 83
Golden Mean, 64
Greed, 103-04

H

Head & shoulder formation, 58
Hedge ratio, 13
Hedger, 13, 44-45
Hope, 104-05

Hubris, 103
Hunt Brothers, 69
Hypothetical trading, 109, 115
Hysteria, 140

I

IBM, 12, 78
Ideal System, 113
Index(es), 18
Indicators, 49
Inge, Charles, 97
International Monetary Market (IMM), 6
In-the-money options, 4
Intrinsic value, 4, 8

J

Japanese Candlesticks, 98
John Deere Stock, 6
Journal, trading, 101

K

Kappa, 15

L

Law of Probability, ix, 21, 22
Leonardo of Pisa, 64
Leveraging, 21
Liquidity, 121
Local, 122
Logical Information Machine, Inc., 116
London, 140

M

Macintosh, 110
Margin, 7
Market Information Machine, 116
Mark(ing)-to-the-Market, 7

Market-on-close, 17
Market-on-open, 17
Market selection, 86
Market view approach, 65
MATIF, 5, 6
McCarthyism, 140
Mean, 73
MidAmerica Exchange, 19
Money management, 88
Moving average, 59-60, 80

N

National Futures Association (NFA), 128-
    30
National Security Dealers Association
    (NSDA), 128-30
"Naughty Nineties", 1
NFL, 147
New York Cotton Exchange, 5
New York Stock Exchange, 132

O

O'Connor, William, 116
Oedipus Rex, 103
Offsetting position, 2
Omega, 14
Open outcry, 5
Options
    Advantages, viii
    Definition, vii
    General, 9, 14
    Stock vs. Futures, 6, 10
    Use, viii
    Valuing, 67
Orders, 16
Oscillators, 63-64
Osler, Sir William, 83

P

Philadelphia Stock Exchange, 12
Plans (planning), 83, 84

Point & figure charts/systems, 61
Price Modeling, 67
Pre-Arbitration Agreement, 132
Probability, 70-71
Prodigy, 126
Psychological rules, 90 Put, 1

R

Random Walk Theory, 68
Regulations, 127-136
Relative strength indexes, 64
Reparation, 132
Resistance areas, 57
Rewards, unlimited, ix
Reuters, 5
RHO, 15
Risk
    Limitations, ix
    To reward, 88, 101
    Transfer of, 21
    Spread, 39
Rules, 83

S

Scalpers, 121
Scholes, Myron, 68
Seasonals, 62, 79
Security Exchange Commission (SEC),
    40, 109, 125, 129, 130
Sellers, 3
Selling options, 2
Settlement, 7
Sigma price, 15
Silver, 7
Sistine Chapel, 64
"SOFTSware", 152
Software features, 113
Soybeans, 78
Speculators, 21
Spreads, 27, 29-36, 40, 94
Special double, 37
Standard deviation, 74
Stock options, 6

Stop loss order, 43
Straddles, 32-34, 151
Strangles, 34-37
Strategies, 21, 25, 26
Strike (striking) price, 1
Structural analysis, 61
Sugar trading, 138
Support areas, 57

T

"T" list, 124
T-Bills, 6, 82
Technical analysis, 25, 51-66
Terminology, 1
Theoretical option price model, 67
Time, 29
Time value, 8
Trade distribution, 23
Trading diary, 102
Trading process, 150
Trading rules, 91
Trading software, 107-09
Trading systems, 97,99
Transaction costs, 2, 8
Trend following systems, 59
Trendlines, 56

U

Uncovered option writer, 42
Underlying entity, 14
United States Department of Agriculture
    (USDA), 77
United States Postal Service, 127
UNIX, 110

V

Vega, 15
Volatility, 15, 29, 67-82

W

Wasendorf Composite Index, 81
Wasendorf Trading System, 109
Wave principle, 62
World War II, 139
Writing options, 39

Z

Zeta, 15

About the Authors

Thomas A. McCafferty's involvement in the cash commodities and futures industries goes back to 1973. He has traded futures for his own account and supervised brokers who traded for others. Additionally, he has a strong background in sales and marketing and is the author of *In-House Telemarketing: A Master Plan for Starting and Managing a Profitable Telemarketing Program* (Probus, 1987). Currently, Mr. McCafferty oversees the branch office system for Wasendorf & Son Company, an introducing broker, and manages its marketing effort. He is also on the marketing faculty of Upper Iowa University and a consultant for the Small Business Administration.

Russell R. Wasendorf has been totally involved in the futures market since he took over the reins, in the late 1970s, of the Commodity Education Institute, which trained hundreds of futures brokers and traders. By the early 1980s, Mr. Wasendorf had developed his proprietary indexes and began the development of his index analysis system. By the mid-1980s, he had written *Commodities Trading: The Essential Primer* (Dow Jones-Irwin, 1985), began a newsletter to track his trading system, *Futures and Options Factors*, and launched a commodity price charting service, *Pocket Charts*. Currently, he manages his own introducing brokerage firm, Wasendorf & Son Company. Most recently, he has founded Peregrine Financial Group, Inc., a futures commission merchant.

Together, Mr. McCafferty and Mr. Wasendorf have also authored *All About Futures* and *All About Commodities*.

Dear Reader:

We hope you've enjoyed this book. More importantly, we hope you've received a solid overview of exchange traded options.

If you'd like to learn more, please contact us for a free trial to our weekly news-letter, *Futures and Options Factors*. It chronicles the Wasendorf Trading System, includes our market commentary and our option trading recommendations. The classroom section is designed to further your understanding of futures and op-tions trading. You'll even find a recap of our trading track record on Page 8 of this newsletter.

Sincerely,

Thomas A. McCafferty and Russell R. Wasendorf

P.S. To begin your free trial to *Futures and Options Factors* newsletter, mail the coupon below or give one of us a call at 1-800-553-1711.

_____

Yes, please start my free, no risk trial to *Futures and Options Factors* newsletter.

Call 1-800-553-1711. Or mail this coupon to:

Wasendorf & Son Company
802 Main Street, P. O. Box 849
Cedar Falls, IA 50613

Name _____

Address _____

City _____

State _____ Zip _____

Phone (____)_____

Other Books in the "All About . . ." Series